Give wisely +
invest
proactively!

Best

John

A Passion for Giving

A Passion for Giving

TOOLS AND INSPIRATION FOR CREATING A CHARITABLE FOUNDATION

Peter J. Klein
Angelica Berrie

WILEY

John Wiley & Sons, Inc.

Published by John Wiley & Sons, Inc., Hoboken, New Jersey.
Published simultaneously in Canada.

For general information on our other products and services or for technical support, please contact our Customer Care Department within the United States at
(800) 762–2974, outside the United States at (317) 572–3993 or fax (317) 572–4002.

Wiley also publishes its books in a variety of electronic formats. Some content that
appears in print may not be available in electronic books. For more information
about Wiley products, visit our web site at www.wiley.com.

Library of Congress Cataloging-in-Publication Data

Klein, Peter J.
    A passion for giving : tools and inspiration for creating a charitable
 foundation/Peter Klein and Angelica Berrie.
        p. cm.
    Includes index.
    ISBN 978-1-118-02387-7 (cloth); ISBN 978-1-118-22195-2 (ebk);
    ISBN 978-1-118-23204-0 (ebk); ISBN 978-1-118-23577-5 (ebk)
        1. Charitable uses, trusts, and foundations—United States—Popular works.
    2. Endowments—United States.   I. Berrie, Angelica.   II. Title.
    KF740.K57 2012
    3361.7'632068—dc23   2011039268

Printed in the United States of America
10 9 8 7 6 5 4 3 2 1

To Claire: Your lessons will not be forgotten and your legacy will continue on—this honor, with its weighty responsibility, I accept and embrace with an open mind and a full heart. You are missed but will always be in our hearts and minds. Rest well my friend.

—P.J.K.

For my husband Russ, whose generous spirit transformed the lives of so many and changed mine forever.

—A.B.

Contents

Preface

If philanthropy is the cure then private foundations are the actual inoculation or pill that one takes to achieve this cure. Philanthropy, as broken down from the ancient language derivation, means "the love for mankind, the love of people." Although a private foundation is by no means the only method by which to illustrate or execute one's love for people, it is certainly a primary choice of many individuals and families when considering a philanthropic gifting program; a program that can incorporate the entire family—for generations to come. A private foundation is much like a family orchard or vineyard; the seedlings are planted and cared for and then passed down to the next generation to continue this care and harvesting.

In this book we have attempted to take the reader on a journey; a journey that starts in the world of concrete science and information and ends up in the world of passion and heartwarming stories of philanthropic successes.

In Part I this journey starts with a hypothetical couple who serve as the vessel through which the reader learns about the basics of estate planning, charitable giving, and private foundations. Once the reader becomes aware that this hypothetical couple chooses the private foundation as their favored "vessel" for their philanthropic giving, the journey is moved along to gain an understanding of the in's and out's of a private foundation.

Starting, maintaining, and investing for a private foundation is a broad, well-researched topic. There are scores of excellent books and journals that interested parties can busy themselves with for years to come. In this book, however, it is our goal to provide an overview and a template to get the potential foundation thinking about the issues involved in managing a private foundation. This is by no means an exhaustive journey into the inner workings of a private foundation but it does serve as a primer for any potential philanthropist considering such a vessel.

At the conclusion of this first part, the reader is invited to continue this journey into Part II—the private foundation world; namely the "why." Although the reader has received much information and a defined template on how to manage and invest a foundation's assets, he or she has not learned the "why" yet. "Why should one embark on a mission of philanthropy?" "Why should a private foundation be used to make a difference?" "Why even consider this—what difference can it make?"

These and other why's are answered through the anecdotal accounts of several leading philanthropists. Through many years of "toiling in the private foundation world" we have been able to provide the reader with a continuation of the journey and to warm their hearts along the way. To learn about such visionary philanthropists as Ken Behring, Peter Karoff, and Peggy Dulany is in itself a lesson to be cherished. There are a myriad of additional lessons that can be gleaned from these pages—the importance of being inspired and challenged like those stories from Lisa Nigro and Ken Behring— whose names may not be household fodder but who have certainly moved mountains and dreams along their journey.

It is our hope that this book provides the reader—whether a budding philanthropist or a family member with new found philanthropic responsibilities—with a good understanding of how to invest a foundation's assets and manage its operations effectively while understanding why it needs to be done: for the common good.

Peter Klein and Angelica Berrie
October 2011

Acknowledgments

Peter Klein

My first thank-you goes to my co-author on this project—Angelica Berrie. Angelica, without your inspiration and passion for giving, this book would have never come to fruition.

There are many fantastic people who assisted in the writing of this book—professional colleagues such as Jon Abbondanza, Lawrence Davidow, Lawrence Doyle, Adam Gottlieb, Michael Fontanello, Brian Iammartino, Robert Larocca, John Murcott, David Okorn, Christopher Petermann, David Sterling, and Steven Stern. A special thanks to my team for their indefatigable support and guidance: Robert Limmer, Trisha Flanagan, and Jane Voorhees.

There were also several private foundation experts who were instrumental in guiding this work: Christine DeVita, Dr. Nancy Rauch Douzinas, Dr. Mark Fasciano, Ann Gambling, Val Green, Amy Hagedorn, Richard Kandell, Ilan Kaufthal, Daniel Komansky, Celeste Land, Linda Landsman, Thomas Lawrence, Karen Outlaw, José Rivero, Long Island Community Foundation, Greg Siegrist, Roy Tanzman, Mitch Tobol, and Michele Cohn Tocci. A special thanks to The Association for Small Foundations and Foundation Source for their indefatigable efforts in advocating for, and fostering, stronger, more efficient private foundations.

A special thanks also to those clients who devoted their time to assist and provide feedback for this work—these individuals (and their families) understand the meaning of giving back and building a sense of philanthropy into their daily lives. They include Gene Bernstein, Don Hill, Isaac Mekel, Ronald J. Morey, Nancy Payne, David Rosen and Bill Schoolman.

Many people I have come across while conducting research for this book embody the essence of philanthropy—these are givers, thinking long term and setting in motion legacies that will far out live them: Steven Acunto, Anthony Bonomo, Bert Brodsky, Stephen and Beth Dannhauser, Charlie Hammerman, Doug Hammond, Anita Kaufman, Gary Krupp, Michael Leeds, Howard Maier, Barry and Marilyn Rubenstein, Stanley and Phyllis Sanders, Roger Tilles, Paul Tonna, Paul and Gail Watson, Andy Whitehead, and Eli Wilner.

Finally, I would like to express my love and gratitude for my family and friends. My wife of 20 years and my three children light the fire that is my fortitude each and every day—it is with them by my side that I remain resolute and confident that any mountain can be climbed and every river crossed.

Angelica Berrie

Often writers don't see the whole clearly until the book is finished. Listening to experienced voices with a "beginner's mind" helped me reflect on my own practice, to realize what I still have to work on to get out of my comfort zone.

My heartfelt thanks to everyone who contributed not just to this book but to my learning curve.

To Peter Klein, whose idea it was to provide a narrative companion piece, and for his practical advice on starting a foundation— thank you for risking your reputation with a neophyte writer.

To my philanthropy guru, Peter Karoff, who came into my life when Russ and I were seeking advice on becoming strategic givers, shaped my education in philanthropy, coached me through the growth period of the Russell Berrie Foundation and continues to influence me in so many ways. Looking back at a decade's worth of copious notes from my sessions with him provided the inspiration to curate a conversation about philanthropy and extract clear messages that readers could apply in their own practice.

To my fellow philanthropists, practitioners, and innovators in the art of giving who, as mentors, coaches, and role models, contributed to my own transformation.

To my sister, Issa, my exacting editor and midwife to my writing labor pains. Her patience and encouragement helped me get through writer's block, to stop trying to perfect every sentence and just let go!

To the trustees and staff of the Russell Berrie Foundation, my partners in learning and fellow travelers on this journey toward wisdom.

A Passion for Giving

PART
I

SO YOU WANT TO BE A PHILANTHROPIST

*To me, money is a means to do good. I reached a point in my life where
I enjoyed tremendous business success that afforded my family everything
we could possibly want. My wife and I then decided that we could use our
wealth to make a difference. So we created the Broad Foundations to do
four things: to improve urban public education, to support innovative
scientific and medical research, to foster art appreciation for audiences
worldwide, and to support civic initiatives in Los Angeles.*
                    —Eli Broad, philanthropist and businessman

---

Setting: An office of a wealth management firm in suburban USA.
Financial adviser, Mr. Emmett ("Em" for short) Pathy, is sitting down to
a meeting with one of his longstanding clients—Mr. Phil Anthony. Phil
requested the meeting to discuss with his trusted advisor of many years his
changing estate planning objectives.

"Hi Phil, good to see you again. How's the family—is young
Charlie finished up at college yet?"

"One more year in his six-year MBA/JD program," Phil replied.
"Everything else is fine, I am glad we were able to meet on such

short notice—there is something on my mind that I wanted to speak with you about."

"I figured it was important when you called," said Mr. Pathy, an industry veteran. "You are never around here during the summer; usually you are at the beach house."

"Well yes, but this has been something that has been pestering me and I wanted to get your advice," said Phil.

Phil, a wealthy businessman who sold his self-made business a few years ago to a large corporation whose shares (some of which Phil received in the buyout) have appreciated substantially in the past two years (to that end, Phil has been involved in a liquidation strategy, most recently thinking the shares have peaked), goes onto discuss his interest in charitable giving. He tells his financial advisor that he is concerned about making sure that his family does not get "lazy" with their inheritance and continue to work hard to build something—just like Phil did. He says he is worried about his grandkids, too—will they become spoiled rich kids—"trust fund babies" like the ones who used to turn their noses up at Phil while he was working his way through college? These are not the values Phil wants to leave his kids and grandchildren.

Also Phil, now retired for a couple of years and never much of a golfer or sailor, has become restless himself. He wants to try to do some new things—get involved with projects—and use his contacts and his resources to help others.

Phil and his wife Mary were never much for charitable giving—it just seemed like a waste to simply write a check—and they always wondered where the money went. How did they know it did some good? Being a control-oriented person, Phil was bothered that he lacked control when giving in this manner. Sure, it was fine for the one-off minor checks—but now that they have amassed serious wealth they are more interested in being active in their giving.

A friend at the club had started a private foundation for his philanthropic interests—he maintains a portfolio of investments for the foundation and has his family involved in deciding which nonprofit organizations to provide grants to each year. But he always seems to be complaining about this form or report, the requirements of the Internal Revenue Service (IRS) and other legal entities. Phil wondered if this might be the right vehicle for his and Mary's interests; he liked the idea of maintaining control of the portfolio but the minutia of the administration worried him. But maybe there are systems that he could put in place to make the administrative tasks easier to deal with—perhaps with careful planning and execution he could make a private foundation work?

What is actually involved with starting a private foundation? How does one initiate a foundation? What paperwork is involved? How about the continued compliance that is involved—taxes, conflicts of interest, and other related requirements? These are the questions that Phil and Mary have been mulling around in their heads recently. In addition to the legal and tax requirements there are also the soft issues that need to be addressed—which nonprofits would we focus on? How would we state our mission statement? Would the foundation have a spend-down policy over some number of years or a perpetual, legacy format? These questions were also front-of-mind for Phil and Mary.

So Phil came to the office of his financial advisor, someone who he has worked with for more than three decades and has always respected his counsel and friendship—he liked that Em really cared—he "got" Phil—he understood what made him tick.

"Charitable giving is a big area and a big step—one that we need to not take lightly," said Em.

"I realize this and you know me well enough to know that I am not interested in doing something halfway; the more I read about this philanthropy stuff the more excited I get. Think about the legacy opportunities here—my children are all fairly well off—Mary and I made sacrifices along the way to ensure that they received a good education and understood the value of a dollar. But we worry that they will inherit a substantial amount of money—more than we ever conceived, and that worries us—and that they can get off track. And how about the grandkids? We want to make sure that they receive these same values despite being part of a world that moves so fast and is so focused on the here and now—it is very easy to lose one's way."

Emmett suggested that he, Phil, and Mary embark on a journey through the maze that is philanthropy—from the basics of nonprofit research and "packaged products" to more specialized planning and private foundation management. Em said that he would provide a report on each stage along the way so Phil and Mary can be fully aware and comfortable about their decision.

Emmett explained to the Anthonys that his report would take them through the basics of estate planning with a focus on charitable vehicles to better understand the differences between private foundations and other platforms for charitable interests. Em also expects to discuss the importance of understanding how nonprofits work and what to look for in the due diligence process—the key signposts as well as the caution flags. Private foundations are a science onto itself and Em's report will go into how to start and manage a private foundation—the issues with respect to developing a mission statement as well as an approach toward philanthropy. Of course, there is more to running a private foundation than that—there are possible staffing issues, investment management functions, and the circumstances surrounding legacy and sustainability. Em was confident that his analysis of the field would provide his clients with a working model to effectively make their decision and implement their plans.

"Eyes wide open," Phil said, "I like it—let's get started."

"Great," said Em, "but first we will need to update some of your financials and talk—broad strokes—about yours and Mary's interests with respect to charitable giving."

The three of them sat in Em's conference room—yellow pad and pen in hand—and started to update the Anthonys' net worth statement—much of which Em already knew. But there were some new nuances that came to light. For instance, Phil and Mary were always major advocates of education for their children—Em can recall how, early on, they sacrificed on some extravagances to instill in their children the importance of gaining an exceptional education. Vacations were limited—school always came first. There were high expectations and the Anthony children responded nicely. Phil and Mary now wanted to use some of their wealth to establish an "educational legacy" for their grandkids and great-grandchildren. In this way, the burdens of a strong, well-thought-out educational plan that has increased substantially in the past several years would become more manageable for the next generation of Anthonys. Not to say that shared sacrifice is not an important virtue—clearly it is—but Phil and Mary did not want education to become something that had to be thought about but rather something that was built-in, "hard-wired" as Phil would say, into their plans from the get-go.

Phil took some notes and already had some ideas with regard to this "segmented educational legacy portfolio" that would serve the family for generations to come. There was also the issue of the beach house that they would need to address. This purchase, on Long Island's East End, was Phil and Mary's first "big ticket" splurge.

Years ago, realizing how important it was to them to have their kids together and how each of them enjoyed the splendor that is Long Island's East End, Phil and Mary, to the total surprise of their friends and neighbors, purchased a lovely home that has become their "family home." It was important to the Anthonys that "Sandy Haven" was kept in the family—a home for generations to come to gather and maintain the bonds between them. Call it a "family compound" or "beach house"—it didn't matter to Phil or Mary. It was important to them that it stayed in the family—equally owned by all immediate family members and maintained in part through a trust of some sort so that it would not become a major financial burden to keep up. "I have heard of these types of arrangements so I am sure they exist," said Mary. "Of course, there are trusts and methods by which this can be accomplished," replied Em, adding that there are potential tax savings along the way as well.

Emmett, a proactively minded financial advisor, continued in this vein, discussing and updating his files on the Anthonys' current situation—both financially as well as emotionally, for Em knew that much of his work is clearly "science-based" (finance and economic science) as he calls it, but the soft or emotional side of his practice—"the art"—is as critical if not more so in many cases. Em confirmed that Phil and Mary, who also worked for the company for many years, receive a sufficient income from their accumulated pension benefits to maintain their lifestyle (which included a robust travel/vacation schedule) and that their balance sheet was free of debts of any kind. Their health was excellent and Phil and Mary were quite proactive in maintaining their healthy lifestyle—walking, cycling, and even taking a few yoga classes each week. That said, Em updated his files on their insurance portfolio—both own fully paid up life insurance held in trusts as well as long-term care policies to ensure that they were cared for in case they were to become incapacitated.

It seems apparent that Phil and Mary were very attentive to their family's educational needs as well as their own financial ones. "The new thing on our list, as a consequence I guess from the sale of the business, is this interest in doing something in the charitable world—something where we can maintain some control and be active in the process," said Phil. "As we mentioned, a friend has set up a private foundation but he seems to have some issues with management and administration so we were not sure that would be the way for us to go," said Mary.

Emmett assured Phil and Mary that there were methods one could incorporate into their private foundation management that would ease the administrative burdens, but agreed that running a private foundation is no small matter—it requires time, energy, and a strong interest in the charitable work underpinning its mission.

Em sat back and listened (something he does more than speaking in these meetings where his goal is to gain an understanding of his clients) as the Anthonys described their interests in this next phase of their lives.

■ ■ ■

Em knew the next steps started with an examination of the basics of estate planning and charitable giving. As he began to lay out his report, Em focused on the glide-path that would be the journey that he and his clients would take over the next several weeks—from estate planning and charitable giving to the basics and operations of a private foundation to investing protocols for private foundations.

CHAPTER 1

Estate Planning and Charitable Giving

*I will continue to distribute blankets, sleeping bags, warm clothing, and
food on a regular basis, in the hope that my modest efforts will give some
comfort to those people we are able to help.*
　　　　　　—Mohamed Al-Fayed, philanthropist, businessman

Em was nodding his head—he knew his client and understood
exactly where this was going and he liked the big picture very much.
To start things off, Em developed a detailed report including the
reasons—why, from an estate planning perspective, someone would
look at charitable giving as an instrumental part of their estate plan.

Starting from the beginning—estate planning is the process by
which an individual sets up his or her (or in case of a married couple,
their) estate (what remains after they are deceased). In the United
States, taxpayers may be subject to an "estate tax" on the value of their
assets upon their death—it is the minimization of these taxes that is
often the initial reason why someone embarks upon charitable giving
(of course, the person also has to have an interest—a "calling"—to
give back to society).

Although charitable giving is not solely a U.S. phenomenon, its
magnitude is to such an extent that it very well could be. Case in
point, private giving in America is in excess of 2 percent of GDP—
the highest of any nation, with the United Kingdom number two at
0.7 percent of its GDP. From a scope perspective it is also huge. The

IRS has certified 1.5 million organizations as satisfying the requirements for tax exempt status under sections 501(c)(3) and 501(c)(4)
of the federal tax code (which define charitable and mutual benefit organizations, respectively), as well as another 353,000 religious
organizations—churches, mosques, synagogues—which are not
required to seek IRS certification for tax exempt status.[1] Of course,
what is not listed here are the multitude of organizations that are
not "institutionalized" or formatted under said standards—just simple groups of people doing good work in helping others and their
communities. So why are Americans so infatuated with giving?

The answer to that question might stem from the early history
of Colonial America, where religious oppression and lack of freedom
persuaded these early colonialists to brave the rough waters of the
Atlantic for the new world. This spirit of freedom laid the framework for the institutions that the colonialists established here in
the United States. Their first order of business once on these free
shores was to establish self-governing religious congregations, which
provided schooling as well as worship and other services without any
governmental body as an overseer. It was this penchant for indepen-
dence that led to the formation of other organizations—again without the support or interference of some government body—which
in turn led to the affinity groups (be it religious, racial, ethnicity,
etc.) that now take on the label of nonprofit organizations.

These efforts in philanthropy took on a whole new vigor once
the tax laws made it such that donations were not only a good thing
to do (and often a mandated thing to do within a given group, like
the tithing requirements of the Protestant religions) but also a tax-
advantaged thing to do.

Going back to the early part of the twentieth century, 1917 to
be exact, the IRS established rules with respect to allowing deductions of gifts to charitable or nonprofit organizations. These gifts
may be cash, financial assets (stocks, securities), as well as real property, artwork, or clothing—although the deductibility of nonfinancial assets differ from those of cash and financial assets. Gifts of cash
and other noncapital gain assets (those assets that cannot appreciate
while holding) are only deductible up to 50 percent of the donor's

---

[1]Joel Fleishman, *The Foundation: A Great American Secret* (New York: PublicAffairs/
Perseus Books, 2007), 15.

adjusted gross income (AGI) whereas capital gain assets (i.e., real property, artwork, financial assets) are limited to 30 percent of AGI (the reason, in part, for this is a capital gain asset has already enjoyed the "deduction" from the perspective that the donation avoids the capital gain tax as well as the deduction).

Going back to 1917, the federal government, worried that increased tax rates would dissuade private charity, introduced the deduction to gifts to nonprofits and charities. To minimize the loss of tax revenues, the government limited deductions to 15 percent of taxable income on individual returns (corporations were first permitted to make tax-deductible contributions in 1935). Part of the thinking at the time had to do with the need to subsidize the programs of nonprofit organizations and to essentially minimize the onus of these programs on the federal government. In essence, the federal government "leaned" on the goodness of the American people and their long-standing commitment to community and charity by providing them a tax incentive to continue to give and support these important organizations, and in turn, their services to those most in need. For the most part, these incentives for charitable giving, legislated by the federal government through the tax system, have remained fairly consistent—except during the Reagan administration, when a cut in federal spending for many programs led to tax deductibility of charitable gifts even for those taxpayers who didn't itemize their deductions (1981–1986).

But it might have been more than a simple "passing the buck" exercise—evidence suggests that private charitable giving is superior to direct government support.[2] By providing a tax deduction and essentially promoting charitable giving without having to do it itself, the federal government avoids potential conflicts of interest that could arise when a religious organization provides food and shelter to the poor (separation of church and state). There is also the belief, shared by many, that the government may not be as efficient or effective in its giving as a privately run charitable organization would be—especially if this organization is "competing" against other organizations for contributions.

---

[2] William C. Randolph, "Charitable Deductions." In *The Encyclopedia of Taxation and Tax Policy*, ed. Joseph J. Cordes, Robert D. Ebel, and Jane G. Gravelle (Washington, DC: Urban Institute, 1999).

There are many reasons why the government supports this initiative of private giving through tax deductions. Clearly, stronger efforts in education and religion can go a long way toward a stronger, safer, more civically responsible society. Education in scientific research can reduce the incidence of disease and result in higher standards of living for the society on the whole. Bottom line—the tax deductibility of gifts to nonprofit organizations has helped continue to foster the importance of charitable giving in the U.S. psyche.

Estate Planning 101

During a lifetime, people accumulate assets—from intangibles like investments (stocks, bonds, etc.) and cash balances (in all accounts—like checking, CDs) to tangible assets like artwork, jewelry, and operating businesses. These assets comprise one's estate upon death. There is a fairly in-depth process that occurs when someone dies, where an inventory of the assets is developed and an understanding of where those assets are to go now that the owner is no longer alive. For assets where there is a direct path to new ownership—a Joint Account with Rights of Survivorship, an account designated as Transfer on Death, an annuity or retirement account, where there is a beneficiary designation form already executed by the now deceased former owner, there is a clear glide-path to the destination of those assets. All other assets, be it your favorite necklace or a 1967 Chevy, need to be probated (which is from the Latin term meaning to "prove").

The Probate Process

The probate process uses the decedent's last will and testament to prove where these assets should go now that the owner has passed away. Of course, like any legal process, probate takes time (it could be years if there are litigation issues to contend with) and can be costly (although there are statutory guidelines, which vary by state). Other expenses, again governed by statutes, are the commissions paid to an executor or executrix who handles the entire estate process.

Once the will is admitted to probate and the executor (or executrix) is given the Letters Testamentary from the Surrogate Court, the probate process begins. The executor is charged with the responsibility to marshal all of the decedent's assets, pay all creditors and manage the affairs of the estate in a fiduciary conscious fashion. A detailed accounting of all activities—both from a balance sheet (assets and liabilities) as well as an income statement (income and expenses) perspective is compiled. Next step? Taxes.

An estate tax is a tax on the fair market value of the decedent's assets on the date of death (or actually, the executor has a choice of using the date of death valuation or the entire estate's valuation six months from the date of death). Typically, the executor will choose the lower valuation in order to mitigate any taxes on the estate; however, in doing so, the decedent's income tax return might be impacted (because the value of an asset on the estate's tax return becomes the new basis for the asset for income tax purposes). Understanding these somewhat complex issues is tantamount to the responsibilities of the executor and therefore it is advised that the executor seek professional counsel (an attorney specializing in trust and estate law) when embarking on such decisions. These somewhat complex legal matters, like many things in life (from the important, like investment management to the mundane, like haircutting) are best not to do alone but alongside professional counsel; making a mistake can be life-altering, or in the least, embarrassing.

The estate tax return is due within nine months from the date of death and it can have tax rates as high as 35 percent of the assets in the estate (because of this somewhat quick time frame families are often forced to sell assets quickly to pay the estate taxes, which is where the term "estate sale" originates). Which assets are included in this taxable asset inventory? Well, most are (yes, including that necklace and old Chevy!) with the exception of assets in specially designed trusts (irrevocable trusts). It is important to note that assets that pass to a surviving spouse are not taxed and there is no limitation to the amount that can be passed, estate tax free, in this manner, but, of course, when the surviving spouse passes all of the assets in her name (unless she remarries) will be estate taxable (hence the insurance policy known as "second to die," which is triggered when the surviving spouse dies and the taxes are then due).

In calculating the estate tax, the IRS provides a coupon for a certain amount of assets in the decedent's estate that are not taxed—this is called the *unified credit* (with the Bush-era tax cuts being extended for two years, the unified credit amount was increased to $5 million per person) and only assets above this amount are taxable in the estate. Please note that in the above we are discussing federal estate taxes—there is also, in most states, a state estate tax with substantially lower unified credit levels and tax rates.

Besides irrevocable trusts (trusts that can't be changed or terminated in contrast with revocable trusts), which "shelter" assets from estate taxes (because assets in these trusts are typically considered "outside a decedent's estate" and therefore are not estate taxable), the other tool for reducing one's taxable estate is the concept of gifting away assets. Anyone may give assets to anyone else—and these gifts are, up to an annual limitation per person, not taxable as gifts (gift tax exemption) and are not counted as assets in the grantor's estate. The gift tax limit, as of this writing, is $13,000 annually—gifts above that amount to any one person is taxable as a gift (gift tax rates are in the 35 percent range). A grantor can avoid this gift tax by reducing his or her unified credit amount—but that will have implications when it comes to estate tax minimization as well. Of course, without this gift tax construct, anyone would simply gift all of their assets to his or her family and die with a smaller estate and avoid the estate tax.

In addition to the $13,000 per person ($26,000 for a married couple) per year that someone can give to anyone else and have it exempt from gift taxes and reduce one's taxable estate, are donations made to public or private (foundations) charities. A public charity is a 501(c)(3) exempt organization, while a private foundation is typically governed by section 509(c)(3). Grantors in these cases do have limitations from a tax deductibility perspective—they can deduct on their personal income taxes a donation up to 50 percent of adjusted gross income (AGI)—and an additional amount can be carried over, and utilized as deductions, for five years. With respect to private foundations the bar is set at 30 percent of AGI—again with a carry forward provision. Once individuals max out their contributions to a private foundation, typically they can still make a tax deductible contribution to public charities. Other types of assets—real estate, artwork, and so on—can be donated to a foundation, but are subject to limitations.

In the estate planning process, professionals counsel clients seeking to reduce the value of their taxable estate to enter into a yearly gifting program to those individuals to whom they want to pass their capital, as well as to make donations to charity. In each case the taxable estate is reduced and, all other things being equal, that would mean a lower estate tax bill. Estate planning is made infinitely more difficult, from an estate tax minimization goal, once the person passes. Upon death the individual is no longer an entity (although they will have to file a personal income tax return for the period between the beginning of the year and their date of death) and the "estate of the decedent" begins. So, the gifting exercise ceases to be useful as a means by which one can reduce the value of the estate (you can't give a gift if you no longer exist).

The Anthonys were somewhat well-versed in this area—they had sought the counsel some years ago of an estate planning specialist—an attorney who was actually recommended by Emmett. It was this attorney, together with Emmett, who suggested the long-term care policies that Phil and Mary purchased several years ago, as well as the Irrevocable Life Insurance Trusts (ILITs) that house their life insurance policies (using an irrevocable trust removes the asset from their taxable estate and allows the proceeds to pass down to the kids in a trust set up for their use). "I am pleased to learn that we have executed the initial phase of our estate plan in an effective format," said Phil.

But what about the bequests made in one's will? The bequests (gifts written into the will and only come into play once the will is probated) are income tax-free to the recipient and, for the most part, are not deductible on the estates' income tax return. Nor do these postdeath gifts (the definition of a bequest) reduce the value of one's estate. But what are fully deductible on the estate tax return (in other words, what we can use to reduce the value of one's taxable estate) are donations made in a will to a public charity. They may also be partially, up to an AGI limit, tax deductible on the estates' income tax return.

Gifting Techniques and More Advanced Estate Planning

There are advanced gifting techniques that are beyond the scope of this work—establishing trusts like GRATs and GRUTs, where the donor provides a gift today for future return of either a terminal value or cash flow, and in doing so is able to discount the value of that gift for estate tax purposes. Why? Because the value of a future gift is less than the value of a current gift and therefore the IRS permits discounting (the reduction of value due to a stated interest rate and time) when calculating the value of that gift for estate tax purposes. There are also family limited partnerships (FLPs), which are set up to "house" business interests where the donor is a general partner and therefore is able to discount these assets because he or she no longer owns 100 percent of the asset. The vehicle known as a Qualified Personal Residence Trust (QPRT) works in a similar fashion—discounting the value of a residence or real property for estate purposes because it is being gifted to a trust. This trust is held usually for the benefit of the grantor's children. "This could be an excellent tool to keep Sandy Haven in the family," said Mary excitedly. Em agreed.

There are also more everyday techniques that permit reductions to one's taxable estate. The IRS permits prepaid funeral expenses as deductible from one's estate for tax purposes. Also, qualified educational expenses are exempt from gift taxes and therefore can be paid (reduction of assets) without incurring gift taxes. There is also the concept of "accelerated gifting," with college 529 plans being the most common of these programs. Gifts to these plans—which allow for tax-free growth if the invested capital is used for secondary educational expenses—can be accelerated by five years without incurring the typical gift tax liabilities. For example, if Grandpa and Grandma Jones are seeking to reduce their taxable estate and are contemplating a $26,000 gift ($13,000 per person) to each of their five grandchildren, essentially removing $129,000 from their taxable estate, they could make that gift of $129,000 per grandchild today (removing $645,000 from their taxable estate). That capital gets invested today and begins to compound tax-free in the 529 plan (outside their estate but still controllable by them), which can make a big difference in the terminal value years in the future. There is a catch, however; the IRS requires that the donor in this advanced gifting program live for the five years after the gift is made in order to remove the entire gift from his or her taxable estate.

Phil and Mary both saw the light immediately with using 529 plans to establish their multigenerational educational legacy—"this would be a perfect way to insure that our grandkids and even their kids would have a means towards higher education," said Phil. "As the rules are written today, 529 plans enjoy tax-free growth if used for higher education expenses, and the value of this account would be outside of your estate but you can control the disposition of the assets—truly a win-win," said Em. "In addition," Em continued, "the beneficiaries of a 529 plan are fungible, which means that if one grandchild receives a full scholarship to a school of his or her choice and therefore does not require the capital from the 529—the beneficiary can be changed to another grandchild who might need greater assistance for say graduate school." The issue of ensuring a multigenerational legacy can be achieved through naming successor trustees to each 529 to handle the next generation after Phil and Mary are no longer around.

When all of these techniques, both the easy and the advanced, are maxed out, the estate's remaining value is assessed upon death and the tax is levied as described. The estate tax return is compiled, which lists all of the assets that comprise the taxable estate, and the resulting tax is calculated.

Responsibilities of an Executor

The executor (or executrix) is the person who has been chosen by the decedent, and specified in his or her will, as an "agent"—to carry out the wishes after his or her death. The executor administers the estate and has a wide spectrum of responsibilities and powers as detailed below:

Immediate Actions

You learn that someone close to you (a family member, a friend, a client) has passed away. You believe that you were designated as his executor (of course, there can always be the case that the will was changed and a new executor was named)—so what do you do now? First things first, you need to—together with the family—arrange for the decedent's funeral and burial. The person who is arranging this may only be the "nominated executor," which means that the court has not yet accepted the will for probate (on doing so, the designated executor named in the will receives Letters Testamentary, granting him or her the powers and responsibilities of managing the estate).

Probate

The will is filed with the Surrogate Court and the estate process begins. Once accepted, the court issues Letters Testamentary to the executor granting him the powers over the estate and its assets. The responsibilities of the executor are wide ranging—from marshaling assets and disposing of debts to adhering to the wishes of the decedent via the will as to bequests and the residuary assets (what's left after the bequests). Which assets does the executor handle?

(Continued)

For the most part it is all of the assets but it is important to denote the differences between the gross estate and the probate estate's assets—the differences are the assets that pass by operation of law—that is, those assets held in joint accounts or transfer on death accounts or those with a beneficiary agreement (IRAs, annuities, life insurance policies). These assets are not under the control of the executor or the estate, for they automatically pass to the designated party through an operation of law upon death.

Sixty Days from Date of Death

In the first 60 days, the executor must transfer all of the decedent's probate assets (those that did not pass by operation of law) in the name of the estate (typical titling: "The Estate of Robert Jones") and under the control of the executor. The executor then must ascertain the liquidity needs of the estate—the bequests in the will, creditors to be satisfied, and any expenses and taxes, and to that end perhaps sell assets to raise the cash needed. With respect to taxes, there are three returns that the executor will potentially need to sign off on: the personal income tax return (from start of year to date of death), the estate income tax return (may be required if the estate generates substantial income, and is due within 3½ months after the close of the estate's taxable year), and the estate tax return. There will probably be a federal set of these returns as well as a state set.

Within Six Months from Date of Death

The executor needs to make a decision on what valuation date he is using for the estate's assets—the date of death or the value six months from the date of death. As discussed, this decision can have consequences for the other tax returns and therefore should not be taken lightly.

Within Nine Months from Date of Death

The estate tax return is due as well as any tax liabilities. Also, the estate must file an inventory of assets in the estate with the probate court. Finally, in order to obtain the court's approval on the completion of the administration of the estate the executor will need to file a complete and formal accounting with the probate court. It is only after this accounting is approved can the executor be compensated—receive his commission, which is based on statutory calculations and vary from state to state. In New York, for example, an executor's commission is fixed by law. The applicable law is New York Surrogate's Court Procedure Act, Section 2307. Commissions are based on the size of the estate and are computed as follows: (1) 5 percent of the first $100,000; (2) 4 percent of the next $200,000; (3) 3 percent of the next $700,000; (4) 2.5 percent for the next $4,000,000; and (5) 2 percent for amounts exceeding $5,000,000.

The Estate Planning Process

"Okay, so what does this have to do with charitable giving?" Em can hear Phil asking himself when he reads this report. Well, the report continues, any donations, gifts, or transfers to qualified charitable organizations are estate tax deductible. (See Exhibit 1.1 for

Exhibit 1.1   Gifting Scenarios in Estate Planning

	Scenario	Personal Income Tax Return	Estate Income Tax Return	Estate Tax Return
During Lifetime	Person gives gift to someone else	Not deductible and if above Gift Tax exemption amount could be subjected to gift taxes	Not Applicable	Not Applicable
	Person gives donation (cash) to public charity (including a Donor Advised Fund)	Deductible up to 50% of Adjusted Gross Income (AGI) with a 5-year carryforward	Not Applicable	Not Applicable
	Person gives donation (securities) to public charity (including a Donor Advised Fund)	Deductible up to 30% of Adjusted Gross Income (AGI) with a 5-year carryforward	Not Applicable	Not Applicable
	Person gives a donation (cash) to a private foundation	Deductible up to 30% of Adjusted Gross Income (AGI) with a 5-year carryforward	Not Applicable	Not Applicable
	Person gives a donation (securities) to a private foundation	Deductible up to 20% of Adjusted Gross Income (AGI) with a 5-year carryforward	Not Applicable	Not Applicable
After Death	Decedent gives gift to someone else in their will (a bequest)	Not Applicable	Not Deductible	Not Deductible
	Decedent gives gift to a public charity in his will	Not Applicable	Possibly fully deductible—depends upon the proportion left as a residuary clause in the will	Fully Deductible—no restrictions
	Decedent gives gift to a private foundation in his will	Not Applicable	Possibly fully deductible–depends upon the proportion left as a residuary clause in the will	Fully Deductible–no restrictions

an overview of the various scenarios.) That means that it reduces your estate, which has the ultimate outcome of fewer assets and less taxes. So those individuals or families that are particularly charitably minded can receive a benefit—a tax benefit in death or while alive—by making donations to their favorite charities. The donations reduce the taxable estate and therefore the tax levied against the estate. "All well and good," Phil would say, "but our interests are more aligned on the charitable side—the actual giving—than the saving on taxes, although that does seem to be a nice additional benefit." Emmett knew his clients were more interested in setting up a plan to provide their children and grandchildren and even great-grandchildren with a duty or legacy for charitable mindfulness rather than schemes to reduce taxes on their estate—although the concept of maintaining more assets (paying less taxes) for these charitable efforts would not be lost on them.

Case Study—Estate Planning 101

Fact Pattern:

- Mr. and Mrs. Robert Jones, married for 55 years, 4 adult children, 10 grandchildren.
- Sold private business two years ago—net worth is greater than $16 million, $11 million of which is liquid investments.
- Considering changing their current basic "I Love You" will, which leaves all of their assets to each other and then to the children in order to reduce the likely estate taxes on their passing.
- Advocates of the importance of education for their children and grandchildren.
- Charitably minded—Juvenile Diabetes Research Foundation has been a favorite charity for many years (since their youngest was diagnosed at 15 years old).
- Objectives: A simple plan (nothing too complex) that reduces or at least minimizes the estate tax burden for the next generation, to augment charitable giving, and to provide heirs with a good education and about $10 million in assets (in total).

There are many ways to go here—from the elegant and complex estate plan to a simpler plan that might accomplish the same goals. (See Exhibit 1.2 for a simple flow chart of the various paths available.) Given the Joneses' interest in "keeping it simple" the following solutions are offered:

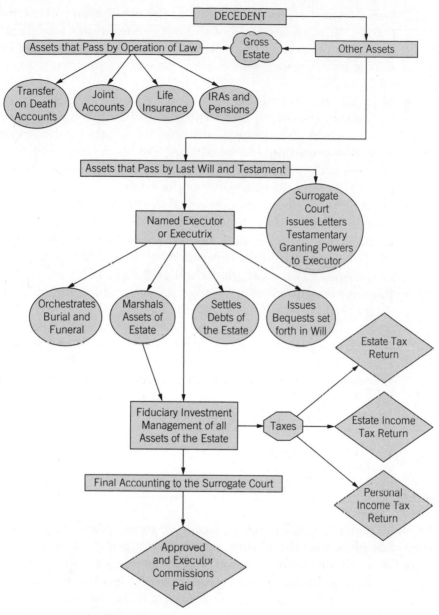

Exhibit 1.2   The Estate Flowchart

- Retitle assets so that each has at least $5 million of assets in their name. These accounts, again keeping it simple, can be designated as Transfer of Death (TOD) accounts for each of their children (this is a simple, cost-effective way to move assets from one party to another). These assets will be included in their estate, but due to the exemption will not be taxed (although the issue of the next generation's assets and their eventual estate tax is why one should consider a more detailed estate plan with trusts that can shelter assets from estate taxes).

- Maintain the remaining assets in a Joint with Rights of Survivorship account. Enter into an annual gifting program to each child and spouse (and possibly to other relatives or friends)—providing the maximum gift each year, which is gift tax exempt and reduces (or maintains, depending on the growth of the estate) the value of the estate.
- Make 529 contributions—five years' worth ($26,000 per grand-child times five years, times 10 grandkids equals $1,290,000 of assets out of their estate, assuming they live the five years). These assets remain fully controlled by Mr. and Mrs. Jones and are designated for each grandchild's education.
- Pay any educational expenses as they arise, which reduces the estate further—without any gift tax exemptions.
- Make charitable donations to Juvenile Diabetes Research Foundation (other charities) up to the maximum of 50 percent of AGI each year. These will be fully tax deductible on the income tax returns and will also reduce the value of the taxable estate.
- In the will, designate probate assets (that is the amounts above the TOD accounts and the joint account) to go to charity of the Joneses' choice. This bequest is fully tax-deductible to their estate's tax return.

Summary

In this chapter we learned the basics of estate planning with an emphasis placed on the gifting aspects in the estate planning process. Gifting has its immediate tax benefits to one's estate, but there are also the considerations of control and the level of flexibility a donor expects in his or her gifting program. In the next chapter we dive further into this gifting issue with a deeper examination of charitable giving—the vehicles available to achieve one's stated charitable gifting goals.

CHAPTER 2

Charitable Giving

Charity is a supreme virtue, and the greatest channel through which the mercy of God is passed on to mankind. It is the virtue that unites men and inspires their noblest efforts.

—Conrad Hilton, hotel titan and philanthropist

Emmett met Phil for lunch the next week, after Phil had the chance to review Em's preliminary report on the reasons one would or should consider charitable giving in the estate plan. But Em already knew that Phil had a grasp on estate planning and that he and Mary had seemingly forged an effort to become more charitable in their giving, but in a way that was not as simple as writing a check to their favorite charity.

"Well, what I am hearing from you is that you would like to embark on a project focused around philanthropy—to provide your kids and their kids with the lessons and tools to help others and to be grateful that they can do so," said Em.

"Spot on! You always did get me, Em—but I just don't want to give my capital away, I want to make it a long-lasting family project where we are all involved and the lessons of our value system are firmly front and center," said Phil.

"What might fit the bill is a private foundation," said Em. "But before we get there we should discuss the other options—simpler, less institutional, less costly ways to conduct this philanthropic exercise."

Emmett Pathy, financial adviser, went on to discuss in detail the different ways one can embrace charitable giving. Now that Em understood the reason for Phil's visit he was able to develop a report that indicated all of the various options available to Phil and Mary as they embarked on this journey in charitable giving. Although it seemed to Emmett that a private foundation would be the best option, he wanted to take Phil and Mary through all of the vehicles and tools available so that they were well briefed and could then make the best decision for their objectives.

Em's report started with the basic tool of charitable giving—simply making a donation, large or small—either now and/or in their wills—as a bequest to a charitable nonprofit organization. The report indicated that this is the most "efficient" way to make a charitable gift because it does not require much of anything besides the capital and knowing the nonprofit (or nonprofits) that they wanted to support. According to Giving USA,[1] individual contributions and bequests were estimated to be 83 percent of all charitable giving, to the tune of $216 billion. In 2005 individuals donated $200 billion of the $260 billion total received by not-for-profit organizations. This figure dwarfs foundation contributions that year (between $30 billion and $33 billion).

The direct gift, although elegant in its ease of use and efficiency, leaves the donor in a noncontrol position. There are many examples where the spirit of the gift, for whatever reason (new leadership at the nonprofit organization, economics of the time, or marketing opportunities), is replaced with a new mandate—one that may be fervently opposed by the original donors or their families—and there is nothing the donors or their families can do about it. One example of this is the high-profile fight that went on in 2000 between Marylou Whitney and the Whitney Museum. Mrs. Whitney, a daughter-in-law of the museum's founder and a director and a member of the museum's national fund-raising committee, together with other family members took issue with the use of Nazi iconography in a planned exhibit. The museum dismissed their concerns and went through with the exhibit. This is a good example that even having your name on the door doesn't grant you

---

[1]Giving USA, "Giving USA 2006," 2006.

the control of an endowment or a previously given large gift—you have lost control.

Although there are many other examples of this loss-of-control issue (Yale's return of a $20 million grant to Lee Bass because he wanted "too much control of the gift"; St. Luke's Roosevelt Hospital and the Smithers Alcoholism and Treatment Center; the Central Park Zoo and one of its "named benefactors"), the results are the same— once the gift is given, the control is lost.[2]

Em can only imagine what Phil and Mary would say to that. He knows that Phil is a control-oriented person and that Mary seems to be set on certain charitable interests—and that they would not take kindly to someone using their capital and doing with it what they pleased, especially if it is something that they are firmly opposed to. Em realized that although this is an important issue to understand and be familiar with, a direct gift and the loss of control that comes with it is not what Phil and Mary would want.

What Is a Nonprofit Entity?

That opened a discussion on nonprofits entities: What are they and how could the Anthonys know which ones are better than others?

First a definition: a nonprofit is a tax exempt entity under 501(c)(3) of the Internal Revenue Service (IRS) code. In order to receive that special notation under the code, an organization must complete certain tax filings. These are known as Form 990s, but there is more to them than a form—much more.

An organization that qualifies under Section 501(c)(3) of the IRS code—either as a public charity or a private foundation—must be organized exclusively under one of the eight exempt purposes and operate primarily for such purpose:

- Religious
- Charitable
- Scientific
- Testing for public safety
- Literary
- Educational

---

[2]Roger Silk and James Lintott, *Creating a Private Foundation* (New York: Bloomberg Press, 2003).

- Fostering of national or international amateur sports competition (as long as no part of its activities involves the provision of athletic facilities or equipment)
- Prevention of cruelty to children and animals

Private foundations can also make donations for scholarships and grants directly to individuals as hardship, emergency, or medical assistance but they need to meet certain IRS rules.[3]

It is important to ensure that the organization you are considering making a donation to—either as an individual or as a private foundation—is in full compliance with the IRS and its charitable agencies. If an organization is not a tax-exempt entity—and the rules requiring 990 filings have just been revamped and now require charities with donations of less than $25,000 annually to complete and file their required 990s in order to remain tax-exempt entities—then your donation is not tax-exempt. This, of course, can develop into a major to-do—think about the refiling of tax returns, not to mention the embarrassment factor for a private foundation. So beware budding philanthropists: do your homework and make sure the entity you are looking to support is indeed a 501(c)(3).

Due Diligence

Okay, so now we have found a charitable organization that not only appeals to the issues that we are concerned about—be it world hunger, medical research, or building libraries to teach and inspire children to learn to read—but it is also in full compliance with the regulatory bodies and has a 501(c)(3) status. What do we do next to make sure that we are dealing with a solid organization—where does our due diligence begin?

Conducting proper due diligence in any project is a critical first step—the jumping-off point. With private foundations, which are geared to support nonprofits, it is even more so. Remember (and never forget) that this capital is not "yours"—the foundation's board members are stewards of this capital (yes, even if you were the one that made the money and contributed it—once it is

---

[3]Foundation Source, *14 Terms Every Foundation Should Understand* (Fairfield, CT: Foundation Source Press, 2004).

Checking on Charities

The first piece of data you are looking for is to make sure that the nonprofit is registered as a 501(c)(3) organization.

Using the IRS Website

Go to www.irs.gov/app/pub-78/.

When you input a charity, a screen will come up. The code indicates the type of charitable organization and the deductibility afforded to contributions to this particular organization—essentially indicating that the nonprofit has 501(c)(3) status.

There are also other resources that permit the search and exploration of nonprofit organizations. GuideStar (www2.guidestar.org/) and Charity Navigator (www.charitynavigator.org/) are some of the best known resources on the Internet.

in a private foundation it is no longer yours—it now belongs to the "common good" as directed in the founding papers of the foundation). So from that standpoint, the due diligence process in determining and vetting nonprofits that are worthy of support takes on a greater sense of gravitas. Furthermore (and we should never forget this one either), a private foundation is not so "private" insomuch as the rest of the world (anyone with Internet access) can see what we are doing and what grants we are making—Big Brother is watching!

Em continued with this dialogue, drawing on his own personal experiences as a board member of a local private foundation. He felt that it was especially important to go deep into this issue of nonprofit due diligence, for if his clients were indeed going to embark on this new world of philanthropy, it would need to be a cornerstone of their future work. Emmett Pathy takes his work seriously and as a steward of his clients' hard-earned capital he has the ultimate responsibility to guide them—especially when entering new fields of interest. For Em, investment management is not just asset allocation or hot stock tips, but rather fully understanding and advising on his client's holistic objectives—from estate planning and their philanthropic interests to understanding them on an emotional and intergenerational level.

"Many board members, myself included, believe that this heightened awareness is a good thing and keeps the members of the private foundation sector on their toes," said Em. According to Hope Consulting, only 35 percent of donors (not only private foundations, but all donors) do any research before making a donation and only 10 percent use outside information sources to gather data on the nonprofit *before* making a donation.[4] This survey did have a bright point however; 85 percent of the people responding stated that knowing something about a charity's effectiveness was important—putting in the time and effort to find that data was apparently another story.

Due diligence is like detective work—it requires some digging and some thinking, and also casting a skeptical eye toward motives and expenses. There are no definitive rules with respect to proper due diligence in this area, but a few items are important to keep mindful of. In the nonprofit world, donors can often be lulled into a state of complacency, where all work seems to be "good work" and where some faults and inconsistencies are swept aside. Just because the nonprofit's staff is passionate for their cause does not mean they can be lackadaisical with respect to running the organization.

Furthermore, many times we see a wonderfully run nonprofit with expensive office digs (even if it is donated it may raise some eyebrows—think what the same donation in cash could do for the cause at hand) and hefty salaries. While this is the United States and certainly an economy that runs on capitalism, in the nonprofit world it is not business as usual. Heightened scrutiny and a vengeance for keeping expenses low—all expenses—are critical aspects of a well-run nonprofit. This does not mean that we are only looking for volunteers to run this nonprofit enterprise and that they must use technology that is three generations old, but a balance needs to be struck and a mindfulness of the ultimate beneficiaries of this capital must remain tantamount to its mission.

One of the things a donor can do to determine if a particular nonprofit entity is well respected and well managed is to search for other donors to the same nonprofit—specifically, foundation donors. "Program officers at foundations—private or corporate—tend to be very thorough and careful before making grants, so if the charity you are interested in supporting has received foundation

---

[4]Hope Consulting, "Money for Good," May 2011.

grants, it means someone has vetted it very thoroughly," says Eileen Heisman, CEO of the National Philanthropic Trust.

Digging Deeper

Em knew that Phil and Mary were taking this philanthropy role seriously and to that end they would indeed embark on the non-profit due diligence process with the verve and dedication that they are demonstrating in their journey into the philanthropic world. So he felt it was important to provide them with a bit more information and education on the red flags to watch out for with respect to evaluating nonprofits, as well as some helpful hints along the way.

Financial issues are the first place we should start. Not that they are the only things we need to study and evaluate, but knowing where the cash comes from and where it goes is a critical part of the evaluation of any enterprise—perhaps even moreso in a nonprofit (where the importance of the mission can sometimes obscure financial issues). The materials that we are going to want to study in this regard are the nonprofit's federal filing (990s) as well as their financial statements. The 990 forms required by the IRS provide a snapshot of the charity's assets, liabilities, revenues, and expenses. They are not the easiest to decipher (stacked in the typical federal filing notation), but they are the primary piece of data that we require when making our judgment of a nonprofit. The additional piece of financial documentation that we need is the nonprofit's annual financial statement, which lays out assets, liabilities, and the amount spent on fund raising and programs related to the nonprofit's mission—essentially the same information as the 990 but in a more typical accounting format. This data should be easy to get from the nonprofit (they should be expecting you to ask for it and is often found on its website), and there are also independent web sites—the IRS site, GuideStar, and Charity Navigator, just to a name a few—that provide this info as well as a bunch more helpful data.

What are we looking for in these financial documents? Well, there are several red flags that we hope not to see—things like losses, low or no reserves, or high operating expenses. Now, like anything, many of these red flags may need further exploration—that is, they cannot be taken fully on the surface, for oftentimes the data may be misleading. For example, looking strictly at the financial forms one would take notice of a charitable organization where only about 44 percent of its funding goes toward the programs the nonprofit is set up to support—earning it a failing grade by an outside rating service. But on further due diligence the "philanthropic detective" (and surely the nonprofit would point this out as well) learns that this nonprofit acts like a clearinghouse or a hub for other affiliate organizations. It is on these affiliate organization's financial forms where the majority of the funding (from the larger nonprofit) is accounted and detailed. Therefore, it is not prudent to rely solely on the financial forms—often we need to dig further and deeper.

Other flags to be on the lookout for include an overemphasis placed on fundraising and marketing. Fundraising is an important part of the nonprofit organization but the nonprofit's board needs to make sure that it doesn't lose its focus—that is, the programs, people, and issues that are the focus of their mission. There can also be some trickery in trying to hide these figures—for example, a nonprofit can slap on a paragraph or two about its mission onto an "educational flyer" and call the expense involved "program funding" rather than what is "fundraising," and in doing so show more capital going toward programs than there really is ("program inflation").[5]

Also, a basic businessperson's assessment of the figures is an important part of the puzzle. Are there losses? Why? What is the status with respect to reserves? Finally we need to be mindful of the source of the funding—Is it from a government grant? What's the term? Is a majority of the funding coming from one source or is it widely dispersed? These are important considerations with respect to the sustainability of the nonprofit—after all we would not want to invest (and in the end of the day that is really what we are doing—investing in a charitable enterprise) in a losing venture—a sinking ship.

The next study area in this due diligence process is management—that is, the board of directors of the nonprofit. What we are most concerned about here are any conflicts of interest that might exist between the members of the board and the charity. Perhaps the charity is in a building that is owned by a member of the board. What

---

[5]Mary Pilon, "How to Donate Like a Pro," *Wall Street Journal*, December 4, 2010.

happens if the board member leaves the board or decides to sell the building? The charity can find itself out on the street, so to speak, or at the least, sidetracked with finding new digs, most likely at an increased cost (unless the charity was paying an above market rent to the board member—a serious breach of fiduciary responsibility).

Governance in the board of directors "suite" is also of major importance. How are the rules addressed with respect to decision making? Do some directors hold a greater vote or sway over the board than others? Is the board itself made up of independent thinkers who are knowledgeable about the mission of the nonprofit, or are they simple "yes men" for the lead director? How about the policies with respect to expenses and travel? It is important from where we sit—as funders of this nonprofit—that the board doesn't function as if the assets of the nonprofit are their de facto piggy bank. There need to be checks and balances in place—more so in smaller nonprofits than larger, more institutionalized ones—to ensure that the assets (and reputation) of the nonprofit are protected.

There is also the issue of successorship that needs to be addressed. What happens when the leader of the nonprofit, someone who built it and ran it for decades, retires? Does the nonprofit have a "deep bench" to permit a new set of leaders to step in and run the organization seamlessly? It is an important part of the sustainability issue that many funders battle with—being mindful of the long term and making sure that today's grants are not lost in the future. Philanthropists think not in years but in decades, if not longer, so sustainability of the mission becomes an important issue to address.

During the due diligence process we have looked at the finances and the management of the nonprofit—what's next? Well, asked a different way—what first attracted you to this particular nonprofit (most of the time it has to do with their stated mission)? The nonprofit's focus is typically what first attracts others to it. It might be battling a disease that you have a personal connection to or a particular social issue that you are passionate about. Either way, the mission of the nonprofit is a strong lightning rod for the professional funder and the occasional check writer alike. That said, how can we evaluate the nonprofit on this, its ultimate objective? The finances might look fantastic and the board top-notch and beyond reproach, but how can we know if the mission is being accomplished? What qualitative metrics can we employ to discern this all-important fact?

Going grassroots and getting personally involved in the non-profit by volunteering can serve the philanthropist well. By seeing firsthand what the organization does and how it does it, you can not only get a sense of its level of efficiency but also gain an important perspective on its most pressing needs. Getting a sense of any "mission drift" that might be under foot is an important data-point that often is undetected before it becomes too apparent—and too late (often times a large grant can change the focus of the nonprofit— for whatever reason—while the funding base has no idea it is occurring). By speaking with the beneficiaries of the nonprofit, be it the homeless that are trying to restart their lives or the kids who want to learn how to read, we can gain a powerful front-row seat to the work of the nonprofit. One philanthropist I know, whose family members are all involved in the foundation he started, requires each board member of the foundation to volunteer at a nonprofit of his or her choosing each year and report back to the board what he or she has learned. In many cases, he tells me, this has been an impetus to some of the board's best and long-lasting grants.

Okay, so now we have a sense of what to look for in a nonprofit and how to look for it (although we will explore this issue in greater detail in the private foundation chapter, where its attention is of an even greater import). Getting back to the giving side of the equation,

---

A Tool to Use When Evaluating a Nonprofit

Em wanted to condense the concepts of due diligence into an easy-to-remember (especially in light of the younger generations that he knew Phil and Mary wanted to teach and motivate) mnemonic device. In juggling around the main points he arrived at a cute little tool—"BIG$"—that not only allows recall of the important pieces of the due diligence process, but also the gravity of the capital involved, and hence the importance of the due diligence process in the first place.

B = Board evaluation: management, governance, conflicts-of-interest, successor-ship.
I = IRS status: 501(c)(3), full compliance.
G = Grassroots: volunteering at the nonprofit to gain insights in their successes and issues.
$ = Financial: 990s, financial statements, losses, reserves, donation base diversification.

it would seem that the downside of the outright donation is that it is not "institutionalized," that is, not a family affair. Even if the whole family gathered and decided on the nonprofit to support, it would still be Phil's and Mary's decision—the rest of the family would not have a true vested interest. And what happens after Phil and Mary are gone? The will can state the donations they want to make, but what then of the legacy that they wanted to create for the kids and grandkids? An outright gift, even a substantial one, would not serve as a constant teaching tool to further propagate the morals and values that Phil and Mary wanted to instill in their kids and grandkids.

Donor Advised Funds (DAFs)

Em's report went further in this vein, searching for a solution that would serve the Anthony's "legacy interest." It started to discuss the advantages of a Donor Advised Fund (DAF). DAFs have become more popular in the past few years. A DAF is an irrevocable gift to a public charity (the fund) and is set up in the name of the donor—so in this case, for example, it might be the "Phil and Mary Anthony Family Fund." The fund is run through another organization (often an investment firm or a nonprofit entity hoping to capture a donation—although it is not required) that serves as the "back office" for these donations.

In a DAF, the grantor receives a tax deduction in the year the donation is made (typical carry forward applies) and has as long as he or she likes to dole out the capital to acceptable nonprofits. Here is where one of the advantages of DAFs versus private foundations comes in: the adjusted gross income (AGI) limitations are equal to those of any gift to a public charity and therefore are more favorable than that of a contribution to a private foundation. This favorability is not only with the AGI limitations but also with respect to the acceptance of appreciated property other than publicly traded stock (donations of securities are limited to 30 percent of AGI, more than the 20 percent they are in private foundations). The DAF—and often these entities are named "Foundations," which can be confusing—seems like an easy way (with substantially less paperwork and costs) to act as a private foundation.

Prior to the Pension Protection Act (PPA) of 2006 (signed into law by President George W. Bush on August 17, 2006) there did not exist a legal definition of a DAF. As a matter of fact, the term cannot be found in any federal legislation until the Katrina Relief Act of 2005, where it was mentioned as a type of gift that did not qualify for the accelerated 100 percent of AGI deduction. Consequently, there had been episodes of misconduct with respect to the use of DAFs—schemes whereby promoters would offer donors the opportunity to shelter capital and give it away (with the tax deductions as well) to scholarships and "charities" that donors indeed benefited from ("economic benefits"). It was in large measure due to these issues that the IRS defined DAFs as part of the PPA of 2006.

DAFs are defined as a fund or account:

- That is separately identified through reference to the contributions of a donor or donors by including their names in the fund.
- That is owned and controlled by a sponsoring organization.
- In which the donor or person appointed by the donor has or reasonably expects to have advisory rights with respect to investments or distributions.

Penalties for noncompliance with the above definition and rules (and, of course, the all-important "spirit of the law") are substantial: "a penalty of 125 percent of the value of the economic benefit, other than an incidental benefit, to a donor, adviser, or related parties can be levied on the person recommending the grant (the fund adviser) or the person who received the benefit. And fund managers are subject to a 10 percent penalty of the value of the economic benefit if the manager knew the distribution would result in such a benefit. Unlike other penalty taxes, these penalties are not paid to the charitable organization; instead, the taxes are payable to the United States Treasury."[6]

So, basically, DAFs are a way to increase a taxable deduction and reduce the required paperwork and regulations compared to contributions to private foundations. It is to this end that a debate has been waging in philanthropic circles about the potential problems that can occur with DAFs versus private foundations. It comes

---

[6]Laura Hansen Dean, JD, "Donor Advised Funds: New Provisions in Pension Protection Act of 2006," September 12, 2006.

down to control: who has it with respect to the ultimate grant to a qualified nonprofit? Does the DAF, in its attempt to satisfy the interests of its client (the donor), honor the donor's requests of nonprofit entities? If so, then one can see (and the IRS has been studying this exact issue for the past few years) how the donor circumvented the rules regulating private foundations and still, seemingly, maintains control. Congress made it quite clear in the Tax Reform Act (TRA) of 1969 that it considered control over a private foundation to be a privilege, and in exchange for that privilege, foundations had to adhere to a complex set of requirements and limitations.[7]

Many DAF providers have made it clear—at least on paper—that they, not the donor, control the capital in the fund and its eventual path toward 501(c)(3) nonprofit organizations. But one has to wonder if that is fully accurate; there are clear conflicts of interest involved in this arrangement. After all, why would the donor donate his assets—irrevocably—to DAF if it was not going to permit his navigation of the donation to the charity of his choice? The question that the IRS is tackling is: How often do DAFs actually agree to the donation requests made by their clients? That data point leads to further investigation of the question—Who really controls the choice of nonprofit donations from a DAF?

The answer to that question could have important ramifications for the donor to a DAF. If the IRS were to determine that donor advised funds were not a public charity, donors would lose deductions and owe interest and penalties. Furthermore, the fund itself could be subject to penalties, which would further reduce the assets to the donor. Obviously this is not a good outcome for the charitably minded donor.

The History of Donor Advised Funds

The first DAF was established by a local community foundation in Winston-Salem, North Carolina, in 1931. However, its history can actually be traced back further, as an outgrowth of the first community foundation, established in Cleveland, Ohio, in 1914. Either way, one can agree that DAFs have been an important part

---

[7]Roger D. Silk and James W. Lintott, *Creating a Private Foundation: The Essential Guide for Donors and Their Advisors* (Princeton, NJ: Bloomberg Press, 2003).

of the philanthropist's toolkit for nearly a century. DAFs received a turbo boost to their growth in the 1990s when for-profit financial investment firms began to establish affiliated nonprofit organizations to maintain DAF accounts. Typically, these commercial DAFs hire an affiliated for-profit investment firm to manage the investment of the assets in the accounts for a fee that varies based on the balance in the account and the number of annual transactions.

There were two major court decisions that shaped the DAF landscape during this period. In *National Foundation, Inc. v. United States* (1987), the court held that "an organization that raised and distributed funds to other charities and administered a wide variety of charitable projects, mostly recommended by its donors, qualified for exemption under Section 501(c)(3). The court found that National Foundation Inc. (NFI) would refuse to administer a project if it did not meet five stringent standards: (1) that it be consistent with the charitable purposes specified in Section 501(c)(3); (2) that it have a reasonable budget; (3) that it be adequately funded; (4) that it be staffed with competent and well trained professionals; and (5) that it be capable of effective monitoring and supervision by NFI. The court also found that donors had relinquished all ownership and control over the donated funds or property to NFI and that NFI exercised its discretion in authorizing charitable distributions of the funds."[8]

The other case (*New Dynamics Foundation v. United States*, 2006) offers a stark contrast to the actions and policies of NFI in the above case. New Dynamics (NDF) did not qualify for exemption because it permitted donors to use the funds to serve private interest (e.g., to allow the donor to attend retreats, conferences, or seminars; to research investment opportunities; to save for retirement; to provide scholarships for family members; to pay donors' children for performing charitable work). The court found that NDF was designed to "warehouse wealth," that is, to allow donors to "contribute" property and cash to their foundations, control the investment decisions of those resources, and then, allegedly, to have the income and corpus grow tax-free.[9]

---

[8]"Donor Advised Funds Guide Sheet Explanation," IRS, July 31, 2008.
[9]Ibid.

So much happened between those two court rulings and many skeptics would suggest that the commercialization of DAFs caused, in some way, a good thing to lose its way a bit. Of course, the good thing is the "democratization of giving" that DAFs had brought to the forefront. Prior to the growth and market acceptance of DAFs, individuals interested in charitable giving—even a modest amount—would be without a simple, formatted product offering to assist them in this giving exercise. Private foundations were seen, and rightly so, as a tool of the wealthy (though less so now, this stigma is still very much a part of private foundations due in large measure to their costs and ongoing administration issues) and not a part of the average giver's lexicon. Did DAFs go too far in their marketing efforts? Does it make sense to be able to contribute capital to a DAF, receive an upfront tax deduction as if you gave it to a public charity, and have as much time as you like to direct ("advise") grants to charities of your choice? It seems like the marketing machine got a little ahead of itself, although many would agree much good probably came from the vast majority of these contributions to DAFs—and still does.

A DAF makes philanthropic giving easy—one simply asks the fund to distribute a portion of its fund to any approved nonprofit (and the DAF often has databases that list nonprofits to ensure complete compliance of the IRS code). Em could imagine the Anthonys gathered around their dining room table a few times a year—with all of their kids and grandkids—to decide, together (although that might be a difficult consensus to come to) how the fund should be distributed. What causes are better than others? Which organizations seem better suited given their reach and depth than others that might be more grassroots organized? Or maybe the grassroots organizations, given that they are operating with volunteers, could use the donation more? These are the same types of questions that will be discussed at any philanthropic group's grant-making meeting—the difference here is that it is not cut in stone; that is, it might change from period to period as the grantor's interests change. Furthermore, there are no assurances that the DAF will accept the family's wishes with respect to which charities to fund at any given time. It comes down to a loss of control—something that is not likely to sit well with Phil and Mary.

With a DAF, unlike with an outright gift, the Anthonys can attain the legacy issue that has been such a critical component to this project. DAFs permit successor trustees to run the advisory side of the DAF, and as such a DAF is considered perpetual if this is the intention of the donors. After Phil and Mary are gone, the next generation can maintain the grant advice function, and to that end, the lessons of philanthropy and giving back continue. The DAF may suggest that Phil and Mary make distributions from their fund to smaller funds in the names of the children and grandchildren. In this way, family members will have their "own" fund to distribute as they see fit (which many grantors might see as a negative, for these future donations do not have to meet the requirements and areas of interest with which they initiated the fund years prior). Again, the trade-off here is one of simplicity and ease for loss of control. With a private foundation, the donor can shape and define the mission and the policies with respect to grants that are to be followed for generations to come. Bottom line: One can create a legacy of giving and leave a mark for future family members.

Another major downside of DAFs is their lack of investment flexibility. Investment inflexibility is a major issue for many active investors who prefer to invest their capital—and have, in many cases, decades worth of experience in doing so. For seasoned investors to give up the reins with respect to this potentially large pool of capital is no easy task—they are used to having control of their portfolios, and giving that up is not an easy thing for them to do. Most DAFs offer a series of homegrown funds as the vehicles to which this capital will be invested. Often these funds carry fees ranging from 0.50 percent to 1.1 percent, not including any possible sales charges to financial advisers. Although these fees are not overly egregious by any measure, the issue again is loss of control; seasoned investors, especially those who have large pools of capital at their disposal, are interested in maintaining control with respect to investments.

The bottom line with DAFs, as Em's report states, is that they are good in many instances when a donor wants a simplified philanthropic vehicle where he or she can request a donation be sent from the fund at any time (although, as stated above, these requests do not have to be adhered to by the DAF). The tax deduction advantage over a private foundation is certainly significant, but the loss of control, legacy issues, and investment inflexibility all make the DAF option not optimal for what the Anthonys are trying to accomplish.

Community Foundations

Similar to a DAF—but on a more localized level—is the community foundation. Community foundations, which have their roots in the early part of the twentieth century, serve as an excellent tool for those who are philanthropically minded with a local bent. Do you remember the board game Monopoly? The Community Chest? Well that is what a community foundation is: a charitable pool of assets focused on making donations, on the behalf of the donors, to local causes or charitable projects. Of course, as we have learned earlier, all giving must be made to a 501(c)(3) organization to be in compliance with the tax laws. So donations cannot be made through a community foundation for a new car for the town's mayor—although they might be used, depending on restrictions, to further local government through a 501(c)(3) arm that is often set up by local governments.

The first community foundation was established in Cleveland, Ohio, in 1914, and within five years, community foundations were being formed in many other cities around the country.[10] In the years that followed, as these and other community foundations were established and grew, a myriad of Americans from all economic backgrounds cast their vote—be it in the form of time, money, or both—along the side of the local community foundation to help meet the needs of their local communities. It reminds one of the early days of the new world, where colonists established their own local schools and churches and supported these institutions and the works that they did in the community—not with government subsidies, but rather with independent giving.

Community foundations went on a growth spurt after the adoption of the TRA of 1969, which increased the regulations on private foundations and consequently made community foundations a favored vehicle for many philanthropists focused on local issues. The TRA of 1969 permitted lifetime gifts of certain types of appreciated securities to receive full tax deductibility (at fair market value) when granted to a community foundation, but not to a private foundation. In addition, the annual limit for deductions is higher for gifts given to a community foundation than to a private foundation. There is also the fact that a private foundation must

---

[10]http://communityfoundations.net.

pay an excise tax on its assets, reducing the appeal of such vehicles versus a community foundation, which does not have any such tax requirements.

A community foundation accepts two types of donations: restricted and unrestricted. In a restricted donation, the grantor has placed a limitation on what type of charitable nonprofit organization can receive a grant from his or her pool of capital held at the community foundation. In this case, philanthropically minded local businesspeople might start a "fund" with the local community foundation to support educational efforts in their community or environmentally friendly initiatives in the community. It then becomes the onus of the community foundation to ferret through the maze of causes and nonprofits in their local community working on these issues and to help the donor arrive at a good, effective course of action within their areas of interest. Often the community foundation will embark on an expansive (and expensive) study on a particular issue to arrive at the best course of action. This is part and parcel to the benefit of working with a community foundation; the foundation knows the local issues and can offer the best, most effective solutions for the donor's capital.

Community foundations can also make unrestricted grants from donors who do not place restrictions on the use of their funds. This is the lifeblood of the community foundation's work because here it can really make a difference in a community by supporting some of the most needed but less understood or less "sexy" issues. The professionals who work indefatigably at local community foundations really know their stuff—they have committed countless hours to understanding the major issues affecting their communities and are an excellent resource for the charitably inclined. It is often recommended that local philanthropists, those managing their own private foundations, become active in their local community foundations, for it is an excellent way to better understand not only the important local issues but the institutional techniques and policies with respect to grant administration and nonprofit due diligence.

Clearly there is a place in the philanthropic world for community foundations—often an excellent vehicle for the charitably inclined individual or family that is unsure of the needs of a particular community (even if they live in that community, often these "critical needs issues" go unnoticed and identifying these is one of the greatest values of community foundations) as well as more engaged philanthropists who grant a pool of capital to a community foundation due in large measure to their efficiency and expertise in a local community.

Community foundations are not free. The fees charged to the pools of capital they receive are levied along a sliding scale depending on asset size. Taking a $1 million account, for example, the average community foundation fees range from as low as 0.64 percent to as high as 2 percent with averages between 1.06 percent and 1.43 percent.[11] These fees include administrative as well as investment management costs and, as we will see, are fairly in line with costs for these functions in a private foundation. Again it comes down to control—control of grants as well as the management of the investments.

■ ■ ■

Emmett Pathy went through the above report, highlighting the issues and differences between DAFs, community foundations, and private foundations for his clients, Phil and Mary Anthony. "As I said," Em continued, "the major issue comes down to control, and knowing that you guys do not want to be simple givers, but rather active participants in your philanthropic giving, it would seem that a private foundation is the way to go." Phil and Mary agreed with Em's analysis, suggesting that, "We will begin to explore the issues involved in establishing and managing a private foundation in my next report." Phil added, "I would like to become more active in my local community foundation, it seems like an excellent way to gain a better understanding of philanthropy, nonprofits, and the most pressing local issues." "Music to my ears," said Em, who sits on the board of a local community foundation. "There is no better way to gain a strong foothold in this new area of philanthropy than to join the advisory board of a local community foundation." The Anthonys and their trusted financial adviser, Em Pathy, agreed to explore in earnest the establishment of a private foundation as well as participation in their local community foundation, of which they may consider establishing a fund as a small offshoot from the

---

[11]Foundation Source, "Private Foundations, Community Foundations & Donor Advised Funds: A Comparison," 2011.

foundation. They asked Emmett to continue his work in this regard and to report back to them, as he had done thus far, on the considerations and issues of initiating a private foundation.

Summary

In this chapter we explored the different vehicles used to effectuate giving as part of one's estate plan. As illustrated, there are simple approaches—those that require a perfunctory contribution and little more—and there are solutions that require a more active involvement. It is in this latter camp that we find Em Pathy's clients, for they want to be active participants in their giving rather than simple check writers. It is to this end that the concept of a private foundation arises. In the next chapter we further explore the process by which one starts a private foundation, and the issues involved.

3

Starting a Private Foundation

True happiness is not attained through self-gratification, but through fidelity to a worthy purpose.

—Helen Keller, author, political activist, and lecturer

It is easier to make $1 million honestly than to give it away wisely.

—Julius Rosenwald, the Rosenwald Foundation

What is a private foundation anyway? I mean I know it is not very private—I was able to look up my friend's foundation online and actually learned what charities they made grants to and even the salaries of the officers and staff," asked Phil. "But what is it really—and which set of rules and regulations govern private foundations?"

"Well," said Em, "that is exactly the next step in our journey—to learn about private foundations for I do believe a private foundation is the best vehicle to accomplish your philanthropic goals."

Em continued in this vein in his written report. F. Emerson Andrews, in his seminal work on private foundations (*Philanthropic Foundations*) developed the definition that the philanthropic industry still uses today:

A foundation is a nongovernmental, nonprofit organization with its own funds (usually from a single source, either an individual, family, or corporation) and program managed by its own trustees and directors, which was established to maintain or aid educational, social, charitable, religious, or other activities serving the common welfare, primarily by making grants to other nonprofit organizations.[1]

Essentially, a private foundation enjoys the tax-exempt status of other nonprofit entities—like charities—but is controlled by a board of directors or trustees who can exact the foundation's mission statement in various ways. It is this control and flexibility that differentiates the private foundation from other philanthropic vehicles.

There are several labels a private foundation can go by—fund, endowment, or trust, and sometimes just "Inc.,"—which can often add to the confusion and mystique around it. There are also different ways to set them up (via a trust or a corporation) and a host of different types—from corporate to private—but in the end, private foundations all share the major attributes of control and flexibility in their charitable giving.

The History of Private Foundations

No one in the private foundation field would dispute that the first private foundation was set up by none other than Plato. On his death in 347 B.C., he left income from his estate for the perpetual support of his academy. Even though control passed from heir to heir, the academy continued its work, as designated by its founder and through the use of his largess, until the Roman emperor Justinian terminated it for spreading pagan teachings in A.D. 529. A nice run under any circumstances (nearly 900 years!); amazing when considering the time period.

Probably the first private foundation in the United States was that of our statesman/Founding Father, Benjamin Franklin. Franklin left 1,000 pounds of silver to the cities of Boston and Philadelphia upon his death in the late eighteenth century, but in such a way that only adds to the brilliance and prescience of this great man. Franklin directed that some of the earnings should be used as loans to young married couples, but that the principal and interest should

---

[1]David Freeman and The Council on Foundations, *The Handbook on Private Foundations* (New York: The Foundation Center, 2005).

compound (he obviously understood—like another genius to follow him, Albert Einstein—the power of compound interest, as "the
most powerful force in the universe") and its initial use should be
100 years after his death. Thus the endowment permitted the establishment of important institutions of learning such as the Franklin
Institute of Philadelphia and the Franklin Institute of Boston, and its
remainder continues to grow today.

The next major figure in U.S. philanthropy is probably best
known in London, England, where his Peabody Donation Fund,
established in 1862, built model dwellings for impoverished work-
ers. Although Peabody's name is affixed to Baltimore's famous con-
servatory and museums in New England, he is much less well-known
than other U.S. philanthropists who came a generation or two after
him. Peabody's lifetime giving totaled about $10 million, clearly
diminutive when compared to the amounts of later donors, but his
education fund made its own stand in U.S. philanthropy.

The Peabody Education Fund, started in 1867, created the first
foundation in the United States fully engaged in addressing major
national policy issues.[2] The issue at the time—one that was near
and dear to Peabody's heart—was his hope for a national reconciliation after the Civil War, as well as his lifelong ardor for education. Peabody's modus operandi, if you will, the fund's "competitive
advantage" was its adoption from its inception of a strong board.
The fund attracted such American luminaries as Presidents Ulysses
S. Grant, Rutherford B. Hayes, Theodore Roosevelt, and Grover
Cleveland; as well as several members of the Supreme Court, and
governors, wealthy businessmen, financiers (J.P. Morgan was a
board member), and prominent educators and clergymen. I guess
you could call the Peabody Fund the first network for the affluent
and wise, and perhaps it was this "first mover advantage" that gave
the fund a mystique and attracted top-notch men to join.

No matter if it was indeed this mystique of membership or
the stated vision of George Peabody himself, the fact remains it
worked—ultimately the foundation thrived for 47 years, closing its
doors in 1914. During the Peabody Fund's last few decades, however,
the United States was undergoing a level of fantastic change. With the

---

[2]James Allen Smith, *Foundation Fundamentals* (New York: The Foundation
Center, 2008).

Industrial Revolution and the advent of small communities becoming an integral part of a larger landscape, through railways and the telegraph, the government responsibilities and burdens on all levels also began to change. This sea change forced the public charitable organizations—foundations—to also change, to become more efficient, more professional, and in the end, more scientific in their approaches to social and economic problems. It is during this period that the "American Foundation" as we now know it began its work. The large foundations established in the first two decades of the twentieth century—Russell Sage (1907), Carnegie (1911), Rockefeller (1913), Rosenwald (1917), and Commonwealth (1918)—shared the vision of making philanthropy more efficient and scientific.[3]

However, in seeking a more efficient protocol for their philanthropic giving, these wealthy donors often made the job of their successor trustees very difficult. Under the heading of making written guidelines too strict, we have the stories of Stephen Girard and Bryan Mullanphy.

Stephen Girard endowed a Philadelphian orphanage in 1832. His intentions were simple and perhaps even genuine, but he did not think in terms of decades and having an impact well into the future. Girard specified that the orphanage was to only accept "white boys from the age 6 to 10 who could produce birth certificates as well as parents' marriage certificates (to prove they were not illegitimate)."[4] First off, these exclusionary instructions left out girls, nonwhites, children of single mothers, and older children, but leaving that aside for a moment we can see the impact of Girard's restrictive instructions when looking through the lens of history. Orphanages themselves became antiquated as they were replaced with foster care and adoption, so Girard's institution became less and less relevant, making it harder and harder to fill the 300 beds in the orphanage. It took a decision by the U.S. Supreme Court in 1968 (138 years after the orphanage's founding by Girard) to strike the exclusionary language from the original document in order to permit Girard College (as it was later called) to continue (some would say start) its mission of helping less fortunate children.

---

[3]Smith, *Foundation Fundamentals.*
[4]Roger Silk and James Lintott, *Creating a Private Foundation* (Princeton, NJ: Bloomberg Press, 2003).

We can debate the reasoning behind the changes made to the original document, with some saying that it was Girard's wishes to exclude those he did and therefore changes to this mandate should not be allowed. Others, ourselves included, feel that the perpetuity nature of foundations dictates a dynamism that warrants interpretations in order to stick with the spirit of the donor. In this case, Girard could not have foreseen the changes in society that rendered his original instructions futile in his attempt to solve a societal problem.

In the case of Bryan Mullanphy, we can also see how it is impossible to know the future and how changes in society and technology can render one's intentions today useless tomorrow. Mullanphy was mayor of St. Louis in the late 1840s and as a lifelong resident of St. Louis, was familiar with its history. In the early 1800s, many travelers heading west in covered wagons became stranded in Missouri due to lack of funds. Unable to return home or continue west, many of these families were in an awful predicament. In 1850 Mullanphy started a foundation with the stated purpose to "provide help and assistance to worthy travelers in covered wagons on their journey west";[5] in his eyes this was a great way to continue America's expansion westward as well as to help stranded families that he was sure to have witnessed growing up in St. Louis. The problem, of course, was that advances in technology rendered covered wagons obsolete soon after the establishment of this endowment, which made it difficult for Mullanphy's trustees to carry out his stated mission. Eventually, at no small cost, Mullanphy's will was challenged and the court finally ruled that the funds could be spent on all types of travelers in St. Louis.

The above cases illustrate the importance of not making one's foundation documents too restrictive. It is important to maintain a longer term view of your stated mission so that those who are left to run the foundation after you are gone have considerable flexibility to maintain the spirit of what you have intended. However, this cuts both ways—you don't want to leave too much to the imagination of the trustees. Clearly there is a balance that needs to be struck between providing too much in the way of instructions and mandates and leaving nearly none.

_____

[5]Silk and Lintott, *Creating a Private Foundation.*

Leaving a Stated Mandate for Future Generations

Without stated instructions, trustees and directors of a foundation are left to interpret the donor's charitable intentions and develop a mission statement accordingly. That often is not so much of a reach given that most donors have an established track record of charitable giving during their lifetimes. It's these track records that provide a blueprint for the trustees and directors to follow. However, as we will see, there have been occasions where donors have not left clear instructions or a stated track record of charitable giving to impute one's intentions, rendering the foundation to a difficult position.

One of the most famous of these lackadaisical mandates was John D. Rockefeller Sr.'s instruction (if you could call it that) to serve "the well-being of mankind." Fortunately, in this case, Rockefeller's trustees and successors had a fairly well-defined track record to refer to in order to develop a mandate for the foundation's charitable giving. The trustees left to decipher the intentions of John D. MacArthur and Henry Ford did not have it so easy. MacArthur and Ford both left little in the way of instructions with respect to their charitable intentions or a stated track record that could be referred to for guidance. As a result, their foundations have been accused of funding programs that are actually antithetical to their founders' interests and desires.[6]

MacArthur's successors and trustees had only one line of guidance from their founder: "I made the money, you guys figure out what to do with it." Given that he did not have a charitable track record during his lifetime, these trustees were presented with a difficult task. The MacArthur Foundation's "genius grants" are unrestricted grants with no required reporting and are awarded to "creative individuals regardless of field of endeavor." Many advocates of strict donor intent have complained that these grants—and the selection of the grantees—would only serve to embarrass John D. MacArthur. Others, like MacArthur's son Roderick, are pleased with the foundation's freedom to pursue its own vision.

> This (the private foundation) is the only institution in our society that does not have constituencies that it has to keep looking to. All others have to worry about pleasing a lot of people, so they are

---

[6]Silk and Lintott, *Creating a Private Foundation.*

bound to tend toward conventional wisdom, respectability, and the lowest common denominator. . . . Foundations should be striving to do the things that that the government cannot do. I repeat cannot do—things that are politically unpopular, things that are too risky, things that are just too far ahead of what the public will put up with. . . . A private foundation, where the board of directors is answerable only to itself, is in a completely different situation, and if it doesn't take advantage of that uniqueness, it's just blowing its opportunity, and perhaps even its moral obligation.[7]

Henry Ford initiated the Ford Foundation for estate tax reasons and to keep the Ford Motor Company in family hands after his death, and to that end he never regarded the foundation in a positive light. He did not provide any guidelines, and because he didn't have a charitable track record during his lifetime, the trustees had little to guide them. Conflicts between the foundation and family members ensued, with the latter stating that the foundation was demonstrating an anti-business bias through the projects it funded. All shares of the Ford Motor company were sold by the foundation (once its largest shareholder) in the late 1970s and no Ford family member has sat on the foundation's board since then. Today, the company and the foundation have little, if any, connection. Although perhaps Henry Ford would not have cared two nickels about the Ford Foundation, many would argue that its work has far surpassed that of the Ford Motor Company when it comes to societal impact and serving the common good. It is sad that Ford's family is not involved in this wonderful charitable institution—sad for the foundation that could have benefited from a more involved donor family, and sad for the family who could have redeemed their patriarch's lack of charitable interest.

Em could hear Phil saying to himself, "This stuff is fascinating but where are the concrete data—the laws and regulations that actually shaped the foundation concept in America many years ago?" Em decided to get into the more modern history of the private foundation, especially those congressional investigations and ensuing laws that defined the modern private foundation.

---

[7]Silk and Lintott, *Creating a Private Foundation.*

Modern History of Private Foundations

The era of the modern private foundation came about—and was actually defined—as a consequence of the Tax Reform Act of 1969. Beginning with the the early days of the twentieth century, at the outset of the formation of the Rockefeller and Carnegie foundations, public and congressional scrutiny of foundations increased. The U.S. Commission on Industrial Relations of the U.S. Congress—known as the Walsh commission for its chairman—launched the first investigation of independent (the term private foundation was introduced in the Tax Reform Act of 1969) foundations in 1915, looking into charges that wealthy capitalists were using the foundation form to protect their economic power, but no major legislation or restrictions resulted. Two subsequent world wars and the Great Depression produced a relatively quiet period for foundations, as Congress focused on other issues.[8]

During the 1950s, a period of strong growth for the formation of new foundations and the growth of existing ones developed as a consequence of increasing wealth and a more attractive tax structure. Foundations began to be targeted by the U.S. Congress once again, this time in a series of investigations (the Cox Committee of 1952 and the Reece Committee of 1954) focused on the concern du jour: "Un-American activities" (What can be more American than giving back?). Fortunately, this silliness died down, as did this dark period in the U.S. Congress' history, without any major restrictive legislation.

In 1961, however, an open-ended investigation into foundations was initiated by Congressman Wright Patman, chairman of the Select Committee on Small Business. This investigation, coupled with the U.S. Treasury Department's study on foundations, led to a new legal and regulatory framework for foundations in the Tax Reform Act of 1969. This act created the private foundation designation and included company-sponsored foundations and the rules governing them. It set forth special rules that (among other things):

- Prohibit certain transactions between foundations and "disqualified persons," including their donors and managers, as "self-dealing."
- Restrict foundation ownership and control of private businesses.

---

[8]Smith, *Foundation Fundamentals*.

- Limit the percentage of an individual's annual income that can be donated to a private foundation as a tax-deductible contribution.
- Regulate foundation giving to individuals, other foundations, and nonexempt organizations.
- Ban grants or other activities to influence legislation or support political campaigns.[9]

During the 1980s, the Reagan administration, while making substantive cuts in areas like arts, education, housing, childcare, and health care, turned to the foundation sector to step-up its efforts to close the gap in these areas. It was this push toward volunteerism that was a hallmark of the administration—and its policies reflected the administration's view of smaller government especially in areas like the National Endowment for the Arts. Fortunately, the foundation sector stepped in, and in a big way. They were helped during this period by favorable tax policies (between 1981 and 1986, charitable gifts were deductible even if you did not itemize your deductions) that further increased their reach (the upper middle class were becoming more intrigued with the notion of a private foundation—it was not just for the über-wealthy any longer). Also, there were favorable operational changes—foundations were no longer subjected to the complexities regarding administrative costs, the change in required payout, and the option to reduce the excise tax to 1 percent.

"What a fantastic report! I really enjoyed learning more about the history and background of some of the most well-known private foundations," exclaimed Mary Anthony at Em's office.

"Yes it was interesting, I am as excited as ever to get started on this new venture! What are the next steps?" asked Phil.

"Well now that you are familiar with the some of the basics of a private foundation we can get into the actual mechanics of starting a private foundation—the how-to, if you will," said Em.

"Great let's do it," chimed both Mary and Phil.

So Emmett Pathy, financial adviser (and so much more), went back to work and developed a report for the Anthonys' consideration that went through the steps in creating a private foundation.

---

[9]Smith, *Foundation Fundamentals*.

Creating a Private Foundation

The first thing that needs to be addressed is determining if the foundation will be set up as a trust or as a corporation. No matter the choice—and each has its own set of nuances—a foundation is treated the same for tax purposes.

When setting up in a trust format, you do have more limitations than in a nonprofit corporation. In a trust, the founder must document his gift to the foundation and designate one or more trustees. This is not so different from forming a trust in basic estate planning (be it a simple credit shelter trust or a charitable remainder trust); written instructions and named trustees are the first order of business. In addition, the founder needs to develop the terms of the trust, which can be in a narrow (restrictive) or broad language. In this way, the grantor of a trust-based private foundation has more control (it is harder to change the terms of a trust than that of a corporation).

Trustees, like directors of a corporation, can receive reasonable compensation for services, although many states limit these amounts more in a trust format than in a corporation format. These trustees can generally select their successors, and to that end, can essentially create an extended family affair with respect to managing the private foundation into the future. The biggest issue, however, may be the heightened fiduciary requirements in a trust versus a corporation. In a trust, the trustees are held to be fiduciaries (where in corporations directors are held to a business judgment rule), which may open them up to lawsuits by beneficiaries of the foundation if there are questions about their work. Furthermore, due to this heightened care requirement (and the threat of lawsuits), it becomes harder to attract good candidates to serve as trustees of a foundation.

Setting up a private foundation as a corporation is the favored approach. While a corporate structure will provide less control for the founder, it will make it easier to run the "business" of making grants by attracting better candidates to serve as directors. Like setting up a for-profit corporation, setting up a nonprofit corporation is fairly straightforward. First, a filing is made with the state (the Secretary of the State's office)—a certificate of incorporation—and then bylaws are drawn up and adopted which detail the inner workings of the corporation, the rules of the road. Rather than having shareholders, as in a for-profit corporation, nonprofit corporations have members who elect a board of directors. It is this board of directors (akin to the trustees in a trust set-up) that appoints the officers of the corporation, as well as electing their own successors.

A major benefit of the nonprofit corporation setup is the limited liability that it affords to its officers and board of directors. In addition, a nonprofit corporation has greater flexibility and a greater ability to make changes to the foundation's mission as the environment might dictate. Also, a nonprofit corporation can have perpetual life, which is prohibited in most states for foundations set-up as trusts. Like a trust, a nonprofit corporation can compensate its officers and directors a reasonable amount and can also delegate investment management and administrative tasks to professional advisers. However, like a for-profit corporation, nonprofit corporations also must maintain records of board meetings (minutes) and other formalities that are required by any corporate structure.

"I like the idea of the meetings and the minutes—it can provide our children and grandchildren with a good sense of the workings inside the corporate board room," said Phil.

"Indeed, an invaluable lesson," replied Em. "So, now that we have determined that the corporate structure is best for your private foundation, the next step is to determine which type of private foundation this non-profit corporation is," said Em.

There are three types of private foundations that the Internal Revenue Service recognizes: standard private foundation, private operating foundation, and pass-through or conduit foundation. Each has its own rules when it comes to the deductibility of contributions, as well as the permissibility of gifts. In addition, each type of foundation has its own set of nuances:

Standard Private Foundation (also known as Private Nonoperating Foundation)

- The most common form of private foundation, where funding has typically come from one source, either in a one-time gift or a series of gifts or bequests.
- The primary function of a standard private foundation is to make grants to public charities and nonprofits—it is a grant-making entity.
- Must spend an amount equal to or more than 5 percent of the average investment assets on qualifying grants or administrative expenses annually.
- A donor's cash gifts to the standard private foundation are deductible up to 30 percent of the donor's adjusted gross

income, with a five-year carry forward in excess of the 30 percent limit. Gifts of appreciated property are deductible up to a 20 percent limit of the donor's adjusted gross income.

- Subjected to an annual 2 percent excise tax on the foundation's net investment income (as shown on line 27b of the Form 990-PF). Some private foundations, if they meet the special requirement of annually increasing the amount of their grant making, can benefit from a lower (1 percent) excise tax. (Note: Senator Charles Schumer, NY-Democrat, has introduced a bill that has been approved by Congress to institute a flat excise tax of 1.35 percent on net investment income on foundations).

Private Operating Foundation

- Typically funded through one source.
- Uses the majority of its resources to carry out its own charitable programs rather than making grants to public charities.
- Operating foundations must spend 85 percent of their annual adjusted net income (not assets) on the operations of their charitable programs.
- Donors to an operating foundation do enjoy a greater deduction on their donation—cash gifts are deductible up to 50 percent of adjusted gross income—like donations to a public charity—and donations of appreciated property is limited to 30 percent of adjusted gross income.
- Excise tax rules are the same as for a standard private foundation.

Pass-Through or Conduit Foundation

- Similar to a standard private foundation because it does not directly operate a charitable organization.
- Not able to build an endowment through its grants; that is, the donor's gifts must be passed through (within 2½ months from the end of the tax year that the donor made the gift) to public charities in the form of grants.
- The tax deductions are more liberal in the pass-through foundation than in a standard foundation—these donations can be deductible up to 50 percent of adjusted gross income (30 percent for appreciated property).

Once we have decided on the structure of the private foundation—in this case, the corporate structure seems best suited—we must then complete the filing requirements. Because nonprofit corporations, and trusts for that matter, are regulated on the state level (state law versus federal law), there are specific state filing requirements that need to be adhered to. First, we need to establish the actual entity. If the founders do choose the trust option rather than the corporation option, they will need to address the following in their establishment of this trust (the trust document):

- The name(s) of the trustee(s).
- Statement of Charitable Purpose—a sort of mission statement that outlines the areas to which the foundation will be making its grants (remember, in a trust setup making changes to these documents is not a simple task, so be mindful of the long-term nature of the entity in crafting this mission).
- Will the trust be perpetual or will it have a dissolution plan?
- Will the trust establish successor trustees?
- A statement prohibiting lobbying, political campaigns, and private inurement.
- A statement that the foundation will abide by Sections 4941 through 4945 of the IRS Code, which discuss the following: self-dealing (4941), required distributions (4942), excess business holdings (4943), jeopardy investments (4944), and taxable expenditures (4945).

The corporation structure of a nonprofit foundation has its own requirements, which are similar to the initiation of any corporation: the articles of incorporation, bylaws, setting up an organizational meeting, and maintaining a book of minutes. Let's take each of these separately:

- Articles of incorporation—This first step in any corporation must be filed with the state's Secretary of State and serve as a formal document that establishes the corporation. In this document you will need to include the basic information about your nonprofit corporation (foundation) like:
  - Name and address of the entity—Either incorporating the family's name into the title or, as some foundations do, highlighting the cause or mission of the foundation.

- Purpose of the organization—Can be as vague as "religious, charitable, scientific, testing for public safety, literary, or educational purposes" (actually, this is the typical language used, for it provides for the greatest amount of latitude); however, some states do require a more detailed description of the purpose.
- Names and addresses of initial directors or agents of the corporation (remember this information will be public, so be mindful of which address you choose; in other words, you may want to use the foundation's address). A registered agent is required to receive service of process if the foundation were to be sued for any reason, so in this case it is typical to list your attorney or accountant as a registered agent.
- Plan for dissolution of the corporation, if any (if it is not going to be perpetual).
- Method to make amendments to the articles of incorporation.
- Clauses prohibiting lobbying, political campaign grants, and private inurement.
- Adherence to the IRS codes 4941 to 4945.

Sections 4940–4945 and 6104 of the IRS Code: The Big 7

The Big 7, as they are known in the Private Foundation world (well maybe only the tax geeks who toil in this sector refer to them as such), are the most important sections of the IRS Code for our work going forward as directors of a private foundation.

Section 4940—Excise Tax Based on Investment Income: This refers to the excise tax that foundations pay, between 1 percent and 2 percent (and recently Congress has passed a law making a "flat" excise tax of 1.39 percent) of their net investment income (more on that in Chapter 4).

Section 4941—Taxes on Self-Dealing: The basic rule is that any direct or indirect transaction between a private foundation and a disqualified person is prohibited, unless it is permitted under a specific exemption. Who is a disqualified person? Officers, directors, trustees, substantial contributors, and potentially family members of the above. What are the transactions that would be deemed self-dealing? They include:

- Sale, exchange, or lease of property.
- Lending of money or extension of credit.
- Furnishing goods, services, or facilities.
- Transferring the foundation's assets or income to a disqualified person, or use for the benefit of such a person. (Exception: Trustees/directors can be compensated for some services and family members can be hired as staff, if both the services and the compensation are necessary and reasonable).*

Section 4942—Taxes on Failure to Distribute Income: The 5 percent penalty rule—a private foundation is required to make charitable distributions of at least 5 percent of its average assets (included in this aggregate figure are certain reasonable administrative expenses, including salaries but *excluding* investment management fees). Failure to do so will subject the foundation to hefty taxes (approximately 30 percent) on the nondistributed amount, as well as an embarrassment factor that might sting even more (consider the potential of a blogger whose diatribe against the foundation for not doing its job goes viral on the web—not pretty for the directors who will have to defend the actions of the foundation).

Section 4943—Taxes on Excess Business Holdings: This rule basically states that the foundation together with a disqualified person(s) cannot collectively own more than 20 percent of any business enterprise. This speaks directly to 4941—where self-dealing is highlighted.

Section 4944—Taxes on Investments that Jeopardize Charitable Purpose: This is one of those rules that you have to sit back and say "Duh!" Of course, as directors of a private foundation we should not invest in anything or anyway that would prevent us from carrying out our stated purpose—that is, to make charitable grants. But I suppose that the lines can sometimes become gray, especially if the foundation was established years before, so from that perspective highlighting this rule make some good sense.

Section 4945—Taxes on Taxable Expenditures: Foundations cannot make certain expenditures, and if they do so, they are then taxed. Examples of such expenditures are as follows: noncharitable expenditures, influencing public elections, and lobbying activities.

Section 6104—Public Disclosure Rules: Recall when we stated that a private foundation is somewhat of an oxymoron because it is anything but private. Private foundations are required to make their books and records available for public inspection—items such as the foundation's Form 990-PF and the initial Form 1023 all need to be made available for the public (which often is done through other services like GuideStar and Charity Navigator but should also be available on your web site if possible).

---

*"How to Start a Private Foundation," Association of Small Foundations, 2009.

- Bylaws—Once the articles of incorporation are filed, the next step is to prepare the bylaws, which are essentially the rules of engagement within the corporation (in a trust setup, the trust document is used in this capacity). Although many of the requirements of a set of bylaws have state influences to contend with, the specific corporation does have some leeway with respect to certain areas (i.e., specific duties of officers, certain fundamental policies of managing the corporation). However, the common elements of all corporations include a list of officers and directors and the meeting schedules of officers and of directors, as well as some definition of their actual duties. Clearly, the directors of a new foundation should seek the counsel of an attorney who is well versed in this area of the law to facilitate these exercises; however that does not mean that the directors are silent throughout the process. They should be intimately involved and have their voices heard, for these are the rules that they will have to live (work) with in the future. That is not to say that bylaws cannot be changed or altered; the amendment process allows for just this, but a vote (typically a supermajority) is required to change a portion of the bylaws (note: any changes need to be filed with the Secretary of State, the IRS, and the Attorney General's office). For similar reasons, the bylaws should be written in easy-to-understand language to promote its constant use and utility for those who need to refer to it from time to time.

"After running a corporation for the last four decades, we have some very specific views on how one should be run, and we would expect to be able to implement these policies in this new nonprofit corporation," stated Phil.

"Of course. I would suggest that you voice your opinions and then have your attorney draw up the bylaws accordingly," replied Em.

"For example," continued Phil, "in order to prevent any attempt to force out or 'gang up' on any one director, we would want a policy that requires a unanimous vote by all board members (excepting the member who is being voted on) to replace any existing one."

"Also, an automatic board position for any direct descendant upon reaching the age of 25. In this way all family members get a voice in the legacy, years—decades—into the future," offered Mary.

"Sounds like you guys have given this some thought—well that's great. I am sure that your legal advisers can work all of these mandates into the bylaws of this new corporation," said Em.

Other issues that are typically addressed within the bylaws include:

- The general powers of the board of directors, including their responsibilities, their term's length, and the method by which they are replaced and selected (as Phil and Mary discussed above) need to be listed. Also, the compensation structure for the directors as well as officers of the corporation should be laid out. It is recommended that the newly formed nonprofit corporation—the foundation—seek out the services of a compensation expert in order to develop a matrix of fair and typical compensation plans for all parties.
- A definitive meeting schedule needs to be developed so that each director and officers are fully aware of their requirements; their attendance, foremost, but also reports that have been requested by the board. These meetings also need to be fully recorded in the corporate "minutes book" that is usually maintained and kept by the secretary of the corporation.
- The bylaws also determine the corporation's fiscal year, the method by which expenses will be repaid, and the committees needed to run the corporation. Even with the establishment of a compensation committee, it is recommended that, given the family nature of a typical foundation, an outside expert is retained to provide insights to the committee. It's a matter of protecting the foundation from unwanted scrutiny from the public as well as the Attorney General's office.

Once the Articles of Incorporation are filed and the bylaws drafted (they need to be voted on before "the motion is moved"), the next step is to obtain an Employer Tax Identification number (EIN), which is done by completing the Internal Revenue Service's Form SS-4, conveniently called, "Application for an Employer Identification Number." We are not done however, for the final form that needs to be filed is the "Application for Recognition of Exemption under Section 501(c)(3) of the Internal Revenue Code" or, as it is known, the IRS Form 1023.

Form 1023

Form 1023 is a comprehensive form (see www.irs.gov/pub/irs-pdf/f1023.pdf for a copy of Form 1023) that should not be completed without qualified legal and tax counsel. The information that is required on this form (and more information and assistance can be found at www.form1023help.com) encompasses a wide range of details on the foundation such as:

- The source(s) of the initial financial support—Was it a one-time gift to the foundation? A bequest? Does the foundation plan to solicit funds from the public?
- Contact information and compensation of directors and officers.
- Type of grant making, highlighting any special plans with respect to international grants or scholarships.
- Current financial picture (revenues and expenditures), as well as a budget for the next two years.

The IRS allows a fairly lenient time period for this form to be filed; Form 1023 is due 15 months after the nonprofit corporation was formally organized (that is, the date when the articles of incorporation were filed or the trust was established) and there is a 12-month automatic extension, bringing the total time to file the 1023 to 27 months. The form grants the nonprofit corporation ("the foundation") a tax exemption due to its charitable activities. You don't have to wait for the IRS response to the 1023 (the Determination Letter, which takes between three and five months from the filing date) to commence activity (a nice thing, as there is no reason to delay).

Next up is the Attorney General's (AG) office. Some might wonder why the AG is involved in this process. The AG of the state has, in his or her jurisdiction, the protection of nonprofit entities of the state—both the receivers of grants and the grant makers (like private foundations). Bottom line, if it has to do with charities, then the AG's office is involved. State laws vary a bit on these rules and procedures, so for the most part the AG's office becomes a critical "partner" with the nonprofit foundation and thus the directors of a foundation must be aware of its role.

Guiding Documents

"Em, you have given us an excellent primer on how to initiate a private foundation—the legal and accounting requirements and such—but we are wondering how we manage this new entity. How do we go from the drawing board to actual giving?" asked Phil.

"I understand perfectly and what I recommend for newly formed foundations is to develop a set of 'guiding documents': intentions and value statements that can be passed down from generation to generation to keep the mission of the foundation in the forefront at all times," counseled Em.

Emmett Pathy went into this topic in greater detail in his follow-up report to Mary and Phil Anthony.

The foundation's guiding documents often include a **Statement of Values**, wherein the founders delineate a set of principles that they have been guided by and which they expect their foundation to follow well into the future. There is often also a **Statement of Donor Intent**, in which the founders detail the reasons for starting the foundation and what they hope it will accomplish in the future. The **Mission Statement** is an outgrowth of the Statement of Values and the Statement of Donor Intent—a sort of a tagline or "elevator pitch" for the foundation where its purpose can be easily identified. Finally, we have a list of "no-no's" that are compiled into the **Code of Ethics** that serve as a guiding conscience for the directors of the foundation long after the founders have passed.

The Statement of Values

The Statement of Values serves as the lynchpin for the foundation. Using an analogy of taking a long journey in a car with the family, the Statement of Values would be the rules that the traveling family will abide by while on the trip—no fighting with the person sitting next to you, no loud music or phone calls that can disturb your fellow passengers, no sardine sandwiches or soft French cheeses all developed with one goal in mind; in this case, getting to the end point of the journey (without someone getting sick along the way).

Statement of Values—The Phoenixville Community Health Foundation, PA

Ethical behavior to preserve the public trust.

Accountable actions.

Compassion for the community, its people, and the organizations attempting to help them.

Responsiveness and sensitivity to the community needs.

Fair, respectful, honest, and professional relations with all who come in contact with the foundation.

Passion in pursuit of philanthropic excellence.

Sarah Beggs and Kimberly Adkinson (ed.), *The Trustee Handbook: The Essentials for an Effective Board Member* (Washington, DC: Association of Small Foundations, 2007).

The Statement of Donor Intent

Going back to our car journey analogy, the Statement of Donor Intent would be the directions or the map (or that person who speaks to you through the navigation system of your car), essentially providing the route to get from where we started to where we want to go. In this document the founders lay out the genesis of the foundation—why they started it and what they expect it to do well into the future—in broad terms. This statement might actually list guidelines for grants as well as choices for (or how to choose) directors or trustees. Bottom line, this document serves as a voice-from-the-grave, engaging future generations to fully understand what is expected of them as stewards of this foundation.

It should be noted that there are no legal requirements to develop these guiding documents—it's simply good practice to do so. Furthermore, these documents and their instructions are not binding from a legal standpoint, although foundations that go awry from the charitable intent of the founders might find themselves the target of charities who feel they have been slighted—and any such press is never a good thing in the world of private foundations. But again, there exist no legal ramifications from funding outside your stated mission.[10]

---

[10]Beggs and Adkinson, *Trustee Handbook.*

Dorothy Koch Family Foundation's Statement of Donor Intent

When I established the foundation, I had several objectives in mind. My wife Dorothy and I have accomplished much in our lives through hard work and good luck. Our children are all doing well, and we want to reinvest some of our family's wealth in our community.

It is my hope that the foundation's giving will make a difference in people's lives. For that reason I would like the foundation to focus on education. Not only is education a lifelong interest for my wife, but it is clear how much our children have benefited from excellent educations. We believe that education can open doors to financial success and interesting lives.

There are many ways the foundation can support education—for example, giving to schools, grants to teachers, scholarships to individuals, or funding to administrators and organizations to educate parents to support their schools. I would like the foundation to favor the third, fourth, and fifth grades. Not only did Dorothy's teaching career focus on these grades, but they seem to be crucial to launching kids on the educational path.

While there are unlimited ways to improve the American educational system, I would like the foundation's giving to focus on communities where Dorothy and I have the strongest roots—Brown County and Indian Hill.

Other objectives for the foundation relate to family. By choosing a family foundation as a vehicle for giving, I hope to encourage family members to maintain contact and work together on a project important to them. Additionally, I hope to encourage family members to become involved in their own charitable giving.

Giving Guidelines

I expect the foundation will usually give away its income every year and will meet federal requirements for foundation giving. The foundation's giving can fluctuate from year to year. Some projects may be funded over multiple years, while others may receive a single year grant. Part of the foundation's income can be used to pay expenses for trustee meetings, but I expect the bulk of the income will be dedicated to giving.

Trustees

Since one of the reasons for channeling our giving through a foundation is for the family to maintain contact with each other, I prefer that the management remain in the family, and that the trustees be family members. For now, that means our four children.

I leave it to the trustees to develop a plan to involve the next generation of the family in the foundation. The trustees should also determine the lifespan

(Continued)

of the foundation. If it becomes a burden on the family, the trustees are free to determine when and how to liquidate the foundation.

While this document spells out my intent in establishing the foundation, things change. This is not meant to limit trustees, and I expect they will make their own decisions, even if they are at variance with what I have outlined above.

Beggs and Adkinson, *Trustee Handbook*. Reprinted with permission from the Association of Small Foundations.

The Legacy Group, Inc.—Writing a Statement of Donor Intent for Future Generations

One of the best resources for developing a statement of donor intent is provided by The Legacy Group, Inc. Their guide can be found at www.legacyatwork.com /pdf/Donor%20Intent.pdf.

The Mission Statement

The mission statement could be seen as the mantra you and your kids are singing during the journey in the car. It sort of answers the question, Why are you taking this journey? But it does so in such a manner to make it engaging and memorable. The mission statement is almost a sort of selling tool, providing the directors and trustees of a foundation with a handy description of what the foundation does. Picture a director of a foundation at a cocktail reception or a seminar, and someone inquires as to what sectors their foundation serves. It is nice to have the mission statement down pat— *"We provide grants in three distinct areas: fine arts, including ballet programs for underprivileged school children; healthcare, focusing on diseases affecting children and the elderly; and tolerance programs, with an eye turned most recently towards stemming the tide of bullying in our schools."*

Can the mission statement change? Out of the four guiding documents, the mission statement is the one that is most fluid or dynamic, and to that end it is likely to undergo changes or revisions as the environment and conditions suggest. As in the previous example, the addition of bullying is most likely a newer piece to the mission statement—while it may have always had tolerance as part of its mission, the foundation's board must have felt the urgency of eradicating bullying in our schools is sufficient for it to be added to the mission statement. Hence, I would suggest that the mission statement is more akin to a living, breathing document than something cut in stone. This can be seen in what is probably the best worded and most well-known of all mission statements (although a little lengthy compared to the sound bite world we live in today):

> We the People of the United States, in Order to form a more perfect Union, establish Justice, assure domestic Tranquility, provide for common defence, promote the general Welfare, and secure the Blessings of Liberty to ourselves and our Posterity, do ordain and establish this Constitution for the United States of America.

It has been suggested that the mission statement should be a well-defined set of rules and procedures for the foundation to follow well into the future. Although there are no set tenets in this area of the foundation "business," it seems intuitive that if such rules were so important to the founders, then they might have considered a trust set-up (rather than the more "liberal" nonprofit corporation) in the first place. Furthermore, such policies and rules can be better organized and adhered to in the Statement of Donor Intent, where the founder's vision is fully developed, as well as in the operations of the foundation. Again, much of this is ethereal anyway in that it is not legally binding. Often the best mechanism to continue the founder's intentions is to choose the best directors and trustees from the outset. It is these good people who can then mold and choose the future directors and trustees accordingly. Bottom line, as in many pursuits, it's the people and not the words that run the show.

Sample Mission Statements

Here are two good examples to help you in crafting your own mission statement.

- The Stelios Philanthropic Foundation, mission statement available at www.stelios.com/about-us/the-mission-statement.html.
- The Wallace Foundation, mission statement available at www.wallacefoundation.org/learn-about-wallace/mission-and-vision/Pages/default.aspx.

Code of Ethics

The final guiding document (and not all of these are required or even suggested) is the code of ethics. Going back to our car trip analogy, the code of ethics is like the mandated laws and policies for driving—the speed limit, changing lanes, and so on. In the foundation world, the code of ethics is like the angel on the shoulder of the director or trustee, telling them how to act and, sometimes more importantly, how not to act. Of course, the prohibition against self-dealing would be foremost in the code of ethics, as would the avoidance of any appearance of engaging in any conflict of interest. Also listed here would be to adopt patience for fellow directors' ideas and passions, to be—tolerant and empathetic throughout the process.

"We have begun to develop some thoughts in regard to our foundation's guiding documents," said Phil.

"And in keeping with the age of technology that we now live in, in addition to writing them down, we actually made a video recording of the both of us explaining each document and its importance so that there will be little to misinterpret," said Mary.

"Excellent! Using video recordings has become popular in the last few years—it does serve as an excellent way to communicate these important ideals and expectations, and does so with a strong sense of personal feelings because it is coming from the founders' mouths," said Em.

"Okay, so what are the next steps? We have the legal and initiation process under our belt, we developed our guiding documents including the Mission Statement—now what?" asked Phil.

"Yes we have completed the so called *set up phase* and now move into the *operation phase* of managing a private foundation," said Em.

"Good so we can start making some grants to some of these very needy and worthy causes?" asked an anxious Mary.

"Well almost, Mary. While I do share your enthusiasm for making grants and doing good, there are some important documents

---

Code of Ethics

A good example to use when developing your foundation's code of ethics is the Surdna Foundation. Their code of ethics can be found at www.surdna.org/about-the-foundation/code-of-ethics.html.

and matters that we really should become more familiar with before fully embarking on a giving campaign, and in my next report I will drive you through the process," said Em.

"Great, drive away!" echoed the Anthonys in unison.

Be Proactive and Know Your Charities

"Not to be repetitive," Em said as he was sitting down with Phil and Mary, "but it is critical to really do your homework when it comes to studying the charitable organizations to which you are making grants." Em continued. "There are several stories like the ones we discussed in our previous meetings where the name on the door, even of a well-known organization, does not tell the whole story. That can lead to some embarrassing situations."

Em mentioned that few institutions in the modern world enjoy more trust than charities—both from the wealthy who give them money and by the public that may benefit from their work. A recent study from American Express illustrated this point—70 percent of Americans trust nonprofit outfits more than government or business to address some of the most pressing issues of our time. A Merrill Lynch survey of rich people found that more than 94 percent trusted nonprofit organizations (businesses won a 68 percent rating and governments a paltry 32 precent).[11]

Em offered the example of the Salvation Army as one such example. "When you think of the Salvation Army," he asked the Anthonys. "What comes to mind?"

"The bell ringing at Christmas time," said Phil.

"Those are the folks who raise money during the holidays to help the less fortunate, at least that is what I assume they are all about," offered Mary.

"Well, they do indeed raise money, and as a matter of fact they were the largest public charity in the United States, receiving $1.4 billion in donations in 1999," said Em. "But when you dig deeper you find that the Salvation Army is actually a church: an evangelical Christian denomination with more than 1 million members, who refer to themselves as soldiers, in 107 countries," said Em to an amazed Phil and Mary. "While that is all well and good, someone's religion is their business," said Em.

---

[11]Beggs and Adkinson, *Trustee Handbook*.

"I couldn't agree more," said Phil.

Em continued, "But in this case the money raised goes to support clergy members who are on-call 24 hours a day and who follow detailed rules on everything from how to save a soul to how to pick a spouse."[12] The point is that one needs to understand where the actual money goes in a nonprofit, and assuming can be very embarrassing.

"Here I figured that these guys were just helping out the homeless and all types regardless of their religion," said Mary. "Wow, that is an eye-opener."

Summary

This chapter focused on the inception of a private foundation, going through the required forms and documents that are necessary for its development. It covered the major considerations that directors of a foundation need to be most aware of and "guiding documents" that serve as a road map for directors long into the future. In the next chapter, we begin to examine the management of a private foundation. How should the foundation be organized? What are the roles of directors and officers? We also look at Form 990 and other required documentation.

---

[12]Silk and Lintott, *Creating a Private Foundation.*

4

Managing a Private Foundation

Is the rich world aware of how four billion of the six billion live? If we were aware, we would want to help out; we'd want to get involved.
—Bill Gates, the Bill and Melinda Gates Foundation

We started our foundation because we believe we have a real opportunity to help advance equity around the world . . . to help make sure that, no matter where a person is born, he or she has the chance to live a healthy, productive life.
—Melinda Gates, the Bill and Melinda Gates Foundation

Okay, now that we have a handle on the foundation's setup—the required filing with the Internal Revenue Service (IRS) and the state's attorney general's office, as well as the mission statement—we can move toward managing the operations of the foundation," said Em to Phil and Mary.

"I am sure it's complicated, but it can't be as bad as running a family business," said Phil.

"In some cases you are right, Phil, but with a private foundation there are several perverse requirements and procedures that we need to study, starting with the IRS's tax form known as the 990-PF," said Em.

"Tax forms? Shouldn't we simply refer those to our accountant?" asked Mary.

"Well, I have found that a deep dive into the 990-PF can provide some important insights with respect to the work that you and your family will be undertaking as directors of this private foundation— even if your accountant and his or her team do the actual preparation of the form," advised Em.

"I agree. Like I always say: knowledge is a powerful edge. Dive away, Em!" said an enthusiastic Phil.

Emmett Pathy started his discussion of Form 990-PF by showing the Anthonys a copy of the 13-page filing with which they will become all too familiar in the not-too-distant future. His report was not meant to provide a complete analysis of the form—after all, they will have professional accountants to provide this service— but rather an overview, albeit one deep enough to get the major points across.

Form 990-PF

According to the IRS, preparing the 990-PF takes, on average, approximately 140 hours to compile the required data and 60 hours to complete the return—indeed no small task. The 990-PF is in desperate need of an overhaul, much like the IRS did with the 990 form for public charities. Many in the foundation world would very much welcome a simplified and cohesive revamp of this somewhat disjointed form.

The goal of the 990-PF (see www.irs.gov/pub/irs-pdf/f990pf.pdf) is to show details of the foundation's qualified distributions (grants and expenses), as well as to calculate its payout requirements; that is, the amount that each foundation must make in grants (or expenses) annually to maintain their tax exempt status. Failure to make the minimum payout requirement in the time allotted (there may be a one-year grace period) will result in a painful 30 percent penalty for the amount you failed to correctly distribute. This is especially painful because *this is not your money, and to that end you have a fiduciary requirement to make charitable grants*. The government takes this very seriously and has little empathy or leeway for noncompliance. The final goal of the 990-PF is to calculate the required excise tax on the foundation's net investment income. No, a private foundation is not entirely free of tax; they are indeed subjected to a somewhat diminutive (although not to those who funded the foundation) excise tax, which ranges from 1 to 2 percent annually.

The 990-PF is required to be filed by the fifteenth day of the fifth month from the end of the foundation's fiscal year. So if your foundation is operating on the calendar year, that is, ending on December 31, then the 990-PF is due May 15 of the following year. If the foundation is operating on a fiscal year ending on, say, June 30, then the 990-PF is due November 15 of that year (which is not a bad choice given the relative slowness of the accounting profession in November and December versus April and May). The IRS grants an automatic three-month extension, and another three months with a written explanation why you would need an extension, so it is relatively easy to get a six-month extension. After that, the penalties start to come into play, and again, given your fiduciary standing, penalties should be avoided at all costs.

Preparing Documents Needed for Form 990-PF

As with any tax form, compiling the required data in a good layout before embarking on the actual return is always a good idea. In the case of the 990-PF, there are several areas where your attention is best focused:

- Investments. Given that a private foundation is typically comprised of investment capital as its main source of assets, maintaining careful and efficient records with respect to the foundation's investments is critical. In a given year there are 13 statements that you will need to have on hand: the 12 monthly statements that span the foundation's fiscal year and the statement prior to the first month (although this data is often captured as "balance from previous month" on the first period's statement). In order to calculate the average assets required in Part X of the 990-PF (to calculate the "average monthly fair market value of securities") you will need to add each month's ending value of assets plus the first month's starting value and divide by 13. It should be noted that this calculation is not just for investment accounts but includes all savings accounts and checking accounts—all liquid assets of the foundation. In addition to the monthly statements, you will also need to have readily accessible all 1099 forms, which detail the dividends and interest paid as well as any realized gains and losses on each account held by the foundation. Be especially mindful of less liquid and special investments (hedge funds, master limited partnerships, etc.) that will often issue K1s (rather than 1099s). These are notoriously late and probably ill-advised for smaller foundations, given that their complicated tax reporting may result in Unrelated Business Taxable Income (UBTI), which is especially problematic for private foundations.

- Expenses incurred in the operation of the private foundation. Here we are focused on the receipts and details of any expense incurred during the fiscal year that was used to create income in the foundation. For example, investment fees and board meeting expenses (only that portion that was used during discussions of the investment portfolio). Separately, due to the different treatment of investment related expenses and other expenses, we will need to gather details on expenses dealing with legal and accounting services and other professional fees. Also, a schedule detailing the amount of excise tax paid in the current year and the amount paid in the previous year (this is helpful when deciding whether to apply any overpayments to the following year). Additionally, a listing of the foundation's employees and board members, the number of hours worked, and their total compensation from the foundation (including deferred compensation arrangements, benefits, and expense accounts), if any, is required.
- Grants and charitable programs. Here we are looking to compile any information on the grants made during the year—a list with the grantee's name, address, and type of charitable organization (i.e., public charity, private foundation) and the purpose and amount of the grant. In order to flesh out any self-dealing issues, it is important to also show any grants made to individuals where there is a relationship with the foundation as a substantial contributor or any relationship with a member of the foundation's board or staff. Also needed is an explanation of how a grant seeker may apply for funding through the foundation—the method of contact, the proposal process, and any restrictions/limitations due to scope or geographical location. Absent this, the foundation would then need to state that they do not accept unsolicited proposals from grant seekers. Finally, we will need to compile a list of

any grants approved in the fiscal year covered by the 990-PF but not yet paid—all the required info for the grants paid will also be needed for these not yet paid grants (that is, a list of contact information, type of charitable organization, purpose of the grant, and the amount of the grant).

In addition to the above files (and it is good practice to develop a database where these three sections are kept separate in order to facilitate compilation come tax time) it is important to maintain a "master" folder or binder of the founding documents of the foundation. These include the articles of incorporation, the bylaws, the minutes from board meetings, a listing of the states in which the foundation is registered, and a database of contacts for advisers to the foundation (legal, tax, and investments).

Diving into Form 990-PF

At the top of the 990-PF is a box that is meant to capture the foundation's basic info: name, address, employer identification number (EIN), and telephone number. It's best not to use a home or cell number, for again, all of this information is available for anyone to see and use on the Internet—typically the accounting firm's main number is listed. Box J in this section, however, is the first major decision that the foundation needs to make regarding the accounting for the foundation. Box J asks what accounting method the foundation is employing: cash, accrual, or other. As a quick primer to this facet of accounting, consider the following:

- Cash method is most suited for foundations although it is not the best choice—more on that below. In the cash method you record revenue and expenses as they are paid. For example, if you were a corporation involved in selling widgets, on the cash basis of accounting, you would only record those revenues when you received the cash from the company you sold it to, and the same applies to expenses. So if you received an order amounting to $100,000 worth of widgets in December (the last month of your fiscal year because you operate on a calendar year), but did not receive payment for this order until February of the next year, then the revenue for this order must be booked in the following year. The same goes for expenses, so if you charge $1,000 for goods in December using a credit facility but pay it in February then the expense is booked in the February year. For a foundation it is especially important because the goal of a foundation is not to manage a balance sheet and cash flow to make a profit— a foundation's "profits" come from its investments—the goal of a foundation is clear disclosure. But, as we will see, the cash method is not the preferred method in private foundations due to the requirement under the cash method to value assets at cost rather than fair market value.

- The accrual method records revenues and expenses as they are booked, rather than when they are paid, therefore requiring a peculiar construct of accounting known as prepaid expenses, accounts payable, or accounts receivable. In the accrual method, revenues are booked when the company receives a purchase order (or, in the percent-of-completion method used in construction industries, when a certain percentage of a job is completed), and expenses are booked when goods or materials are ordered. For example, if the widget company receives an order in the last week of their fiscal year for $100,000 worth of widgets, the revenue is recorded that day. Similarly, if the company orders goods on its credit card but pays for it in the next period it is still recorded as an expense in the year it was ordered. As you can see, the accrual method makes for a difficult examination of the books of an organization (hence the importance of cash flow analysis for public companies, which the vast majority are on the accrual method). The accrual method does have its place, however; it is especially helpful when examining the finances of a nonprofit charitable organization. Think about it: If a nonprofit is having a tough year raising funds (their "revenues," if you will) and to that end have not paid their expenses (deferring compensation perhaps), with the cash method this would understate their expenses and when operating funds did come in, a larger than expected portion of it would be soaked up reconciling the expenses they owe. With the accrual method their expenses are recorded as they are "earned," and to that end, it provides a clearer view of the true expenses of the nonprofit.

- Modified cash method. This is the preferred method used by private foundations, for it captures all of the transparency of the cash method but permits the foundation's assets to be valued at fair market value (FMV), as required on the 990-PF. As previously mentioned and discussed in greater detail later in this chapter, the foundation's assets are required to be shown at fair market value in order to calculate the required annual payout, as well as the excise tax due annually. The cash method requires assets to be shown at cost; hence the "modified" in this version of the cash method. One caveat, for our friends on the west coast: California requires foundations and nonprofits to only use the accrual method, which adds another layer of detective work for the accounting staff as well as the tax preparers in completing the 990-PF—no matter, maybe their good weather and movie stars serve as a consolation prize.

Part I of the 990-PF is the section that captures the revenues and expenses of the foundation—something akin to an income statement. In the first section, the revenues are reconciled for the period. In foundation-speak, revenues means "contributions, gifts, grants, and so on received," and often this first line will be left blank because the foundation had been funded via a one-time gift from the founders (although in that first year the amount of the gift will be listed). If, however, the foundation does receive gifts or grants then this amount needs to be listed—and if the gift is above $5,000 from any one entity then this information will also be required on Schedule B (Line 2).

Lines 3 and 4 of this section seek entries on interest earned and dividends, which can be fairly easily captured by a quick look at the 1099 forms from the various banks or brokerage firms where the foundation has accounts. The tricky part is to break down the various calendar-year tax forms into a useable format, given your potentially different fiscal year—in other words, if your fiscal year ends on June 30 then the full year's 1099 form needs to be reconciled, seeking the dividends and interest that was paid by June 30.

Lines 6 and 7 capture any capital gains or losses from sales of assets in the period covered by the return. The net gain or loss is listed on Line 6a and the gross sales price on 6b—the difference between these two figures would be the cost of the asset. Line 7 shows this net gain or loss in Column (b) of the form, which is the "Net

Investment Income." Line 10 is used if the foundation made any sales of merchandise (i.e., T-shirts, books) with the resulting profit or loss also shown. The "other income" on Line 11 is meant as a catchall line, where such areas as program-related investments (PRIs) are listed.

There are four columns on the 990-PF: Column (a) lists the revenues and expenses per the books of the organization—either on a cash or accrual basis; Column (b) details the net investment income and doesn't include grants or gifts; Column (c) is called adjusted net income and its use is limited to private operating foundations; and Column (d), where disbursements for charitable purposes are listed on a cash basis only (again, this means if you have not paid the bill than it shouldn't be listed). It is this final column that will permit us to reconcile the qualified disbursements—the expenses and grants paid throughout the period.

The next section in Part I captures the operating and administrative expenses of the foundation. The important point here is that not all expenses are treated uniformly throughout the return. Column (a) details all of the expenses of the foundation right from the books of the foundation—no matter what manner they have been accounted for (cash or accrual). Column (b) reconciles those expenses that are directly involved in the production of investment income. Here we will find entries, on Line 13, for the portion of the officers' and directors' compensation that is involved with the production of investment returns (the balance of their compensation will go on the same line in Column [d]). In addition, we will find the costs associated with investment counsel as well as any fees or expenses for the execution of transactions in this column (legal and accounting fees are listed in Column (d) since they are not involved in the production of investment return). So we will see in Column (b) a portioning of expenses—from compensation to taxes (excise taxes are not involved in the production of investment returns but withholding taxes may be) in order to arrive at the correct amount of administrative expenses associated with investment return. Line 27 provides us with a net investment income figure that we calculate by subtracting the total expenses on Line 26 in Column (b) from the total net investment income on Line 12 Column (b). It is this figure—the net investment income—that we will use to calculate the excise taxes associated with the foundation for that given period.

The expenses that are not captured in Column (b)—true administrative expenses rather than those involved in the production of investment returns are shown in Column (d). Lines 13–15 list the compensation of officers, directors, and staff, including pension plan contributions and employee benefits. On Lines 16a and b we list the costs of the legal and accounting work in the given period—and remember this is on a cash basis—so if it had been billed but not yet paid then do not include it. Other expenses include costs of rent, travel, conferences, and printing; all of these are reconciled on Line 24 to provide us with the *total operating and administrative expenses* for the foundation. On Line 25 we will list the actual—again on a cash basis, so only those that have actually been paid—*contributions and grants paid*. Line 26 adds these two figures together to give us a *total expenses and distributions* figure that will become crucial, as you will see, in our analysis of the required 5 percent disbursement rate.

Part II is concerned with the balance sheet of the foundation; that is, the value of the foundation's assets (liabilities are not a major concern for a foundation because of the absence of deferred expenses due to the cash accounting method). We provide data for each balance sheet asset—cash, savings accounts, and investments—from the beginning of the year (Column [a]) and the end of the year (Column [c]). These figures are required to be shown at fair market value (FMV), and it is to this end that many foundations adopt the modified cash method—modified to allow FMVs rather than cost. Part III is a simple—but very helpful and quick—reconciliation of the foundation's year-over-year asset change, showing any unrealized gains on Line 3 and any unrealized losses on Line 5. This quick test could be helpful in getting a handle on the foundation's investment committee's work—has it been posting unrealized losses year after year? There are no loss carry-forwards for foundations (although not a major issue given the low excise taxes), and therefore if you have taken losses then take as much as you can in gains in the same period to offset the losses (use them or lose them) and simply repurchase the shares (there are no wash sales rules for gains).

Part IV works through the calculation of capital gains on sales of assets. A somewhat perverse issue arises in this calculation that warrants some attention. The IRS allows the listing of liquidated positions of property—be it real estate or securities—in a combined fashion, but it is required that a sold security is matched up with a designated purchased lot of that same security. Typically, Last-In-First-Out

(LIFO) is assumed in these matters, but with foundations the actual lot of securities purchased is matched up with the sold securities. It's strange and kind of silly and will probably be changed with any new version of the 990-PF.

Part V is also somewhat on the chopping block given Congress's acceptance of a flat excise tax for foundations (they just need to find a bill to attach it to). Currently, Part V determines if the foundation can use the lower 1 percent rate as their excise tax versus the 2 percent rate. The calculation seeks to ascertain if the foundation has made increased distributions in the current year versus their five-year average rate, and if so, the 1 percent excise tax can be used in that year.

Part VI reconciles the foundation's excise taxes—the tax that is due versus the estimated tax payments made throughout the year. Foundations are typically required to make quarterly tax payments on the fifteenth day of the fifth, sixth, ninth, and twelfth month of the foundation's fiscal year. So if the foundation has a fiscal year ending on June 30, the tax payments would be due on November 15, December 15, March 15, and June 15. Any overpayments of excise taxes are typically applied as a credit to the following year's tax return. The calculation of the excise tax is fairly straightforward—take the net investment income figure on Part I, Line 27b and multiply it by 2 percent (1 percent if applicable), and it is that figure that is on Line 1 of Section VI.

Part VII is a series of yes/no questions aimed at political campaign contributions or support, and on Line 4, a question regarding UBTI greater than $1,000. UBTI is income that would arise if the foundation were to engage in a business that was not related to the foundation's mission. You also see UBTI in partnerships where K1s are issued rather than 1099 forms—and often you are unaware that the investment you purchased actually is a partnership issuing these K1s. UBTI above $1,000, and listed on a K1, can actually be taxable and throw a bit of a monkey wrench into your foundation's accounting; it's best to stay away from these issues if possible. Line 6 speaks to the issue of self-dealing—a big no-no in the foundation world. The way to think of self-dealing is to ask yourself "Am I benefiting from what the foundation is doing?" The most common example of this is the myriad of gala and golf outing invitations offered to foundation heads. The answer is straightforward: say thank you very much and decline the invite. If you really want to attend—to show your support or to simply mingle—then purchase a ticket for yourself from your own funds, not the foundation's.

In Part VIII, the IRS is looking for contact information for the directors, officers, and foundation staff members (if compensated more than $50,000 annually). Again, fair warning: consider using office addresses rather than home addresses. Remember that this information is on the Web for anyone to see, and the last thing you need is a knock on your front door from a charitable organization seeking a grant. Part IX speaks to direct charitable activities (DCAs) that the foundation may be involved in. This involvement (from conducting educational seminars and conferences to research projects beyond the foundation's grant program) is relatively rare, but when applicable it is discussed in this section of the 990-PF.

To calculate the minimum distributable amount (MDA) that serves as a starting point for the foundation's grants program in a given year we turn to Part X of the 990-PF. On Line 1 we enter the *average monthly fair market value of securities,* which we source by adding the starting value to each month's ending value over the year and divide by 13. A simple spreadsheet can provide an excellent data-capturing device, where each month the foundation's balances are aggregated (and it is important to make sure all of the foundation's accounts are used in this calculation) and then summed and divided by 13 to calculate the average monthly figure. Note the calculation shown below:

Time Period	Account Value ($)
Period starting value	12,456,877.00
Value at end of month 1	14,556,874.00
Value at end of month 2	12,445,457.00
Value at end of month 3	13,225,664.00
Value at end of month 4	14,551,145.00
Value at end of month 5	15,445,522.00
Value at end of month 6	16,554,488.00
Value at end of month 7	16,554,422.00
Value at end of month 8	15,885,522.00
Value at end of month 9	13,552,244.00
Value at end of month 10	14,778,899.00
Value at end of month 11	15,669,988.00
Value at end of month 12	17,223,311.00
Total	**192,900,413.00**
Average	**14,838,493.31**

The *fair market value of all other assets* (Line 1c) encompasses real estate and other alternative investments (i.e., hedge funds, private equity funds) and can be valued annually or however is practical. The sum shown on Line 5—*net value of noncharitable-use assets*—is multiplied by 5 percent to calculate the *minimum investment return* shown on Line 6. Note that this is not the minimum amount that must be distributed by the foundation for that period. In Part XI, we take this *minimum investment return* figure and deduct the excise taxes to arrive at the *distributable amount before adjustments* shown on Line 3. Part XII totals the current-year distributions that are counted as part of the annual required distributions—taken from Part I, Line 26 in Column (d), where we added the expenses to the grants made in the year. Finally, in Part XIII this *distributable amount* is compared to the *qualifying distributions* for the year and the resulting *remaining amount distributed out of corpus* (or carry forward) is shown on Line 4e. The carry forward is good for five years—Part XIII, Line 3 actually has a list of the last five years' *excess distributions carryover* and is aggregated on Line 3f. The way to use this information, from a grant-maker's perspective, is to subtract the amount of the carryover for the oldest year—shown on Line 3a, this is the amount that you would lose if not used—from the current year's distributable amount (Line 1d). This is the minimum you would need to make in distributions in the current year. But grant makers are often not minimalist types, seeking to do more than they are required to do, and to this end we would compare the amount of distributions made in the current year to the amount we are required to make. Any excess is then applied to the carryover schedule captured on Line 10e.

In Part XV, the foundation needs to either select the box indicated in Line 2, stating that the foundation does not accept unsolicited grant requests or, if the foundation does accept unsolicited requests, add more information on the application process on Lines 2a–d. This designation can be changed from year to year (although that would seem frivolous and inefficient) without permission from any governmental agency. In Part XV, grants paid during the year are listed; be particularly mindful of the self-dealing issue in the second column—it's best to be answered as "Not Applicable" if that is indeed the case. In Part (b), a list of those grants covered by the 990-PF (so this is not a cumulative list of "pledged" grants) that have been approved in the year but not paid are detailed.

"That is one heck of a long tax form," said Phil.

"I can't imagine preparing this each year," said Mary.

"Well you won't have to. Most foundations have their 990-PFs and other accounting functions prepared by their accounting firm, or one that specializes in 990-PFs," advised Em.

"Either way it is good to understand what goes into the 990-PF so that we can better manage the foundation going forward," said Phil.

"Next up is the all-important governance issue; that is, board membership, orientation, and development," said Em.

The Foundation's Board and Governance Issues

The structure of the private foundation starts with the board, charged with implementing the founder's vision and the foundation's mission. All board members and candidates for potential future board positions should be made fully aware of the founder's guiding documents (as discussed in the previous chapter) and how it relates to the work of the board. Legally, a foundation's board can be limited to just one member: often the founder himself. But most founders want to bring others into the endeavor—especially if they have (which they should, given the nature of the foundation structure) an interest in creating a legacy. It is this opening up of the board that brings the importance of governance to the table.

The board's most pressing issues include defining the roles of each officer (in many occasions, especially in smaller foundations, the directors/trustees also serve as officers), selecting the board (often dictated by the founders in the guiding documents and corporate bylaws), establishing board committees if necessary, and defining the duties of board members. The board of a foundation consists of the people—directors (in the nonprofit corporation structure) or trustees (in the trust structure)—who have ultimate responsibility and authority for the foundation's actions. Depending on the laws of the state, a board may consist of as few as one to three individuals, with no upper limit. Boards are generally required to hold meetings a minimum of once a year, although most meet more often.[1]

The importance of a strong leader on the board cannot be understated. The board's chairperson, who may also serve as the

---

[1]Roger Silk and James Lintott, *Creating a Private Foundation* (Princeton, NJ: Bloomberg Press, 2003).

president, is a leader whose main functions are to create consensus, manage the inevitable dissent (especially in a foundation comprised of family members), manage the legacy of the foundation by being mindful of succession issues, and execute the long-term vision set forth by the founders (which this chairperson/president very well may be—at least initially). In managing dissent, the chairperson is really showing his or her mettle, for it is often these issues that can lead to the splitting of the foundation into smaller pieces run by differing factions of the family. Although that might be okay from a funding or granting perspective (insomuch that each smaller foundation still provides grants), it certainly falls short of what the founders typically viewed as their vision in starting the foundation (especially a family foundation) in the first place. Hence the importance of a strong leader in this primary role—but a leader and not a dictator, for an overthrow is not the objective.

Succession planning is another key function of the chair of the foundation's board. Many family foundations view their children, grandchildren, and other relatives as natural candidates for the foundation's board and that can be a good starting point. However, succession planning should not lose sight of the opportunity in tapping the huge resources of trusted advisers. Although they may not be family members, often these professionals bring as much passion to the board as family members do, usually with greater knowledge and expertise. In this vein, investment advisers, attorneys, and accountants are typically good candidates for board membership. Additionally, former executives from the nonprofit sector are also excellent candidates, given their strong knowledge of the nonprofit marketplace and the important area of navigation of charitable organizations.

Larger foundations might also look to develop committees within the board, breaking into smaller groups to handle particular functions. For example, those board members with particular knowledge in the investment area might be placed on the investment committee and those who are knowledgeable about the nonprofit sector on the grants committee. Of course, the entire board has a vote when it comes to these matters, but it is the function of each committee to do the preliminary work and then report to the board its findings and suggestions on each matter. This is an efficient way to manage an organization, especially one where many of the board members are busy with their day-to-day work.

There is also the issue of formal evaluations of the board members. Developing a set of guidelines for board members to follow and be evaluated against makes for a stronger, more conscientious board. Perhaps there is a committee of board members that will develop this evaluation and will subject themselves as well as their fellow board members (and, yes, even the chair) to its inquiry. This also allows for a reduction, or at least management of potential liabilities, of board members' fiduciary responsibilities. Let's not forget that although board membership certainly has its privileges (prestige in the community, networking opportunities, philanthropic opportunities, as well as potential compensation), it also comes steeped in responsibilities. From duty of care, skill, and diligence in administrative manners (the definition of fiduciary responsibility) to the importance of complying with laws and regulations, the foundation has to be mindful of the risks it takes with those who work for (officers) or represent (directors or trustees) the foundation. It is to this end that a foundation will often purchase an insurance policy—directors and officers liability (a D&O policy) insurance—to mitigate these liabilities. It is definitely a good idea to purchase a D&O policy. These policies are relatively inexpensive and can be a lifesaver in case something goes awry with a member of your board—yes, even if the board comprises your closest family members.

Who Should Serve on the Board, and Board Orientation

As discussed, many family foundations choose their family members to serve on the board. Is this the right way to proceed? Clearly not every family member has the ability (or even the interest) to serve on a board. Often, the founding documents will specify who should be on the board (for example, all blood relatives), but this type of stringent protocol can leave out some very capable individuals (for example, a brother-in-law who just so happens to be an attorney specializing in nonprofits or charitable entities). Therefore, we believe that board membership should be based on merit and, furthermore, that a trial period of membership should be offered initially (rather than full membership), so that an evaluation can be orchestrated to determine the competence as well as the "fit" of this member.

In evaluating a board member, the full board should look at the following factors to judge if indeed the member (or trial member, if the board is employing such a mechanism) is in good standing and worthy of further consideration (by the way, it is suggested that this evaluation process is maintained for full board members well into their terms to thwart any laziness or complacency with one's role):

- Board members should be fully acquainted with the purpose, goals, history, and potential of the foundation.[2]
- Board members are required to attend meetings and should be an active participant in these meetings.
- Board members need to be well aware of the rules and regulations governing private foundations—from a legal and compliance function, as well as the fiduciary requirements as a director/trustee.
- Board members need to maintain open minds when differing views and opinions are offered—open dialogue and intelligent debate are hallmarks of good governance.
- Board members need to maintain excellent communication with each other and the board as a whole.
- Board members are required to understand the issues that are important to the mission of the foundation and to behave as ambassadors of the foundation to the public.

Board orientation is a broad term and can be achieved in many different ways, but there are a few critical items that serve as good policy initiatives to ensure an engaged and receptive board:

- Introductions and networking between members to create a board with deep ties.
- Presentations by either founders or current chairperson describing the history and mission of the foundation.
- Creation of a Director/Trustee Handbook that outlines a board member, responsibilities (complete with a calendar of meeting dates and events) and a primer on the foundation board members' fiduciary duties and the laws and regulations that govern the foundation sector. This handbook should also contain a copy of the foundation's founding documents

---

[2]Anne Morgan, "Characteristics of Effective Foundation Boards," Council on Foundations, March 2010.

(mission statement, donor intent statement, etc.), as well as the bylaws and policies of the foundation.

- A presentation of success stories where the foundation has made an impact in the community or in their stated area of interest. Perhaps a site visit to a recent grantee of the foundation would also serve as an excellent example of the foundation's work.

Orientation meetings can be done in many different ways; at the actual office of the foundation (if it has one), at a board member's office, or during a board retreat (where over the course of a day and a half or so, board members can meet and discuss matters of the foundation without the pressures of day-to-day life getting in the way). The key takeaway from an orientation meeting is for the new board member to become excited to participate and to be well briefed about his or her responsibilities going forward (and that these issues are taken seriously by the foundation's board).

Furthermore, it is important that each new board member realizes the gravitas and privilege it is to serve on this board, and to that end fully understands and accepts what is expected of him or her in this new role. Clearly, this is serious stuff and needs to be conveyed in no uncertain terms to the new board member (typically any new board member is probably already aware of the weightiness of this new role). This is not some club or trade association membership; a foundation board membership carries with it a greater sense of purpose and responsibility.

Board Meetings

Regular board meetings need to be run in such a manner as to balance the time constraints on the board members and the foundation's staff with the matters at hand. It is to this end that these meetings should be as frequent as every month or so (although we cannot stress enough the importance of providing a definitive and electronic schedule of meetings—to promote downloading into calendars— well ahead of time) and that an agenda be deployed and followed at each meeting. Many boards have adopted the strategy of fewer actual meetings (maybe five or six meetings per year), but frequent e-mails briefing each board member to the matters at hand and seeking feedback electronically. With the time-starved schedules of many board

Fiduciary Responsibilities of Foundation Boards

The word fiduciary comes from the Latin *fiducia*, which means to trust. The definition of fiduciary duties has evolved over decades, from case law and common law (see Prudent Man Rule), and has now been legislated by most states. In the most straightforward terms, a fiduciary has the responsibility to serve his or her role in a manner consistent with the duty of loyalty and care. A foundation board member must observe the fiduciary rules and responsibilities insomuch that they must serve the best interests of the foundation, disclose and avoid any conflicts of interest, and manage the assets of the foundation in a manner consistent with the rules set forth in fiduciary duties. These duties are detailed as follows:

Duty of Loyalty

In this duty, foundation board members must understand their commitment to the benefit of the foundation above their own. Breaches in this responsibility can be seen in some of the following ways:

Conflict of interest: Here a board member can find himself in a situation where he or she can benefit from a proposed transaction that the foundation is considering. In this case, the board member's best route is to recuse himself or herself from any discussions or votes in this particular transaction. In addition, full disclosure of these matters is always a good idea.

Self-dealing: In this situation, a board member (or any "disqualified person") is knowingly and purposely benefiting from actions of the foundation. An example of this might be the foundation renting space from a board member at above-market rent (even if it was at market rent, it would be a questionable action from a fiduciary standpoint).

Theft, embezzlement of assets: Fairly self-explanatory. Bottom line: Stealing is a no-no.

Duty of Care:

In this duty, we are focused on the issue of conscientiousness—the awareness of what is going on and not just going through the motions. The following are facets of the duty of care:

Awareness: Board members should be well briefed on the foundation's mission statement, organizational documents, and guiding documents. They should be aware of the foundation's finances (even if they are not on that committee) and staffing issues, and regulations governing the foundation, as well as any pending interactions with government or regulatory bodies.

Obedience: The bylaws are meant to be studied and understood—these are static documents but require a dynamic adherence and appreciation, since as a fiduciary, the board member must ensure the foundation's tax-exempt status. Playing the ignorance card—"it was someone else's job"—is not going to work.

Prudence: Much of the spirit of the fiduciary duties comes from the concept of the Prudent Man Rule from the early 1600s, where the importance of acting in a prudent fashion defined the standard of care that fiduciaries must adhere to in their work. It is not good enough to make a good decision—a fiduciary needs to make a prudent one. A good example of this might be in the area of investing; take a board member who is in charge of the investments for the foundation—the decisions he has made in regard to the foundation's portfolio have earned it a terrific return, substantially above the market's return. But has he acted in a fiduciary-minded manner? Many would say no, given the risks he may have taken to make these outsized returns. It is not just the results that determine a fiduciary responsibility, but also the thinking that goes into getting there.

members, adopting a more time-efficient plan goes a long way to an engaged and happy board (although actual face-to-face meetings can also serve as a good relationship-deepening mechanism). This debate comes down to the nature of a foundation's board—if it is comprised of those with more time on their hands (retired or semi-retired folks) then actual meetings might be a good policy, versus a board of business people who might appreciate a more efficient e-mail exchange and fewer actual meetings.

The agenda as well as any supporting documents (i.e., grant requests, compensations studies, staff evaluations) should be contained in a meeting packet sent to each board member well in advance (a week or so) of the meeting, to promote advance preparation and efficient discussion at the actual meeting. Obviously in smaller, family-based foundations many of the above may not be as necessary, but they also serve as excellent best practices and protocols that can be built upon and offer scalability that might be needed in future years. Additionally, in these smaller foundations, adherence to good board protocol can nicely serve the younger set as an education for which they might be ever so grateful in future years.

The secretary of the board should conduct an evaluation (see Exhibit 4.1) of the meeting immediately after its conclusion (while impressions are fresh in his or her mind) and on occasion, prepare a report on such findings to the board's governance committee.

Exhibit 4.1   Board Meeting Evaluation Form

Objectives	Status	Suggestions for Improvement
The agenda was clear, supported by the necessary documents, and circulated prior to the meeting.		
The meeting facility was comfortable and supportive for the work being done. Refreshments served? Meeting began and concluded on time?		
Preparation of board members—Were they engaged in the discussions at hand? What percentage of board members were in attendance? Any board member habitually not present?		
We covered a broad agenda—receiving briefings from staff as well as committees ranging from general and administrative issues to grant-making and longer-term strategic issues.		
A diversity of opinions was expressed and issues were dealt with in a respectful manner.		
The chairperson's role—Did the chair guide the meeting and maintain the board's focus throughout? Built consensus?		
Next steps and a host of deliverables, complete with a defined timetable were addressed and agreed to.		
There was a noncontentious atmosphere present, whereby the members of the board seemed to enjoy their fellow board member's input and company.		

Board Compensation

According to the Association of Small Foundation's 2006–2007 Foundation Operations and Management Survey, 30 percent of the survey respondents compensated board members for their routine board and committee service. This was distinct from any additional compensation they received for any advisory or staff services. Among this 30 percent, 51 percent paid an annual fee to board members, 35 percent paid per board meeting, and 14 percent compensated using a combination of annual and per meeting fees. As one would expect, nonfamily foundations and those with a higher asset level were more likely to compensate board members.

Although it is clear from the above survey results that private foundations do indeed engage in compensation of their board members, the question remains: *How much was the compensation?* To tackle this all-important facet of board governance it is recommended that the compensation committee (if one exists in the foundation, if not, then the entire board would suffice) conduct a professional compensation study to develop a matrix of annual compensation depending on the role, number of hours worked, and overall size of the foundation. This professional study, orchestrated by consultants that traffic in this sector, will include interviews with each board member—to ascertain their specific roles and efforts regarding the foundation's work, and to compute their relative index within the foundation sector. It is important to have this study completed (and followed) so that if the foundation's compensation policies are ever in question (remember, it's all on the 990-PF form and on the Internet), the board has substantial backup to defend its decisions. To that end, it is also good policy for board members to maintain a log of their hours and efforts to further substantiate their efforts for the foundation.

"Well, that is certainly a lot to think about," said Phil.

"I figured that a certain level of compensation would be justified for our family members serving on the board, but didn't realize that we really can't make arbitrary amounts up," said Mary.

"Nothing is arbitrary in the management of a private foundation," said Em. "Everything needs to be checked, verified, and rechecked."

"Well now that we have discussed board, development and good governance policies, what's next?" asked Phil.

"Can we start to make grants?" begged Mary.

"Yes, the next report will discuss exactly that—how to develop a procedure and glidepath to grant making so that it is done with proper care and precision," said Em.

"Fantastic!" said Phil.

"Finally!" said Mary.

Summary

This chapter focused on the management of a private foundation—from understanding the relative tax forms to the responsibilities of the board of directors. It covered who should be on the board, as well as those members' fiduciary responsibilities and how to evaluate a board meeting. In the next chapter, we discuss the grant-making process with an emphasis placed on how to evaluate a particular charitable organization. Are they in full compliance? Does their mission and expected impact align with ours? How do we evaluate their proposal?

CHAPTER

5

Managing a Private Foundation— Grant Making and Operations

Let us erect a foundation, a trust, and engage directors who make it a life's work to manage, with our personal cooperation, this business of benevolence properly and effectively.
    —John D. Rockefeller, in 1899, at the event commemorating
        the 10th anniversary of the University of Chicago

Okay, so how do we get started making some grants? Do we simply write out some checks and mail them to our favorite non-profits?" asked an anxious and excited Mary Anthony.

"Honey, hold on, I am sure that there is more to it than just writing checks, right, Em?" said Phil Anthony.

"That's correct Phil. Like anything in life, there is a right and a wrong way to do it. Given that we are dealing with substantial capital and will be monitored by the Attorney General's office, not to mention anyone with an Internet hookup, prudence clearly should dictate our actions," said Emmett Pathy.

"I figured as much. Don't worry, Mary, we are almost there!" said Phil.

"Yes, we are—almost. And the best way to ensure an effective outcome is to put in place a robust set of rules and policies—a glide-path that will guide you in this grant making process," advised Em.

"That sounds good. I have always been a rule follower, so I can understand what you are saying," said Mary.

"Okay, but first we need to figure out what kind of foundation you will be—one focused on collaborative projects with other foundations, or an activist foundation that seeks to make policy changes, or maybe one involved with venture projects," said Em.

"That's a lot to think about—let's get into it and see what we come up with," said Phil.

"Right on, Phil. Don't worry, Mary, we will get to the check writing soon—I promise," said Em.

"Fantastic! Because there are many excellent charities that could use our support," said a heartfelt Mary.

Emmett Pathy developed a report for the Anthonys' consideration that focused on several important facets of a private foundation—issues that they will have to consider and define in order to better understand what type of foundation they will become. The first issue is the concept of grant sourcing: how will the foundation get grant requests? Will they sit back and wait for nonprofits to find them? That might be difficult because, like most foundations, they checked the box in the 990-PF form that indicated that they were not interested in solicited grants. But if they were to uncheck that box or, despite the designation, if grant-seeking nonprofits solicited the foundation (which they will), would that be the best way forward for the foundation? Think about it: How could the foundation study this wide spectrum of grant requests? Without a common thread, with requests coming in from all corners of the nonprofit universe, the foundation would certainly be challenged from an efficiency and effectiveness point of view. Even if the grant seekers respected the foundation's mission statement and attempted to craft their requests accordingly, there would still be the issue of controlling the process, which could certainly hamstring even the most ambitious foundation.

Given the above constraints, it is advised that foundations do indeed check the 990-PF "nonsolicitation box" and seek to source their grant requests through more controlled and defined means. These often include the foundation's board and advisers, who certainly understand the mission statement of the foundation that they represent, and to that end can source nonprofits that are in the zone of possibility. Additionally, the leadership of the foundation, be it the board or the staff, can proactively reach out to organizations that they believe strategically fit the foundation's reach and scope. Once this process of sourcing begins it will take on a strength of its own and the foundation should have plenty of opportunities to sort through.

Type of Support: Periodic versus Endowments and General versus Program-Based

Assuming that sourcing is now in place, the next step is to gain a better understanding of the actual support we plan to give—will the capital (grants) be of a periodic nature or an endowment setup? Periodic grants or support consists of smaller grants spread out over time.[1] Endowments are grants in which the donor loses control of the grant, and as we discussed in earlier chapters, even if the nonprofit changes its philanthropic mission the donor cannot rescind the previously given grant. With periodic grants, the donor (the foundation in this case) maintains the all-important control reins, and to that end, has substantial power to continue to effectuate change. Assume for a moment that the nonprofit in question is seeking to diverge into a new area that is counter to its primary mission. The foundation is under no requirement to continue its grant making (even if they have been making such grants for years) and can attempt to shape this new initiative back into something akin to the primary mission. Bottom line, with the checkbook in hand a foundation wields much power to ensure that their interests, and the interests of the charities' ultimate beneficiaries, are met.

We agree that periodic grant making is the preferred method of ensuring that the nonprofit's mission statement is upheld. The other issue that we need to address is the commitment, if any, to these periodic grants. Many private foundations are less likely to commit to "evergreen" funding of a particular nonprofit, where the foundation continues to make grants to the nonprofit year after year. Does this provide the nonprofit with an undesired sense of complacency? If they know that this grant is coming in every year are they as incentivized to continue their fundraising in earnest? How about their projects—does this "automatic grant" usher in laziness in the effectiveness of the programs conducted by the

---

[1]Roger Silk and James Lintott, *Creating a Private Foundation* (Princeton, NJ: Bloomberg Press, 2003).

nonprofit? Many foundations that adhere to periodic grant making embrace a "3 out of 5 year" rule that states that they will only fund a nonprofit three out of five years. In this way, they can see how the nonprofit does in years four and five when they come back for a grant in year six. This kind of protocol eliminates the "sugar daddy" issue that many foundations and nonprofits fall into and motivates the nonprofit to be continually dynamic—never resting on its laurels—always striving to do better.

The next big debate in grant making is the issue of grants directed to general support or those directed to specific projects. General support, also known as overhead, is unglamorous and unexciting, but it is essential to every charity. All charities have overhead, and money for its own operations is usually the most difficult to raise. Program support is support of the charity's specific programs. Here the results are visible and decisive. It's easy to feel that the money is doing good when it is being used for something tangible and dramatic, such as buying blankets that go directly to children made homeless by a sudden flooding.[2]

Clearly, general support is needed in order to run the nonprofit in the first place and many foundations see it as their responsibility to assist in this "unsexy" area of fundraising—for if not them, then who would make these donations? The key for the foundation is to ensure that the general support given is not wasted and is used in the most efficient manner possible. Does the staff of the charity really need fancy offices in the skyscraper? Couldn't they get by with smaller digs donated in part by a generous landlord? Although we wouldn't ever deny professionals their due, we do need to be cognizant of salary levels, and to that end would advocate—for both the foundation staff as well as the charity's—an independent compensation study to ensure that proper levels, are in place. This study cuts both ways—we want to make sure that the compensation program in place is competitive so as not to create a revolving door of nonprofit executive talent. Foundations will be able to ascertain much of this info through their due diligence process, which provides a statistic that compares the expenses of the nonprofit versus their charitable activities—the best run charities typically commit no more than 15 to 20 percent of their income to noncharitable expenses.

---

[2]Silk and Lintott, *Creating a Private Foundation.*

What Type of Foundation Will We Become?

Once we know how we are going to mine for the grants and the type of support we plan to give, we can then move to the next major defining issue of the foundation—What will be the approach of the foundation? There are several approaches that a foundation needs to work through, from a collaborative foundation to one focused on venture philanthropy. Of course, none of these approaches are an exclusive designation—in other words; you can have, as part of your grant portfolio, a number of venture projects and others where you are utilizing a collaborative approach. There are also those foundations whose approach is more akin to "sponging" (in a good way), where they learn the best practices of other foundations and utilize them, maybe after making some changes, in their own grant making. There are also those foundations that employ, typically through pro bono relationships, an expert network to allow them to better focus on the issues in a specific sector and thereby increase the effectiveness of their grants. Finally, an area that has gotten much attention as of late is the program-related investment (PRI), a part of a private foundation's grant portfolio where a foundation makes grants as a secured loan or equity participation in a nonprofit.

Collaboration is a great word—it conjures up a whole host of good feelings—meaning helping each other to grow and attain better heights. In the foundation world, collaboration is also a powerful business model, where foundations of like mind and mission can work alongside each other (no such thing as competition or trade secrets in the foundation world) to ensure a greater outcome for the given nonprofit. It is this partnership platform that permits a greater footprint to be achieved—where often one plus one equals three or even four. There are many foundation networks; that is, networking groups of foundations and other grant-making entities that work on problems in their communities and together ring-fence their resources to accomplish more than one foundation could do on its own. This is the basis of *synergy*—a word that is often bandied about carelessly, but in these cases rings true.

Venture philanthropy combines the interest in giving with the talents of businesspeople and entrepreneurs (many of whom start foundations of this nature) to address an important matter through seeding a new business. In this case, think of the foundation as an incubator—assisting new businesses through their growth and development process. In most cases, the actual businesses that are indeed helped along through the resources of the foundation—and these resources often include more than simple capital like know-how and connections—are linked with the foundation's mission statement and areas of interest. Paul Shoemaker, a former Microsoft executive who runs Seattle's Social Venture Partners, elaborates: "In our case, venture philanthropy means long-term, sustained relationships with nonprofits; imparting business skills and expertise as well as money; a focus on giving general operating grants; and trying to be invested. These organizations need more than money; they need human and financial capital. Each part is necessary but insufficient on its own."[3]

Everyone has heard the old story about a bank robber who, when asked why he robbed banks, stated matter-of-factly, "That's where the money is." Well, the same thinking can be applied to new foundations: Where are you going to go to gain the best insights on grant making and operations? Easy answer: other successful foundations. This concept of "best practices" is utilized by many businesses as well as other entities to gain insights and expertise in matters where they have a similar footprint. We use the phrase *sponging* jokingly, but there is a sense of spending time with fellow foundation heads and their staffs to better understand how they do things in their foundations. Utilizing some of these approaches (and often improving on them) makes for a better philanthropic sector for all players and consequently to the myriad of nonprofits that the foundations support. In the philanthropic sector, unlike the commercial one, fellow foundation executives are more than happy to assist a new foundation, and with this assistance often comes a stronger, more collaborative, relationship—again a win-win for all.

How can a new foundation gain such inroads to other existing and successful foundations? More likely than not, they will find you. Although the private foundation sector is a fast-growing area it is still relatively small—sooner or later everyone in a foundation's geographic or mandate-driven footprint will know each other. There are also networks that have popped up; typically drawn along geographic lines, these groups are excellent forums for the new foundation to meet existing foundations and to develop

---

[3]Silk and Lintott. *Creating a Private Foundation.*

relationships along the way. Usually at these gatherings people around the table introduce themselves and say a thing or two about their foundation, and then a project or issue is introduced for discussion. At the end of the meeting, the new foundation can mingle and network, meet existing foundations that may have a similar interest, and begin to forge relationships. Bring a stack of cards to these meetings and don't forget the sponges!

There is also another type of network that is helpful in the development of a new foundation. Expert networks might have a soiled name on Wall Street these days, but they serve an important purpose and are 100 percent legal in the foundation sector. These networks, or groups of advisers and industry experts, allow foundations to dig deeper on issues where they have an interest in greater understanding and data compilation. A foundation might call on an expert network of environmentalists when considering a project to support a green initiative in a particular area. Or, the foundation might engage a network of civic-minded experts to address (perhaps by writing a white paper) an issue in their local community (i.e., racism, child obesity, educational reform). In both cases, networking, both for internal as well as external reasons, is a major part of the foundation's leadership's role.

Program-related investments (PRIs) have been rapidly growing over the past two decades, due in large measure to the efforts of the Ford and MacArthur Foundations in educating the foundation sector to their benefits. A PRI is an investment made by a foundation that seeks to meet three tests:

1. Its primary purpose is to further the tax-exempt mission of the foundation.
2. Any income or growth must be kept within the confines of what a prudent investor would expect. In other words, a foundation cannot make a PRI with a significant portion of their assets—the basic tenets of fiduciary investment management need to be kept front of mind.
3. The investment cannot be used to lobby or support lobbying.

A PRI can be a loan (most are), social purpose deposit, loan guarantee, line of credit, asset purchase, equity investment, or recoverable grant. The IRS permits foundations to count PRIs as part of the required 5 percent charitable distribution in the year that the

PRI is made. Rates of return on PRIs by definition must be below market on a risk-adjusted basis, and most often are set at low interest rates. There are no set requirements for PRI loan structures, which vary considerably, based on both the needs of the borrower or project and the needs and expectations of the foundation lenders. Terms can range from a few months to more than 15 years (typically having to do with real estate development projects).[4]

"Excellent report, as always, Em. And we have given a lot of thought to these issues and expect to better define our business model, if you will, over the course of the next several months. I assume that there is no rush to lock in just now on these issues," asked Phil.

"Of course, take your time. These issues are more for thought leadership and long-term footprints than anything concrete today—it is just critical that you understand the implications of each," advised Em.

"Understood. And we have discussed these in detail and have taken some steps to define our grant making in light of some of these issues and recommendations," said Phil.

"Now that we have discussed some of the basic tenets that will define this foundation, we can begin to discuss the actual process we are going to go through in making a grant," said Em.

"I have my list of charities ready," chimed in Mary.

"Easy, Mary. I am sure there is a process involved in deciding which grants to make and when to make them," suggested Phil.

"You are right, Phil. This is not like paying your cable bill; there is a process involved that is important to recognize and follow," advised the Anthonys' financial adviser.

"Of course, that makes sense. So, Em, tell us the process, for I am itching to write some checks," said Mary.

"Well, rather than tell you I would prefer to *show* you," said Em, who whipped out a desktop poster board.

"Wow, now that is what I call a glide-path!" said Phil.

"Yes, this flowchart will allow you and your family to maintain proper due diligence and provide a working model of the operations of the grant committee of the foundation," said Em.

---

[4]Francie Brody, Kevin McQueen, Christa Velasquez, and John Weiser, *Current Practices in Program-Related Investments* (Branford, CT: Brody • Weiser • Burns, 2002).

"And the color coded chart, what is that used for?" asked Phil.

"That is a sample spreadsheet that I recommend you folks use in your foundation office to track each nonprofit. Once you start using it, I am confident that it will become an indispensible tool to keep you on track," said Em.

"It looks a little daunting to me. Are you sure we are going to understand it?" asked a concerned Mary.

"Sure you will. Let's get into it now and you will see how straightforward much of this work is," advised Em.

Emmett Pathy, in his sage-like fashion, discussed each part of the flowchart with his clients, the Anthonys. In addition, Em developed a written report that they could refer to in the future and share with other board members as well. In this report Em walked through each piece of the flowchart and operational glide-path in detail.

Sourcing a Grant

Grant requests can and will originate in many different areas, some of which you might not expect—from the neighbor's kid who is working on an extracurricular project to the relative who is afflicted by a particular disease. In each case you may want to help, but often you can't do it all. Having a defined plan of attack with respect to grant-making permits the foundation and its board to say no (often it's couched a little differently—much more euphemistically) to those friends and family who may not understand how foundations operate. Let's be realistic: we can't provide grants to every charitable organization out there—there needs to be a process in place to maintain the integrity of the foundation's giving.

The genesis of a grant can come from friends and family, but more often than not, these grant opportunities will find you (remember everything is on the Internet). The mission of your foundation may be enough to bring a serious bunch of nonprofits knocking at your door (or inbox, as the case may be). In addition, the (charitable) areas that the foundation "management" have been involved with will become an obvious first choice—a jumping-off point—with respect to grant making as well (as seen in Exhibit 5.1). So it is likely that you will not have a dearth of grant-making opportunities—the trick is to research each one carefully and to ensure that your grants make a difference.

As seen in Exhibit 5.2, we start out by tracking each inquiry made to the foundation for a grant by assigning it a tracking number on our spreadsheet. Utilizing this spreadsheet format, each inquiry is logged in and a schedule of tasks is assigned in order to manage the grant-making process. In many smaller foundations, where there may not be a dedicated grants officer, this spreadsheet is often kept

Exhibit 5.1   Grant Management Flowchart

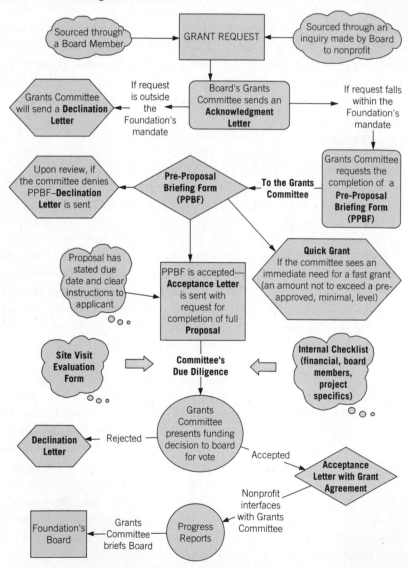

Exhibit 5.2   Grant-Making Operations Glide-Path Spreadsheet

Proposal and Project Background

Nonprofit	Grant Tracking Number	Date Request Received	How Sourced	IRS Web Site 501(c)(3) Status	Applicability to Our Mandate	Declination Letter #1 or Acknowledgement Letter Sent? Date?

Pre-Proposal Briefing Form

PPBF Sent and Due Date	Completed PPBF Received	Grants Committee Study of PPBF	Declination Letter #2	Quick Grant? Amount?	Request for Full Proposal– Acceptance Letter #1 sent?

Grants Committee Due Diligence

Proposal Received? In good order?	Study of Proposal– Evaluation Form Grade	Site Visit Evaluation Form	Financial Checklist

Grant Request–Outcome

Date of Board Vote on Proposal	Proposal Rejected? Date that Declination Letter #3 was Sent	Proposal Accepted? Date that Acceptance Letter #2 Sent with Grant Agreement	Grant Agreement Received?	Check Sent–Date and Check Number

Follow-Up and Progress Reporting

3-Month Follow-Up	Semi-Annual Progress Report Received?	Grants Committee Board Briefing on Grant/Project

in the "cloud," allowing any member (with permission) to utilize the spreadsheet and add a new potential grantee. Another good practice is, on the entry of a new grant candidate, to create a folder with the name and tracking number of the potential grantee so that any information on that candidate can be kept in an organized fashion. A major facet of this "foundation business" is to maintain a sense of organization given the inundation of paperwork that is typical of a grant-making entity. Staying organized and maintaining good files will serve you well with respect to compliance and regulatory issues that may arise when you least expect them.

The Acknowledgment Process

Now that we have entered the new grant candidate onto the spreadsheet and started a file that will serve as the "holding cell" for all of the pertinent information regarding this nonprofit, what's next? Some basic research is in order at this time: Is this nonprofit in compliance with the IRS exemption—the 501(c)(3) status? Does its mission have any relation to our mandate or interest level? The answers to these questions will determine our next step; do we thank them, decline going forward to the next step (nicely, of

Exhibit 5.3   Sample of a Declination Letter #1 (Used On Review of a Grant Request)

Date

Organization
Address
City, State, Zip

Re: Grant Request (<date>)

Dear Mr./Mrs. _____:

The ABC Foundation appreciated the opportunity to review your request for a grant for your organization's efforts to _____.

At the ABC Foundation it is our practice to review all grant requests carefully, and if it meets with our mandate and stringent policy directives set forth by our board of directors, invite the organization to complete our Pre-Proposal Briefing Form. Unfortunately we are unable to invite your organization to proceed to this next step.

Mr./Mrs. _____, as you can imagine, the foundation receives a large number of requests for assistance, only a minority of which proceed to the next step in our process. Of course, our decision is in no way indicative of a negative assessment of your organization or proposal. It merely speaks to the overwhelming needs of our community and to our desire to respond to them in a balanced and equitable manner.

On behalf of our foundation, we wish you continued success.

Sincerely,
The Grants Committee of the ABC Foundation

---

course) and wish them luck in the future, or do we invite them to proceed with the next step in our grant making process?

The answers to these questions will determine the type of correspondence we send. There are two letters that can be sent, each thanking the candidate for their inquiry. In one letter, the declination letter (see Exhibit 5.3), we state that we are unable to entertain their request at this time and wish them success in the future. Short and sweet; there's no need to go into detail on this first go-around. After all, this was just a simple inquiry that might have nothing in common with the foundation's mandate or interests.

The second letter, the acknowledgment letter (see Exhibit 5.4), provides some details to the inner workings of the foundation—its processes and procedures—and invites the nonprofit to complete a Pre-Proposal Briefing Form (PPBF). Now, let me pause here for a moment to state that none of these processes are cut in stone; there

---

Exhibit 5.4   Acknowledgment Letter

Date

Dear _____:

Thank you for your interest in ABC Foundation. We received your letter of inquiry on <date> concerning <some brief description of the matter or project for which they are seeking a grant>.

Your project may fall within an area of our interest, and to that end we would like to ask your organization to complete the attached *"Pre-Proposal Briefing Form (PPBF),"* which will allow the board to assess the viability of this project—to determine if it falls within the scope of our mandate.

After studying the PPBF, and if it indeed meets our requirements for further exploration, we will invite you to submit a full proposal—details of which will be made available to you at that time. We invite you to visit our web site at www.abcfoundation.org to learn more about the foundation as well as our grant making.

Once we receive the Pre-Proposal Briefing Form back from you, a decision whether or not to invite you to make a full grant proposal will be made within 30–60 days. During the review process, you may be contacted by telephone and/or a site visit may be requested.

Again, thank you for your interest in the ABC Foundation. We look forward to receiving the attached Pre-Proposal Briefing Form back from you shortly.

Sincerely,

The Grants Committee of the ABC Foundation

Note: Letter sent, on foundation letterhead—either hard copy or e-mail—on receipt of a grant request.

are no defined rules or regulations on how to conduct the operations of a private foundation's grant making. These are simply best practices that have been honed over many years and provide a simplified set of tasks to maintain control and order.

It is important that the foundation leadership, staff, and benefactors maintain a healthy sense of skepticism for there are many charlatans out there in this nonprofit sector. Hence, one of the first tasks that the grants committee or the staff should complete with respect to a new grant candidate is to check their federal tax exemption as a 501(c)(3) organization. As detailed in Chapter 2, this is a fairly straightforward and simple process thanks to the IRS web site, which checks through all nonprofits and provides a "thumbs up" or "thumbs down" depending on the nonprofit's standing as a bona fide nonprofit. Doing some additional digging on your own can lead to more information, although be wary of what you might read on the Internet. It is always better to simply go to the source—the IRS, in this case—for the defined data that are required to proceed to the next step. On the spreadsheet, it should be indicated that you have indeed checked the nonprofit's tax-exempt status and have decided to send the nonprofit the declination letter or the acknowledgment letter (with the PPBF) for their completion by a stated due date.

The Pre-Proposal Briefing Form (PPBF)

The PPBF (see Exhibit 5.5) is an excellent tool used by many foundations to gather the most important data about a nonprofit quickly, efficiently, and up front in the process. Many find this a more desirable glide-path versus the inquiry-right-to-proposal process, which can become somewhat muddy and time-consuming.

By utilizing the PPBF (or some iteration of it), grants committees at private foundations are more engaged earlier in the process and can then separate the nonprofit opportunities that meet their interest and mandates without having to go through the more time-consuming process of reviewing a full-blown proposal for funding. There is also the issue of the "grant-making economy" that comes into play, whereby the preparation of a PPBF is a lot less taxing to the already strained staffs of many nonprofits. Of course, a full proposal will be required to make a grant (except in the cases of "Quick Grants" and "Discretionary Grants"), but once this is requested the grants committee already has a good sense of the nonprofit's

Exhibit 5.5   Pre-Proposal Briefing Form

Date PPBF Sent and to Whom _____

Date Due _____

Background Information
Project Title: _____

Organization:_____

Address: _____

Phone: _____

Fax: _____

Email: _____

Website: _____

Contact person: _____

Title: _____

Management and Staff of Organization:

Number _____ Avg. Tenure _____

Size of Board of Directors _____

How often are meetings held? _____

Please provide a complete list of Board members (as well as advisory board members) and their affiliations

How long has the nonprofit been in existence? _____

501(c)(3) Status _____

Please include a copy of your organization's IRS exemption letter

Organization's annual budget _____

Previous 2 years budget _____

Operational (noncharitable) Expenses annually _____

Government funding/year _____

Foundation funding/year _____

Foundations that have supported the organization in the past 3 years

_____

_____

_____

The Project/Reason for the Grant Request
Total cost of the project _____

Amount of Requested Grant_____

Type of Grant Requested (one time or multiyear): _____

Current Project Status:

Start date: _____

Amount raised to date_____

Please submit a 1 to 2 page letter of inquiry that contains the following:

- Purpose and history of the organization
- Goals, objectives, brief description, and the population served by the project

Exhibit 5.6   Declination Letter #2

Date

Organization
Address
City, State, Zip

Re: Grant Pre-Proposal Briefing Form (<date>)

Dear Mr./Mrs. _____:

The ABC Foundation appreciated the opportunity to consider your completed Pre-Proposal Briefing Form regarding your organization's efforts to _____.

While your PPBF was in good order and gave us a definitive illustration of the project, we are, unfortunately, unable to move forward with a request for a complete *Proposal-for-Funding* at this time. We will maintain your Pre-Proposal Briefing Form on file and look forward to hearing back from you from time to time.

Mr./Mrs. _____, as you can imagine, the foundation receives a large number of requests for assistance, only a minority of which we request candidates to complete our PPBF. We utilize, on occasion, our database of briefing forms in order to complete our grant cycle. Of course, our decision is in no way indicative of a negative assessment of your organization or proposal. It merely speaks to the overwhelming needs of our community and to our desire to respond to them in a balanced and equitable manner.

On behalf of our foundation, we wish you continued success.

Sincerely,
The Grants Committee of the ABC Foundation

---

project at hand and can proceed through the due diligence phase quicker.

Upon review of the PPBF, the grants committee may realize that the nonprofit does not meet its requirements—from mission statement (which is typically declined in the earlier inquiry process but sometimes is given a longer leash to see if there is something there that might work for the foundation) to a host of other pre-due diligence issues. These issues can include their finances, board members, or governance that is such that the grants committee decides not to pursue the grant request further. At that juncture, the grants committee should send a letter (Declination Letter #2—see Exhibit 5.6) thanking the nonprofit for their efforts and stating that they will maintain the PPBF on file for potential future revisiting. It is this pipeline of grant opportunities that tends to fill in the blanks in the spreadsheet. There is also the intended consequence of permitting the grants committee to watch the progress of these nonprofits—perhaps going through their own growing pains and issues—to determine if, in the future, they have righted themselves and are candidates for a fresh look.

Before we move to the acceptance process of the PPBF there are two instances where the PPBF serves as the mechanism by which the grant is accepted and processed. These two "skips" are for Quick Grants and Discretionary Grants. A Quick Grant is where the grants committee, on reviewing the PPBF, sees an immediate need for an expedited grant to a nonprofit. Most foundations will only allow a perfunctory amount to be issued under a Quick Grant program; the amounts are relative to the size of the foundation, but the typical range of a Quick Grant is something akin to $5,000 to $10,000. The grants committee needs to be as conscientious as ever with respect to Quick Grants and maybe even more so, given the lack of a full-blown due diligence process, and focus their attention on the legal issues (i.e., 501[c][3] status, conflicts of interest, self-dealing) rather than the nitty gritty that is the typical study of a proposal.

In many cases a Quick Grant can save a nonprofit that finds itself in a cash-flow bind or with an opportunity to grow (if they just had a little more capital). There are also instances where a nonprofit might be coming to the expiration of a challenge grant (when a grant is contingent on raising a certain amount by a given date) and they only need a little more to get over the top and secure a major grant for another source. Typically, like Discretionary Grants, Quick Grants are sourced by board members or those close to the foundation (i.e. advisers, collaborators).

With Discretionary Grants, many private foundations allow their board members and trustees to make a certain number of grants— either within or outside their normal grant making cycle—while again, like in Quick Grants, relaxing the due diligence process somewhat. Some foundations use the discretionary grants pool—a defined amount of capital allotted annually for said grants—as a "reward for service" whereby the board member or trustee can process a grant with limited due diligence and oversight. Here again there needs to be a level of conscientiousness with respect to the legal issues of this grant (i.e., 501[c][3] status), but in many cases the foundation is relying on the board member to ensure that a true need exists and that there will not be any embarrassment factor involved with this grant. In Exhibit 5.7 we see an example of a foundation's discretionary grant policy, which, as illustrated, is quite defined in its approach.

Let's return to the typical glide-path from a PPBF to a request for a full proposal. Once the grants committee reviews and approves

Exhibit 5.7   Discretionary Grants

This document describes our policy and practice in regards to grants made at the request of trustees outside our normal grant making cycle. This policy is intended to help us keep our grant making activities clear and consistent from the viewpoint of those who seek funding from us.

– Each year an overall grant making budget is set and a small amount is apportioned for trustee-advised gifts. This amount should not exceed ten (10) percent of our total grant-making budget. This dollar amount is divided equally among the trustees. Thus, grants from this pool are "exceptional" and out of the ordinary course of business. We should communicate the exceptional, non-repetitive nature of these grants to grantees; not to make them beholden to us but so they understand that we make the large majority of our grant dollars available to the whole community in an open process.

– If during the course of events the grant making budget for a year has to be lowered substantially, the first course of action would be to lower the trustee-advised pool.

– Grants from trustees are limited to $10,000 per agency per year. This limitation is intended to keep these discretionary grants from competing in size and importance with grants awarded through our formal grant making process.

– Grants from this trustee-advised pool should be targeted to the San Diego region. This is consistent with our overall grant making policy and helps to maximize the positive impact our foundation has on our community.

– Trustee-advised grants should generally promote the mission of the foundation to help underserved communities, and focus on the two target areas we have identified as core to our work: Education and Health & Human Services.

– Trustees may wish to focus their trustee-advised gifts toward agencies that submitted requests during our grant making cycle, but were not awarded grants. This helps reinforce the efforts of high-quality agencies that are focused in our areas of interest and geography.

– Any remaining unused pool of trustee-advised giving as of the end of November for a given calendar year will be returned to the corpus of the foundation. There is no rollover of unused dollars toward future years.

– A trustee should provide a brief rationale for each trustee-advised gift that is requested. This document should include the point of contact and contact information for the given agency, a description of the need, and the fit with our overall grant making objectives.

– All trustee gifts are part of our public record. Trustees should note that other trustees will see which agencies are being selected for these grants. More importantly, the grant seeking community will also know where we place our resources, hence the desire to make these trustee-advised grants meaningful, relevant, and credible to the community.

– Trustees are treated anonymously when these trustee-advised grants are executed. No mention of individual trustees, only of the foundation, is made when the grant is communicated to the agency. A trustee can elect to be acknowledged or recognized in these communications if they so choose.

Adapted from Council on Foundations, *The Association of Small Foundations Trustee Handbook.*

the PPBF, it will send an Acceptance Letter (see Exhibit 5.8), where it thanks the nonprofit for its submission and invites them to complete the enclosed proposal form and to return it by a stated date (typically 60 days in the future). It is important to require the nonprofit to return the proposal by a defined date because it will give the grants committee a sense of their dedication to a timetable and a sense of how this potential "partner" operates. In addition, having requests for proposals hanging out in philanthropy-space doesn't do any good—we want to know what we have in the proverbial hopper

Exhibit 5.8   Acceptance Letter #1

Date

Organization
Contact, Title
Address
City, State Zip

Re: Request for a Grant Proposal

Dear <contact>:

We are pleased to inform you that the Grants Committee of the ABC Foundation reviewed your recently completed Pre-Proposal Briefing Form (PPBF) and have decided that your current project warrants further attention by our foundation. To this end please find a copy of our self-explanatory **Grant Proposal Form**.

Please note that in order to be considered in our next grant cycle, the completed proposal, together with all related documents, must be returned to us with a postmark no later than

_____.

During our Committee's due diligence process we are likely to request informal discussions with you, your staff, members of the board directors, and the people you serve in the community. Additionally, a scheduled site visit is a typical step in our progress toward making a decision with respect to your proposal. Your assistance in scheduling these discussions would be greatly appreciated.

Please be made aware that we take our role as a grant-making organization very seriously and expect the same level of professionalism from those nonprofits that we support. We wish you much success in your efforts to complete the requirements of our grant making operations. If you have any questions, please do not hesitate to contact us at the following email address

_____.

Sincerely,
The Grants Committee of the ABC Foundation

Note: This letter is to be sent on foundation letterhead to a nonprofit that is being asked, after the committee carefully reviewed the Pre-Proposal Briefing Form, to complete a full Grant Proposal.

and maintain a careful eye on their progress. Therefore, it is also a good practice to add this piece of data—the length of time it took the nonprofit to return the proposal in good order to the grants committee—to the operating spreadsheet.

With our acceptance letter we should include instructions for the completion of the proposal—some semblance of the specific foundation's set of rules with respect to the grant proposal process. In Exhibit 5.9 there is a set of proposal instructions, as well as a defined application process that sets forth steps that the grant-seeking nonprofit needs to abide by (and a stated due date for the information and materials) in order to be considered for the foundation's due diligence process.

The actual required grant proposal can be in many different forms. Some foundations seek a more narrative approach and others develop their own proposal formats. Most will require the information and documents that are typical in a grant review process

Exhibit 5.9   Proposal Instructions

Application Procedure
The Grants Committee of the ABC Foundation has an innovative approach to grant proposal writing—flexibility. We permit one of two ways to communicate your grant proposal request—either through the utilization of a Common Application Form (one of which is available at www .philanthropynewyork.org) or a narrative discussing each of the following in detail:
– Mission statement of the organization
– Description of the organization and its background and history
– Full description of the program, its goals, objectives, and the population being served
– Clear evidence of the need for the program
– Identity and qualifications of the key personnel involved
– Names and affiliations of all directors or trustees
– Detailed program budget showing all sources of funding
– Latest financial statements including most recent audit reports
– The plan for continuing support after the ABC Foundation funding ends
– Projected organizational operating budget for the duration of the program
– Documentation that the organization's board of directors/trustees support the proposal
– Copy of the organization's IRS exemption letter

Review Process
As described in the cover letter to this correspondence we expect your proposal back in our offices, in good order, by _____. After which time our Grants Committee will study the application and prepare a report and recommendation for the full board's consideration at its next grant cycle board meeting. Grant cycle board meetings are held every 6 months—in May and in October. Applicants will be notified of the disposition of the request within two weeks after the board meeting.

Note: Please be mindful of the protocol, as described in Exhibit 5.9, used by the ABC Foundation in the Grant Proposal process. It remains our contention that nonprofit organizations are inundated with paperwork and to that end we have made our approach to grant proposals quite streamlined.

(i.e., budgets, financials, board members, project specifics), so it is advised that the grants committee maintain a careful filing system in order to maintain these documents (many larger foundations have of course gone digital, and to that end have scanned these documents for easy storage and retrieval). Given the use of the PPBF, many foundations have adopted, again in the spirit of grant-making economy, the use of a common application. This is helpful to a nonprofit that writes many grant proposals so it does not have to recreate the wheel each time, only craft the application to the specific project seeking funding. It is also helpful to the grants committee who are often inundated with proposals, especially if they entertain proposals once or twice a year, and would find it more efficient to have a common format for evaluation.

In addition to the prior exhibits, please see the example of an application for a grant at the following link: www.sparksf.org/pdf/grantapplication.pdf. An example of an application used in New York and New Jersey grant-making entities can be found here: www.bayandpaulfoundations.org/files/NY_NJ_Common_App_Form.pdf.

The Due Diligence Process

Now we have a nonprofit project that the grants committee is intrigued by, has gone through a somewhat more than cursory examination of the PPBF process, and has been invited to complete an application for funding. Upon receipt of the application, with all the requested materials, by the stated due date, the grants committee can begin their due diligence process.

The due diligence process is of critical importance, for it defines the mechanism by which the grants committee is going to study the nonprofit application and make their subsequent recommendation to the board for funding or not. We covered many of the basic requirements—the 501(c)(3) status, board of directors and governance issues, and the basic finances of the organization—in the PPBF process and now we are left with a more granular, in-depth study of the nonprofit and the project at hand. One of the first tools that the grants committee (and typically the committee will assign one of its members to a couple of specific nonprofit projects) has at its disposal is the all-important site visit. As we discussed in earlier chapters, the site visit, getting one's

Exhibit 5.10   Site Visit Form

Date of visit: _____

Visited by:_____

Accompanied by:_____

Name and address of site:_____

Amount requested: $_____

% of 501(c)(3)'s budget _____ Multiyear grant?

Purpose of grant request:_____

Where the grant fits in our mission statement:_____

Initial reaction to the site/first impressions:

_____

_____

_____

Project Background

– Project sustainability—Is this a new project? A new area for the organization? Who at the nonprofit is the driver of this initiative? Who will be our direct contact? Will the staff seek training or consultants if needed?

– Can our assistance lead to further growth in donations/grants for the nonprofit?

– How can we leverage our contacts and nonfinancial resources to assist in this initiative?

– Does the nonprofit receive any government funding for this project? Have other foundations made grants to the nonprofit—in general as well as for this initiative?

– What percentage of the nonprofit's time and resources will this project receive?

– What is the nonprofit's game plan in approaching this project? Its timetable for completion? Is the approach feasible? Innovative? Cost effective?

– Once the project is completed can it be sustained without additional support from grants? Is it self-sustainable?

– Which defined metrics can we use to determine the applicability and success of the project? What kind of interim reports from the nonprofit will we receive? The timing of these reports?

SWOT Analysis

Define the project and/or the organization:

Strengths:_____

Weaknesses:_____

Opportunities: _____

Threats: _____

Summary of Findings

– People: Staff, Management (qualified? visionaries?), Board Members (engaged?)

– Project/Initiative: Fits with our MS? Sustainability? Growth?

– Risks in supporting the program or nonprofit? Is it a contentious issue?

Recommendations

– Full funding/Partial funding/No funding/Increased funding

– Deadline for nonprofit's submission of a formal proposal: _____

– Our due diligence—follow-up with outside consultants/contacts "hands dirty" in the actual work that the nonprofit does, is an irreplaceable element of the due diligence process.

Many foundations adopt a two-stage site visit protocol, one that is scheduled with the nonprofit (the proverbial "guided tour") and one that is not (the "pop-in"). Exhibit 5.10, the Site Visit Form, can assist the grants committee member in maintaining a sense of purpose and skepticism while going through what is likely to be a polished tour. The pop-in or unscheduled site visit can also be telling in that it can highlight the true, unpolished nature of the organization. It is important to be on the lookout for the items that the "tour guides" are not telling you, and to that end the Site Visit Form requests the evaluator from the grants committee undertake a Strengths, Weaknesses, Opportunities, and Threats (SWOT) analysis. The SWOT analysis is a long-standing mechanism used by many analysts of companies to determine the strategic footprint of a particular firm. Of course, in the nonprofit world we are not studying companies per se, but nevertheless the SWOT construct can serve to highlight some specific issues that we can then use to further evaluate the nonprofit as well as the specific project.

Exhibits 5.11 and 5.12, the Proposal Review Form and the Financial Checklist, are instrumental tools for the grants committee to utilize throughout their due diligence work. The Proposal Review Form uses a point system to score the viability and acceptability of the proposal—with a heavy negative weight given to nonprofits that are not in good compliance with the stated regulations and timely satisfaction of the instructions set forth from the outset (we do not want to enter a "partnership" with a nonprofit that is unable to deliver to us, in a timely fashion, the required information and materials we requested). The Financial Checklist is a useful tool to sidestep any potential issue in the nonprofits finances before they become an issue. Think of this checklist as looking for any potential red flags that might exist in the finances of the nonprofit—from cash flow contingencies to litigations and balance sheet issues. For example, one of the issues that often comes up—and it might, on the surface, seem unimportant, is the nonprofit's choice of accounting method. As we discussed in Chapter 4, a nonprofit entity using the accrual method of accounting could "defer" many expenses (i.e., salaries, other expenses), which has the impression of making their books look sounder than they would otherwise seem using the cash method. Again,

Exhibit 5.11   Proposal Review Form

PROPOSAL REVIEW FORM

Name of Organization: _____

Grant Tracking Number: _____

Amount Requested: _____

Eligibility	Circle One		Score: Yes = +1; No = −25
Is the program within one of the foundations's program areas?	YES	NO	
Does the organization qualify as a 509(a)(1) or (2) public charity on their IRS determination letter? (Other organizations can be funded but additional paperwork is usually necessary.)	YES	NO	

Completeness		
Has the organization submitted all required documents?	YES	NO
– organizational history, mission, goals	YES	NO
– specific statement of amount and objectives	YES	NO
– statement of need, target population, and support date	YES	NO
– timetable for the project (including start and end dates)	YES	NO
– staff qualifications	YES	NO
– list of board members	YES	NO
– budgets and other financial information	YES	NO
– IRS determination letter	YES	NO

Programmatic Fit	Poor			Excellent		Score
Will this program fill a need within the community not currently or adequately addressed?	1	5	10	15	20	
Is the organization financially sound after analyzing the 990 tax return, annual budget, program budget, and audit?	1	5	10	15	20	
Is the organization capable of implementing and sustaining the program (e.g. adequate funding, staff, resources, community support)?	1	5	10	15	20	

Merit						
Do we have the ability to make an impact with this grant?	1	5	10	15	20	
Does the request exhibit high quality and stand out?	1	5	10	15	20	
Are there any opportunities to match or leverage the foundation's funds?	1	5	10	15	20	
					TOTAL	

A minimum score of 71 needs to be attained in order to proceed with a recommendation for funding.
Adapted from the "Trustee Handbook," The Association of Small Family Foundations.

Reprinted with permission from the Association of Small Foundations.

Exhibit 5.12   Financial Checklist

- Does the organization have timely audited financial statements available (no more than 5 months after the fiscal year end)?
- Which accounting method does the organization use in their financial statements? If Accrual Method, question if there are any outstanding payables currently being deferred.
- Does the organization have an independent auditor's report or opinion that indicated any serious problems?
  - Outstanding litigation
  - Inability of the organization to continue in business
  - Inadequate record keeping or internal controls
  - Uncertainties pertaining to IRS or state audit adjustments
  - Management omitting required disclosures
  - The auditor's inability to render an opinion
  - An inverse (unfavorable) opinion by the auditor
- Are there warning signs in the balance sheet and income statement?
  - Continuous operating losses or fund deficits
  - Excessive payables and other liabilities with minor or no cash
  - Erosion of endowment and reserves to fund operations
  - Excessive cash and investments
  - Large amounts in miscellaneous expense categories
  - Excessive administrative or payroll expenses
  - Reliance on one or two funding sources only
  - Poor yields on investments
- Are there signs that indicate the organization is financially healthy and well run?
  - Operating profits
  - Building up of endowments and reserves
  - Increases in pledges
  - Administrative expenses generally below 20%
  - Ability to add new programs and projects
  - Attractive yields on investments

Reprinted with permission from the Association of Small Foundations.

the importance of being beyond reproach in our grant making is of the utmost importance and the ultimate purpose of the due diligence process—and checklists such as this one provides this all-important sense of comfort to the grants committee and eventually to the board itself.

Once the due diligence process is complete, the grants committee can either reject the application (typically for some missing piece of data, an issue with the site visit or a glaring inconsistency that was not made clear in the PPBF) or pass it along to the full board for a vote on funding or not (the grants committee will include in this report its recommendation on the project—should it be funded, the amount and the term of funding). The Declination Letter in Exhibit 5.13 can be used to reject an application at either

Exhibit 5.13   Declination Letter #3

Date

Organization
Address
City, State, Zip

Re: Grant Proposal (<date>)

Dear Mr./Mrs. _____:

The ABC Foundation appreciated the opportunity to study your proposal seeking a grant for your organization's efforts to _____.

At the ABC Foundation it is our practice to study all grant requests carefully—from potential site visits and a robust SWOT analysis to a full examination of the organization's governance and financial issues. The foundation's grants committee will then make recommendations to the full board regarding the prospect of funding. The foundation's board then votes on the applicability of said grant request, the result of which will determine the grant proposal's outcome. Unfortunately, we are unable to fund your grant request at this time.

Mr./Mrs. _____, as you can imagine, the foundation receives a large number of requests for assistance, only a minority of which proceed to the next step in our process. Of course, our decision is in no way indicative of a negative assessment of your organization or proposal. It merely speaks to the overwhelming needs of our community and to our desire to respond to them in a balanced and equitable manner.

On behalf of our foundation, we wish you continued success.

Sincerely,
The Grants Committee of the ABC Foundation

the grants committee level or the full board vote level. Note, that unlike the previous Declination Letter (#2, Exhibit 5.6) but similar to Declination Letter #1 (Exhibit 5.3), we are not inviting the nonprofit to maintain future contact with the foundation and basically wishing them luck in the future. The reason for this somewhat harsher language has to do with what is likely a glaring issue with the nonprofit and/or the project in question, whereas in the Declination Letter 2 there might only be a minor issue or more likely having something to do with capacity for funding at the current time. This info becomes helpful to the grants committee in so much that they can highlight a particular project or nonprofit as "problematic" and avoid future consideration—hence increasing the efficiency of the grant-making process.

Now that the grants committee has organized the applications (with executive summaries) and their funding recommendations for the full board's consideration, the grants cycle vote can be held. A grants vote meeting is an exciting process that all board members of the foundation should attend (and members not in physical attendance should be permitted to review the "grants packet" and offer their vote accordingly). Essentially, what one would witness sitting in a grants vote meeting is a whole lot of back and forth debate (that is a good thing) and a big list (more likely on a finance committee member's laptop) of committed dollars. Besides the debate focused on a specific nonprofit or its project there are also the discussions, often heated, about how much to award each project or nonprofit. Cries of capacity issues or sustainability of a particular program can frequently be heard in the next room, but at the end of the day (and these meetings can last for hours) board members usually exit the meeting with a wonderful sense of accomplishment and excitement for the future.

The grants committee then organizes the votes and the committed dollar amounts and begins the process of awarding said grants. Exhibit 5.14, Acceptance Letter #2, illustrates a letter of notification to a nonprofit who has been awarded a grant from the foundation. Notice that the check is *not* enclosed but rather the nonprofit will find a Grant Agreement (Exhibit 5.15), which the foundation requires to be executed by the nonprofit's board before any funds are released. The Grant Agreement sets forth certain requirements with respect to the grant—such issues as ensuring that the capital is put to use in the manner that the proposal indicates, that any changes within the nonprofit or the project itself should be brought to the attention of the foundation immediately, and required progress reports at specific intervals. Once the Grant Agreement is signed and returned, the foundation will process the check quickly and efficiently (noting all dates and information in the operating spreadsheet for easy retrieval in the future).

Mary Anthony put up a cheer—"Finally I get to write some checks for needy charities," she exclaims.

"That's right, Mary, once the process is completed the check writing can commence," said Emmett Pathy.

"That's all well and good, Em, but how do we know if our capital is being put to good use? I mean which metrics can we use to determine if any of this is worthwhile or not?" asked a skeptical Phil Anthony.

Exhibit 5.14   Acceptance Letter #2

Date

Organization
Contact, Title
Address
City, State, Zip

Re: Request for a Grant Proposal

Dear <contact>:

We are pleased to inform you that the Board of Directors of The ABC Foundation accepted the favorable comments of our Grants Committee with respect to your organization's grant proposal for <project>_____ and consequently have approved a grant for <amount>.

Enclosed you will find a **Grant Agreement** that explains the responsibilities and expectations of both parties in our grant relationship. Please sign the Grant Agreement and return the original to me within ten (10) days of receipt. Please keep a copy for your records. Once the Grant Agreement is received in our office, the grant monies will be dispersed.

As indicated in the Grant Agreement, the Foundation's board will expect to be kept abreast of all milestones and issues regarding this funded project. Additionally, we would like to be made aware of any material non-project specific matters regarding your organization. As it certainly must be clear to you by now, we take our grant making responsibilities very seriously and expect our "grantee partners" to do the same. Please don't hesitate to contact the foundation with any questions that may arise for as in any partnership, communication is of the utmost importance.

On behalf of the board and staff of the foundation, please know that we are happy to support the important work you are doing. We wish you as much success in your efforts as you undertake the responsibilities of this grant.

Sincerely,
The Board of Directors of The ABC Foundation

"Good point Phil. What many foundations do is to require progress reporting over the year that the grant is made, so as to further evaluate the work of the nonprofit and the potential for future grants," said Em.

"I assume you are going to tell us how to do that as well," asked an anxious Mary.

"You know you can always count on me," said Em.

Progress Reporting and Evaluation

Exhibit 5.16 illustrates a Grant Evaluation Report that can be utilized by members (or the primary member who championed this particular grant) of the grants committee while interviewing the nonprofit

Exhibit 5.15   Grant Agreement

It is The ABC Foundation's policy and grant-making style to try to establish a good working relationship with each grantee. We approach each grant as both a critical investor and a partner, and see each as an opportunity for the nonprofit and the Foundation to make progress toward our own individual organizational missions and goals.

This letter outlines the mutual agreement between **<nonprofit>** and The ABC Foundation to provide a grant in the amount of **<amount>** for the **<project>**. The grant for this project will be allocated in **<number>** payments over the next **<number>** years.

Please read this agreement letter carefully to assure that there is mutual understanding about the purpose of the grant and all the terms thereof.

Conditions:

1. The grant is to be used solely for the project as described in the Grant Proposal dated **<date>**.
2. Grantee is an organization that is both exempt from tax under Section 501(c)(3) of the Internal Revenue Code (IRC) and an organization described in IRC Section 509(a)(1) or (2). The grantee has confirmed such status by filing its determination letter with the foundation. Grantee will furnish to The ABC Foundation any information concerning a change or a proposed change in the grantee's exempt status.
3. If grantee's exempt status changes, The ABC Foundation reserves the right to have all remaining grant funds immediately returned.
4. Any funds not used or committed for the specific purpose of the grant within the specified term must be returned to The ABC Foundation unless otherwise authorized in writing.
5. Grantee agrees to provide a written grant evaluation report to the foundation on the grant's annual anniversary.
6. Unless otherwise agreed to, the grantee agrees not to recognize the foundation, its board members or staff or this grant with certificates, plaques, or similar mementos.
7. If this grant is publicized in any way, we request that you share such materials with the Foundation.
8. The grantee will not use grant funds to intervene in any election or support any political party or candidate for public office, or engage in any lobbying not permitted by section 501(c)(3) of the IRC or, if applicable, IRC sections 501(h) and 4911.

During this collaborative effort, the Foundation's program office will contact you to review the progress of the project. The reporting process is an opportunity for both organizations to review the project's challenges and successes. We will work with you to assess progress toward the agreed-upon outcomes, and will review any obstacles you have and how you are addressing those obstacles. It is crucial that the project director be forthcoming and candid when communicating with the Foundation regarding the project's activities in their verbal and written reports. **All reporting should provide the Foundation with the grant's activities, challenges, outcomes, successes and expenditures.** The following is a summary of the reporting requirements for the grant:

1. Approximately three months through the grant year (and before the release of any additional payment) a verbal update with the program office will be required.
2. An interim, six months from the date of the initial grant, written report including a narrative and financial update will be required.
3. Within 60 days after the end of the grant period, a final written report with a grant narrative on the project and final financial report will be required. With respect to multi-year grants, this final report is required prior to the release of any additional grant checks. In addition, we request an audited financial statement covering the grant period when it becomes available.

(Continued)

Exhibit 5.15   (Continued)

If this letter correctly describes your understanding of the terms of this grant, please indicate your organization's agreement to such terms by having this letter signed by an appropriate officer(s) of your organization and return the original signed letter to The ABC Foundation.

Payment of funds will commence following our receipt of this signed letter. Keep a copy of the signed agreement letter for your files. Please refer to the grant tracking number: **<grant tracking number>** and project title: **<project title>** in all communications concerning this grant.

Feel free to contact our offices with any questions you may have or to request grant-related assistance, advice, or suggestions throughout the grant period. We look forward to working with you on this project.

ON BEHALF OF THE ABC FOUNDATION BOARD OF DIRECTORS, ACCEPTED AND AGREED:

_____   _____

<name>   Date

President

The ABC Foundation

ON BEHALF OF THE **<NONPROFIT ORGANIZATION>** BOARD OF DIRECTORS ACCEPTED AND AGREED:

By Staff:

_____   _____

Signature   Print Name

Title _____   Date_____

By Board:

_____   _____

Signature   Print Name

Title_____   Date_____

Adapted from the Rauch Foundation's Grant Agreement Letter.

Exhibit 5.16   Grant Evaluation Report

As we conclude the first year of our grant to your organization, the Board of The ABC Foundation is seeking certain data and commentary in order to evaluate the effectiveness of the grant.

Project Information

1. Were the objectives of the grant proposal met? Was the project on schedule? Describe the progress (including challenges and obstacles) toward accomplishing your objectives.
2. What do you consider your most notable project accomplishments during the past year? Please provide any success stories—no matter how seemingly inconsequential they might seem.
3. What other organizations/coalitions did you work with to initiate and implement this project?

Financial Information

4. Was the project completed on or under budget? Please provide projected versus actual expenditures to date. Describe any budget changes or other financial adaptations required by any unforeseen situation(s).
5. Please attach a copy of your most recently completed monthly financial statement as well as, if available, your audited financial statement.
6. With respect to sustainability, please indicate how this project will be funded in the future. Has this project and the foundation's grant assisted in increasing your organization's footprint or gleaning any additional financial donors?

Interaction with The ABC Foundation

7. How would you rate your interaction with The ABC Foundation? Were we receptive to your questions and helpful as a steward in guiding your organization?

General

8. Attach copies of any significant materials, newsletters, brochures, or articles that shed light on the projects or your organizations activities.

---

about their experiences with the foundation as well as their successes and challenges with the funded project. As detailed on the Grant-Making Operations Glide-Path Spreadsheet (Exhibit 5.2) there are three levels of interaction with respect to evaluating the project post-funding. The first is a verbal, touch-base call that a grants committee member places to make sure everything is progressing and the project is underway. The committee member's notes on the interaction should be noted in the file, as well as indicated on the spreadsheet (the date of the discussion and the person who held the discussion should also be noted on the detailed report and placed in the folder).

The next level of progress reporting is a full blown six-month progress report that will go into much more depth—indicating the use of funds thus far, the reach of the project, any favorable (or unfavorable) third-party reviews, and any road blocks that the foundation could help relieve. The out-take from this report is to provide a sense of the accomplishments after six months, answering the questions that focus on the ultimate mission of the project and the progress thus far in reaching those ultimate goals. It is this six-month report, together with a 10- or 11-month additional review, that will form the basis of the annual report to the full board at the anniversary of the grant (typically a month or so before the next grants cycle meeting).

"That seems pretty straightforward," said Phil.

"While I understand the importance of evaluating the progress of our grants, I would hope that it will be more apparent, more palpable, than a report in some file," said Mary.

"It very well might, Mary, but that doesn't relieve you and the board from your fiduciary duties with respect to monitoring the capital in the foundation. You need to be sensitive to these duties, and to that end, having defined reports is always a good idea," advised Em.

"That sounds right. Hey, speaking of fiduciary duties, shouldn't we talk a bit about investing these funds that will be in the foundation," said Phil.

"Phil, I can't believe my ears! You have been investing for decades and now you are asking about how to invest . . . it sounds very strange," said a surprised Mary.

"Phil is right to question the procedure for investing in a foundation. Investment management of this type does take on a specific and defined methodology that is often very different from how you would normally invest your own funds," said Em.

"Well that's why we have you I suppose," said Phil.

"Spot on, Phil! The topic of our final report is just that—Investment Management for Foundations," said Em.

"Well, with you stewarding us through these rough waters I am confident that we will be just fine," said a confident Mary.

"Thanks for the vote of confidence folks," said Em.

"Well deserved," the Anthonys replied in unison.

Summary

This chapter examined the inner workings of a private foundation—the actual operations and the how to. We introduced several forms and flowcharts to assist you in managing a private foundation. In the next chapter, we discuss the all-important asset management function of a private foundation. It is of critical importance, given that the assets of the foundation are what make it all work; without the assets, there would be no foundation. Understanding the particular tenets of investment management, especially for private foundations, is most critical.

CHAPTER

6

Investment Management for Private Foundations

Over a three-year period I gave away half of what I had. To be honest, my hands were shaking as I signed it away. I knew I was taking myself out of the race to be the richest man in the world. But the world and life have been mighty good to me. And I wanted to put something back. But you have to learn how to give.

—Ted Turner, cable television entrepreneur

Obviously I understand the basics of investing, but I also know that there is a heightened fiduciary component to investing for a foundation *and* specific methodologies that should be employed," stated Phil.

"You are correct, Phil. Of course you have had the good fortune to have been investing for a long time—and quite effectively if I do say so myself," said Em.

"Thanks to you!" chimed in Mary.

"Thanks. But you are correct in your judgment that this type of investing takes on more of an institutional approach, largely due to the heightened oversight," advised Em.

"And to that end we need to be mindful of some of the policies and procedures that come into play when dealing with a private foundation rather than an individual," continued Em.

"We have relied on your considerable expertise in building our wealth and now will continue to do so in this next phase of giving it away," said Phil.

"Well, you know I appreciate your continued vote of confidence, for it means a great deal to me. Let's begin talking investment management for foundations," said Em.

Emmett Pathy developed an in-depth report for the Anthonys—a report that they could utilize throughout the process of managing the assets for this new private foundation.

The Investment Management Process

As developed in the previous chapter, a process provides the groundwork and stability to nearly any exercise—in this context, from grant-making operations to investment management, having a defined process will certainly serve the foundation well. The process of investment management for private foundations (Exhibit 6.1) is not unlike the process that a proactive individual seeking a solid investment protocol might undergo. The differences between the two—between the institutional and the individual—are grounded

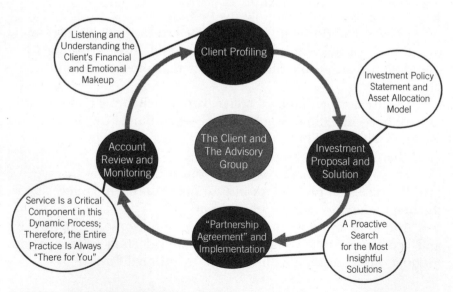

Exhibit 6.1   The Investment Management Process

more in the granularity of implementation than in the process (which can be thought of as a "30,000 foot view" rather than a micro-examination of investment management).

The process begins with a diagnostic (much like what a physician or auto mechanic might employ in their assessment of the issue at hand) in order to arrive at an answer to the questions—"Who (what type of investor) are you? What are your constraints with respect to investments?" The answers to these two questions provide the investment practitioner with the data that are needed to further develop a plan for this particular client.

The "Who" question provides us with an assessment of the type of investor, the objectives and risk tolerance, as well as an eye to our inner investor's emotional quotient or EQ. It is this EQ that allows the investment professional to grasp a sense of our appetite for certain investments. As seasoned investment professionals know, it is not enough to say on a questionnaire that you are able to accept risks for potential greater returns. You need to really mean it, and the only way we can definitively know is to glean the investor's emotional state with respect to money.

How is this emotional probing done? Enter the "art" of the investment management process—where investment advisers seek to uncover, through a series of sensitive discussions and "what-if scenarios," the investor's psychological background with respect to investments. It might seem that the concept of an "art" in the investment management process would more likely apply to individual investors than their institutional brethren. The view that institutional investors (foundations are typically lumped in this category) are without emotion when it comes to investing could not be more wrong. The emotions circling around the investment committee's (IC's) decision process may be less focused than in each committee member's personal balance sheet, but clearly it is still there. Concerns like "Is this the right decision?," "Can we trust this adviser's counsel?" and most poignantly, "Will we be able to maintain the foundation's grant-making long into the future?" are palpable even if not explicitly voiced. It is the wise investment professional who understands the EQ of an institution such as a private foundation for its implications will certainly be important.

Although the art portion of the investment diagnostic provides some concrete data—objectives, risk acceptability—it also provides an important emotional footprint of the private foundation. The science portion of the investment diagnostic equation gets granular with the actual concrete data; from objectives to risks and other constraints. A proper assessment of a potential client—the diagnostic examination—must encompass both the art and the science forms of the investment management exercise. Once we have ascertained the stated objective(s) and risk measures of a given investor we can parse further by seeking data inputs on such constraints as time horizon, liquidity, taxes, and any other unique circumstances. It is these data that allows the investment professional to formulate the primary document in all professional investment management engagements—the investment policy statement.

As shown in Exhibit 6.1, the data from the diagnostic exams—both the art and the science—fill a yellow pad of notes that the investment professional then uses to develop the customized investment policy statement. This in turn leads to an investable asset allocation model. Armed with the asset allocation model, we then turn to the implementation phase of the process, which requires a careful assessment of the economy and markets in order to properly and tactically implement the investor's investment policy statement and asset allocation model. The final part of the investment management process is the all-important communication phase—a phase that is so critical to the entire process that it is the primary reason why clients leave one adviser for another. It is not enough to have some communication with your adviser—it must be effective communication so that you, as the IC of a foundation, can fully articulate to the board where the portfolio is and what they should know about it. For many, this communication phase will be more focused on the education front and for others, especially those sitting on a foundation's IC (given the assumption that they are more knowledgeable investors than others), it will be more of a portfolio update. Either way, the key is for communication to be front and center, and a defined commitment in your investment adviser's practice.

"Why Is the Investment Management Process Important to Me?"

Why is the investment management process so important to me, the client? Why should I care about this stuff? The answer to these questions, and other like them, are rooted in the fact that, as a member of the foundation's IC (or, in some cases, as the *entire* "investment committee"), you need to understand this process in order to better evaluate the skill-set of the adviser in whom you are placing much trust. Is this adviser simply providing a boilerplate portfolio from his firm's workstation or is he or she asking the right questions? Is the adviser listening to you or only focused on presenting the firm's products? Is his or her output—investment policy statement, proposal, and report—well organized and well presented? Does the advisory have a thesis with respect to the economy and the markets or is he or she relying solely on the information of others? Only through these questions can you and the other members of the IC determine the true sense of an adviser, and given how much weight is being placed on this person, we had better know their level of professional acumen.

The Investment Committee

The IC serves a critical role in the foundation, as well as in the development of the policy statements for the foundation's assets. Recall that as a foundation, the portfolio of assets is our primary, and in most cases, only asset. Without this capital we would not exist, so you can imagine the importance in getting this IC member role correct. Many experts would suggest that the IC is the most important committee in the foundation—even more so than the grants committee (for, again, without the capital there can be no grants). Therefore, it is suggested that the members of this committee have more than a basic level of investment knowledge, and perhaps some legal and accounting knowledge as well (although it is a good idea to have some nonfinancial types serving on the IC as well, as it permits them to increase their education on financial matters and reminds the financial types of the actual charitable mission at hand).

Furthermore, it is implicit on these members to continually educate themselves on the matters of importance in the finance and investing fields. If that requires an occasional conference on such matters then so be it—it would almost certainly yield some positive results. Additionally, the members of the investment committee should be permitted, through the foundation, to subscribe to investment journals and important studies on investments for foundations. Again, this is a critical component of the overall foundation's net worth so making an investment in its knowledge base is well worth it.

The following points of guidance should also be taken under consideration when developing an effective investment committee:

- The size of the IC should be such to prevent constant infighting and nonproductive arguments, but large enough where careful deliberations and discussions can take place. The size of the overall board should dictate the size of the IC, but suffice to say that more than five or six members might become unwieldy. Additionally, unless the board chairperson is completely uninterested in investments, he or she should serve on the IC as well.

- Quarterly meetings should suffice given the predisposition of the investment industry to work on a quarterly basis with respect to their performance reporting. Of course, if there is a major disturbance in the financial markets then it would be a good idea to call a special meeting of the IC to discuss the issues and to gain an insight in the state-of-affairs with respect to the portfolio. At each meeting there should be a report generated from the managers, advisers, or consultants the foundation has hired that indicate the portfolio's performance, as well as a host of other important statistics (see Communication section below).

- At each meeting, after the IC discusses its stated agenda, it is always a good idea to invite one of the portfolio managers to make a presentation about the markets and the economy through their professional lens. It is often through this type of communication that the IC members gain further insight into the firm and professional they have hired. It can also serve as a cautionary flag if the manager or adviser is unable to address the IC, begging the question—*Why are they hiding?* The IC can also expand on this guest speaker concept by inviting a speaker from academia to provide some insights, maybe once a year at a special meeting.

- Be sure to keep the full board informed along the way. A "briefing note" is a good way to do just that. After each IC meeting a briefing is developed—a report or summary of what was discussed and where the portfolio is at current is sent to the full board for their review. Invite questions from your fellow board members—you never know what can come from an innocent question or comment. Perhaps an opportunity or perhaps a cautionary note that avoids a major problem.

The types of questions the investment committee of the foundation should be thinking about with respect to hiring a prospective investment manager or adviser are as follows:

- What is the adviser's fiduciary status? Does the adviser have a fiduciary obligation to the foundation through the services he or she performs?
- What is the adviser's educational and professional background? Does he or she hold certain industry certifications (i.e., Chartered Financial Analyst, CFA)? How long has he or she been in the investment management business? What does his or her compliance record look like?
- How is the adviser paid? Are the fees transparent? Are there incentives for the advice that the adviser is giving where the adviser is being compensated through these products?
- Which other foundations are clients of this adviser? What are their profiles with respect to size and IC interaction? How long has the adviser been focused on the foundation sector?
- Does the adviser have a fully articulated investment management process? Does the adviser help the foundations he or she works with in developing their investment policy statement?
- What does the adviser's reporting look like? Is it easy to read and understand? Are these reports readily available to the investment committee in a timely fashion?
- Who does the adviser's team consist of? What is their service matrix comprised of?
- What is the adviser's company like? Is it a major, well respected firm or an independent enterprise? What are the custody (of assets) arrangement?

For more information on choosing a CFA, you can view this PDF on the CFA Institute's web site at:

www.cfainstitute.org/about/investor/adviser/Pages/index.aspx.

You can also look at Vanguard's investment committee checklist on the web here: https://institutional.vanguard.com/iam/pdf/IAMMCL_NP.pdf.

Once established, the investment committee's major role is to seek out the best stable of advisers (or perhaps just one) and money managers to help refine and orchestrate the foundation's investment policy statement. How does the IC find these advisers and managers? The sourcing of the folks to manage these affairs is not often a major problem—they very well might find you (given the drive of many in the investment management industry). The question is: *How do we find the right team?* Typically, the IC will seek input through the request for proposal (RFP) process. It is through this initial report that the above questions will be posed, as well as further hard data on the adviser's performance figures and regulatory statements (Form ADV). A typical RFP is shown in this document at the following link: www.cof.org/files/Documents/Education_Collaborations /InvestmentConferenceCall/Handout3SampleRFP.pdf.

The Investment Policy Statement

If the starting point is the diagnostic exam, the results from that exam is the investment policy statement (IPS). It is with this document that we can determine if the adviser really listened and "got us." It is in this document that the foundation's investment objectives, risk tolerance, liquidity, and other constraints are detailed. This is also where the foundation's spending policy (captured typically in the liquidity constraints) is detailed. In addition, if the foundation is a spend-down rather than perpetual foundation this needs to be noted in the IPS (under the time horizon constraint). The often contentious issue of restrictions with respect to industry sectors is also captured in the IPS (unique constraints). Can you imagine how embarrassing it would be to a foundation, focused on the environment, to learn that it owns stock in companies that are perennial polluters? This is why the foundation's IC needs to articulate (the adviser should make the inquiry) these restrictions to their advisers. It is a critical part of the investment management process for foundations: understanding the unique circumstances that make each foundation a different investor.

In addition to the typical information contained in an investment policy statement (i.e., objectives, risk constraints) there also needs to be a section at the end that closes the circle on the total investment management process. Once the policy directives are put in place, the foundation's IC needs to formulate policies and rules that speak to the expectations with respect to communication, an effective asset allocation model, and details with respect to the implementation phase including manager search as well as the basic requirements of the firms to whom the foundation is entrusting their capital. It is a sad commentary on the investment management business that we need to have such a heightened awareness of potential frauds and other breaches of honest behavior. But that is the world we live in, and as board members we have an obligation to look out for what might happen; there is no room for lax oversight here.

There are many ways to fashion an investment policy statement (we provide links to three sample IPSs later in this chapter, as well as full text of two examples in Exhibits 6.2 and 6.3), but many speak to the following components:

Return Objectives

What are you trying to accomplish in this portfolio? Perhaps you are seeking to outperform inflation (*What rate of inflation? Which measurement of inflation?*) plus the 5 percent spending rate so that the foundation's real "spending power" would be maintained well into the future? These are the types of questions expected to be flying around the room where the IC is meeting to discuss the draft of the IPS they are working on for the full board's approval. We also need to remain mindful of what is known as the "wise-guy objective," where the investor states that the objective he is seeking is "greater than the market's with less risk." Clearly, this type of comment is counterproductive and a waste of the IC's valuable time. The IC cannot afford to take its responsibility lightly—this is serious business and the IC needs to address these issues with the sense of gravitas that such matters deserve. The types of return objectives that might be seen in a foundation's investment policy statements are:

- The foundation seeks a return consistent with our risk constraints and spending policies, as noted in the following, and expects to achieve, over a stated market cycle, a total return that permits the real spending power to remain constant, net of annual 5 percent spending rate.
- The foundation seeks to maximize returns over the long term and seeks a portfolio that is consistent with the market's averages.

- Given the foundation's spend-down provisions over the next 10 years, the board is seeking a portfolio that can return 75 percent of the upside of a market-weighted portfolio while only subjecting the portfolio to 50 percent of the market's downside over a typical market cycle.

While the IC members will usually start with the return objectives in their drafting of the IPS, it is really something that they would typically back into given the other policy directives. In other words, you can't have an objective focused on growth when you have a risk tolerance of "ultraconservative" or a spending policy that is not seeking consistent real (that is, net of inflation) distributions. We need, in the development of an IPS, to remain mindful of the full picture, not just pieces of the puzzle. It is this linkage between each part of the investment policy statement that prevents confusion and provides a strong sense of who we are and what we are seeking—for at the end of the day we do not want our investment advisers and managers to get the incorrect or disjointed message.

Risk Tolerance

Every investor defines risk differently. The parent saving for his kid's college years might see risk as not making enough to grow the assets needed to meet the ever-increasing costs of college. To a retired couple, it might be seen as running out of capital before they pass away. It is a truism that every investor sees investing differently, each steeped in his or her own emotions. The risk of volatility is also a primary concern for most investors. It is often this volatility risk that leads investors to sell at the wrong time and buy at the wrong time—the well documented "herd effect," which is an extension of the emotionality of investing. For foundations, the risks might be codified as losing too much of the investment portfolio that prevents the foundation to function as per their stated mission; or not making enough (yes, that can be a risk as well—no one said that this investing game is easy!) and having the portfolio's real spending power diminish over time; or the risk of excessive volatility, which can lead to bad decision making (read: emotions taking over) as indicated above. There is also the "embarrassment risk" that we touched on earlier, where the foundation learns that its portfolio contains securities of companies that might be involved in businesses and sectors that fly in the face of the foundation's mission.

Add to these "quantifiable" risks the ultimate risk: fraud. As stated above, foundation ICs need to be ever mindful of who they are dealing with and what cautionary flags they need to be on the lookout for. *Are the returns too good to be true? Are they consistent with their stated style or sector? Can they defend their results? Are the assets held away from the manager? Which firm is acting as custodian of these assets?* Unfortunately these questions are all too pervasive in today's world of nontransparency and black box investing—the IC needs to be well aware of these risks as well.

There is also the risk of having an overly concentrated portfolio, typically through the donation of a large amount of one company's securities from the foundation's founder. These securities usually hold some emotional attachment for the founder, who will often direct that they not be sold. This action creates a concentrated portfolio that presents the IC with a host of risks to contend with. From sector concentration (the company may be doing well, but if the sector is out of favor then it is likely the shares would decline) to firm risk, if we have learned anything in the past few years it's that anything can happen to any company—no company is immune to risk. Finally, there is the existential risk of the foundation having to shut its doors (or suspend its grant-making exercises) if the shares of this highly concentrated position were to fall substantially. An example of this concentration risk can be found in the experience of Edwin Land with Polaroid Corporation, which made up 100 percent of the assets in Land's foundation. When the high-flying shares plummeted in the 1970s, Land was forced to close the doors of the foundation that just a decade earlier had very substantial assets and grant-making activities. The David and Lucille Packard Foundation was a little better off—it only had to cut its staff by nearly half and decrease its giving plans by 50 percent versus 2001 levels after a steep drop in the HP stock in which the endowment had large holdings.[1]

There was a time when risk was defined by the type of securities or investments that were owned in one's portfolio. All equity

---

[1] Roger Silk and James Lintott, *Creating a Private Foundation* (Princeton, NJ: Bloomberg Press, 2003).

securities were considered "risky" and the favored, prudent investment to own was bonds. However, as professional investment management moved into the middle of the twentieth century this
attitude toward "defined" risk was replaced with a more portfolio-
based definition of risk. The genesis of this thinking goes back to
the 1830 Massachusetts court ruling (*Harvard College v. Armory*)
that spawned the concept of the Prudent Man Rule. The thinking at that time was that investment management should be conducted as a prudent man would invest his own funds and therefore,
should remain mindful of the needs of the beneficiaries, focused
almost exclusively on capital preservation and regular income generation. This led to the exercise, typical throughout the first half of
the twentieth century, whereby certain assets, if considered risky or
speculative, must be avoided at all times. Fortunately, the revision
of the Prudent Man Rule, the Prudent Investor Rule, came about
and went beyond the individual assessment of risk of each asset to
include the concept of diversification and the powerful force of correlation onto a portfolio. The Prudent Investor Rule understands
that one can reduce risk in a portfolio by adding securities that
would otherwise seem risky as a stand-alone investment.

However, the Internal Revenue Code prohibits private foundations from making certain investments that they have codified in
the term *jeopardizing investments*, a rule that speaks to the old thinking of the Prudent Man Rule. The code has become more receptive
as of late to the concept of diversification, and to that end, utilizing
alternative assets in a portfolio that would go a long way to reduce
risk. The list of jeopardizing investments includes:

- Trading on margin (or any use of debt).
- Trading in commodity futures.
- Investments in working interests in oil and gas wells.
- The purchase of puts, calls, and straddles.
- The purchase of warrants.
- Selling short.

Although the IC of a foundation must remain mindful of this
list, the concept of diversification and use of alternative investments
(like derivatives and short selling) to reduce portfolio risk are now
being recognized and respected by the IRS (in several private letter rulings where, for example, the service allowed 100 percent of a

foundation's assets to be invested in a hedge fund run by the foundation's president (potential self-dealing issues notwithstanding), noting the diversification benefits of hedging and short selling).

Liquidity Constraint

In the discussion of the liquidity constraints of a private foundation, we are concerned with the cash management issues, the outflows (grants and expenses) and inflows (donations received), any lockups or other penalties associated with liquidating a position held in the portfolio, and the costs associated with managing the investments of the foundation (i.e., fees, commissions, and custody charges). Requiring a certain allocation to cash and cash equivalents (typically Certificates of Deposit or U.S. Treasury bills) is, despite the near nil return that one can expect on cash these days, strongly recommended. Cash capital is required not only for typical management exercises (salaries, rent, other operations), but also for the business of grant making—and you never know when a worthy nonprofit will come knocking needing a grant to get over some barrier or to seize upon some opportunity. Many suggest having a year's worth of typical grant making available in cash at all times—approximately a 5 percent (maybe a little more given operating expenses) cash allocation. The IC members meet quarterly so they can reassess the cash needs and reallocate accordingly. This is not an endorsement of holding cash on the sidelines, especially with near zero interest rates, while waiting for the market to go lower. This practice, known as market timing, is fraught with danger and is not suggested given the typical foundation's long-term time horizon. However, as we will see in the description of tactical allocation, dialing up the allocation of cash in times of market froth and down in times of market fears, can be a valuable tool in maintaining capital for the foundation—you just don't want to go overboard.

The balance between cash coming into the foundation, in the form of donations or additional gifts from the founders, and the cash going out due to grants and expenses, is a critical part of the work of the IC. The problem, of course, is that the IC typically does not know, in the case of donations, how much cash the foundation might pull in over the course of a given year. Also, most foundations are funded with one-time gifts from the founders and, for the most part, are not in the business of receiving donations on a regular basis. In that case, the capital budgeting process is a bit simpler, given that we know what we have and we know what we want to give, and the costs involved in maintaining the foundation. Things get dicey when we want to grant more or when expenses increase dramatically from what we have modeled. Absent these circumstances, the cash allocation exercise is straightforward—the IC just needs to be mindful of the risks in maintaining an ultralow allocation to cash, no matter how disgusted it gets with the return on that capital.

With respect to investment management, liquidity used to mean the ease of getting your assets turned into cash. Given the increased complexity and speed of the capital markets, that concern has been somewhat minimized. The only time such an issue of actual liquidity (that is, changing paper assets into cash assets) comes into play these days is with alternative assets like hedge funds, private equity funds, and other such "packaged" products. That is not to say that one should steer away from these assets—not by a long shot, since alternative assets provide an excellent helping of low correlation with more traditional assets like stocks, thereby increasing diversification and often returns. However, no IC should place too hefty an allocation in alternatives with lockups or other anti-liquidity features—it's like garlic in a tomato sauce—you want some just not too much.

Managing the costs of investment management services can make even the most focused investment committee bleary-eyed. The IC needs to be aware of the layers and layers of costs that are typical in today's investment products—from mutual funds to ETFs to hedge funds and other alternative products. Once the expenses of these products are parsed out, the IC can turn its attention to the somewhat easier (at least it should be) and transparent (if not then you should be looking elsewhere) costs associated for the investment advice and counsel that your adviser or manager is providing. There are many iterations to these relationships—from the traditional commission-based arrangement (often not the best way to go) to a fee-based arrangement, where the assets are levied an annual fee that includes implementation costs as well as the advice portion. Although these annual fees can vary widely depending on the firm, adviser, and amount of assets in question, a good rule of thumb is to try to stay in the 0.80 percent to 1 percent range annually.

Some of the questions that would permit the IC to ascertain a better sense of the fees and expenses involved in an investment management candidate are:

- Can you provide a fully transparent proposal with respect to your fees for advisory services? Is it a percentage of assets? How is it charged against the foundation?
- Do you receive revenue from other sources given the foundation's assets and investments? Are there overrides, trailers, and sales incentives that exist? How about 12b-1 fees on mutual funds—are they part of your revenue stream? If so, can you estimate how much they may be (in percentage terms and dollar terms)?
- Depending on which investment solutions are utilized in your portfolio, there are additional fees (above your advice fee) for account implementation; please detail these additional fees—do they decrease with additional commitments to these solutions?
- IIow about your firm—What part does it play in the fee picture? Do you simply receive a percentage of the full fee and balance or is the firm receiving additional compensation? Are there "shelf-space" fees that the investment managers or mutual funds pay to your firm? Do you receive any part of these revenues and are they the same for each product?
- Do you accept any gifts or incidental benefits from recommending one product over another? Are you completely "solution set agnostic," and to that end, only interested in the best solution for the client's objectives?
- Are there custody fees involved? Any additional fees that the firm charges (i.e., account inactivity fees) versus our portfolio, unrelated to a transaction? As part of a transaction (i.e., processing fees, ticket charges)?
- How do you disclose the fees? Can you expect a fully transparent annual statement that breaks down all costs—advice, transactions, custody, trailers, expense ratios, and so on—both in dollar and percent terms?

Time Horizon

The question that comes to mind when thinking about a foundation's time horizon is quite intuitive—*Is the foundation perpetual or does it expect to spend-down its assets by a certain year?* It is the answer to this question that would provide the data for the IPS for this category.

As you might expect, a perpetual foundation would be able to accept a greater amount of risk (it has more time to make up any lost ground) versus that of a foundation that is winding down (gifting away all of its assets be a certain date). The issue comes into play when the spend-down policy is not a specific date but some defined future date (i.e., the thirtieth birthday of the founder's youngest living grandchild). We might be unable to definitively state the date for the youngest grandchild because he or she may not yet be born. Furthermore, what prevents a child from adopting a grandchild in order to maintain the foundation's legacy? As you can see, many issues can come into play in this somewhat straightforward policy directive, hence the need to define these issues from the get-go so that there is no confusion along the way.

Why aren't all private foundations perpetual? It seems as if that plays right into the legacy factor that would appeal to many founders of private foundations. Why have "spend-down foundations" become a greater force in the past few decades in modern philanthropy? For the most part, the appeal for the founders is to see the fruits of their philanthropy put fully to work during their lifetimes (or perhaps their children's or grandchildren's). Part of this movement has to do with the fact that many of today's philanthropists are much younger than the philanthropists of a couple of decades ago. A middle-aged (or in some unbelievable cases, 25-year-old) philanthropist cannot envision his future family and therefore figures it is better to have grants made while he can see them and the good that they will undoubtedly do, rather than pass it along to heirs that are not yet in his glide-path. Either way, the key is for this time horizon constraint to be well thought through and fleshed out in the IPS.

Legal Issues

We have already discussed the substantial requirements with respect to prudence, duty, and care in all investment-related activities within the foundation. It is in this section that these requirements and directives get listed and become part of the foundation's official policy statement. There are also the typical host of legal rules and requirements that need to be addressed in the management of any business or enterprise (i.e., discrimination testing, equal opportunity employment, basic employee handbook measures). In this section, we will also address the policies with respect to voting proxies and any potential shareholder activism that the foundation would want to exercise. These measures can often be substantive, given the potential for the foundation to own a sizeable chunk of the outstanding equity in a given company (diversification issues notwithstanding), and to that end can effectuate potential changes within the company.

Tax Issues

What the IPS needs to address in this category is the importance of ensuring that the foundation is not levied any fines or liabilities due to its ownership of assets that can generate Unrelated Business Taxable Income (UBTI). As discussed in previous chapters, UBTI can be detrimental to a private foundation in that the income it generates can be taxable to the foundation and can also cause potential penalties. It's best to stay away from any investments that can generate UBTI. The challenge is that many advisers and money managers become so overly infatuated with an investment (often becoming "married" to a specific stock) that they cannot see the forest through the trees. Hence, it is critical for the IPS to spell this out from the get-go and to articulate such directives to the advisers who should know this anyway (most do not, unfortunately). The other issue is that UBTI can hide in the most unexpected securities—any investment that issues a Schedule K-1 rather than a 1099 is exposed to potential UBTI. Also, investments that are leveraged or funded through debt often generate UBTI. Here we need to remain mindful of the closed-end fund sector, for many of these funds have leverage built into their portfolio and have a tendency to surprise investors with a Schedule K-1 when they were expecting a standard Form 1099. Master limited partnerships (MLPs), a Wall Street darling for the past decade or so, are also a problem for foundations, given their partnership structure (hence Schedule K-1 not 1099). Don't fret however; if Wall Street is good at one thing it is reinventing itself, and new funds have come to market in the past couple of years that own MLPs but issue only a standard Form 1099—perfect for foundations seeking exposure to this interesting asset class.

Of course we cannot discuss tax issues in the IPS without mentioning the excise tax. Although diminutive (and likely to become more so—see Chapter 4), the excise tax is still very much a part of a foundation's investment policy statement—perhaps less due to the actual liabilities that are incurred and more due to the fact that ignoring it, no matter how diminutive, portrays a foundation's IC as lacking expertise in the sector.

Unique Issues

This is somewhat of a catchall section where the IPS lists all and any restrictions that a foundation might have with respect to investments. These can be types of investments; "packaged products," structured notes, or something as wide ranging as mutual funds (which might sound odd given the ubiquitous nature of these investments, but perhaps the IC members of a foundation determine that their assets are substantial enough to engage direct asset managers with greater transparency and less fees than typical mutual funds). Or, these restrictions might have to do with certain sector or industries. The socially responsible investing (SRI) sector developed as an outgrowth of investors, like foundations and endowments that were focused on one particular social or civic issue and wanted to make sure that their investment portfolio complied with the same thinking. As mentioned earlier, can you imagine the embarrassment for a foundation focused on the welfare of animals to have investments in companies that perform animal testing as part of their standard operations? Let's not forget that the typical foundation's board would count its members in the highest echelon of local businesspeople and professionals, so these folks are not likely to take lightly something as embarrassing as that on their watch.

SRI can also move along the glide-path of activist investing, using its portfolio and its bully pulpit to adopt change in society. We saw this in the past decade or so with respect to the apartheid movement in South Africa, where SRI advocates made clear their intentions to go after companies that conducted business in that country. We also witnessed this in the campaigns against teenage smoking and the work these advocates have done to "nudge" the tobacco companies in a direction that is helping to stem this deadly tide.

In the exhibits which follow, we find several examples of the IPS. They take a variety of forms, but all are fairly consistent and share a single purpose: to permit a defined understanding between the foundation's IC and its adviser. Again, it is this understanding that is critical to the long term success of the relationship, as well as the portfolio. Writing an IPS is sometimes more of an art than a science,

Exhibit 6.2   The Investment Policy Statement—The Dental Health Association

INVESTMENT POLICY DISCUSSION

Prepared for the Dental Health Association by Emmett Pathy, *ABC Wealth Management*, February 2011.

WHAT IS AN INVESTMENT POLICY?

An investment policy outlines and prescribes a prudent and acceptable individualized investment philosophy and sets out the investment management procedures and long-term goals for the investor.

The Need for a Written Policy

The purpose of this **Investment Policy Statement (IPS)** is to establish a clear understanding between the Investor and the Adviser as to the investment goals and objectives and management policies applicable to the Investor's investment portfolio ("Portfolio").
  This Investment Policy Statement will:

- Establish reasonable expectations, objectives, and guidelines in the investment of the Portfolio's assets.
- Create the framework for a well-diversified asset mix that can be expected to generate acceptable long-term returns at a level of risk suitable to the Investor, including:
  - Describing an appropriate risk posture for the investment of the Investor's Portfolio; specifying the target asset allocation policy; diversification of assets; specifying the criteria for evaluating the performance of the Portfolio's assets and encouraging effective communication between the Adviser and the Investor.
- This IPS is not a contract. This investment policy has not been reviewed by any legal counsel and the Adviser and Investor use it at their own discretion. This IPS is intended to be a summary of an investment philosophy and the procedures that provide guidance for the Investor and the Adviser. The investment policies described in this IPS should be dynamic. These policies should reflect the Investor's current status and philosophy regarding the investment of the Portfolio. These policies will be reviewed and revised periodically to ensure they adequately reflect any changes related to the Portfolio, to the Investor or the capital markets.
- A written investment policy allows you to clearly establish your investment time horizon and goals, your tolerance for risk, and the prudence and diversification standards that you want the investment process to maintain. A written investment policy also helps identify your need to take risk in light of such factors as your financial objectives and income stability.
- Articulating a long-term investment policy explicitly, and in writing, offers significant assistance to both our clients and their investment advisers in protecting the portfolio from ad hoc revisions of a well-reasoned policy based on important personal considerations. Studies have shown that investors all too often act on emotional responses, generally to their detriment. A written policy helps assure rational analysis is the primary basis for important investment decisions.

INTRODUCTION

The purpose of this Investment Policy Statement (IPS) is to establish a clear understanding between **The Dental Health Association** ("Investor") and Emmett Pathy ("Adviser") as to the investment objectives and policies applicable to the Investor's investment portfolio. This IPS will:

- Establish reasonable expectations, objectives, and guidelines for the investment of the Portfolio's assets.

(Continued)

Exhibit 6.2 (Continued)

- Set forth an investment structure detailing permitted asset classes and the desired allocation among asset classes.
- Encourage effective communication between the Adviser and the Investor.
- Create the framework for a well-diversified asset mix that can be expected to generate acceptable long-term returns commensurate with the level of risk suitable to the Investor.
- Serve as a reference over time to prçovide long-term discipline for an established investment plan.
- Describe constraints that the Investor chooses to place on the investment strategy.

This IPS is intended to be a summary of an investment philosophy that provides guidance for the Investor and the Adviser.

---

in that the adviser really needs to listen to the IC in order to gain an understanding of its particular constraints and stated objectives. There are many examples of relationships (between the IC and the Adviser) that have failed, despite excellent returns, due to the development of a portfolio that has impeded upon the foundation's risk or unique guidelines.

It may be constructive to distill down the IPS to a one-pager that can be distributed to each of the board members for easy referral—placing a copy in the board member's handbook together with the mission statement and other important founding documents. (See Exhibit 6.4.) Why do you use this one-pager format? The key here is to summarize the IPS and plaster it in the board member's materials (meeting agendas, board member's handbooks, etc.) to such a point that the board member is constantly reminded of the directives, so

Foundation Investment Policy Statement—Samples

The links below show two examples of foundation investment policy statements.
www.fi360.com/fa/help/Report_Samples/IPS_Foundation.pdf
www.cof.org/files/Documents/Family_Foundations/Financial-Management/Investment-Policy-1.pdf

Sample University Endowment/Foundation Investment Policy Statement

The link below shows an example of a university endowment/foundation investment policy statement:
http://giving.unr.edu/uploads/INVESTMENT_COMMITTEE_POLICY.pdf

Exhibit 6.3   Investment Policy for a Foundation

Investment Objective	Provide a reasonably stable, growing, and predictable income stream in the form of dividends, interest, and realized gains to fulfill the mission of the Foundation. Make required charitable distributions. Protect the principal in order to ensure long-term viability of the Foundation. Capital appreciation and liquidity are secondary objectives.
Investment Goal	Realize a real total annual return of at least 5 percent based on market value, plus any additional return necessary to protect the Foundation's assets from the effect of inflation or other economic changes.
Investment Philosophy	Invest with discipline and consistency, taking into account events and occurrences considered reasonable and probable. Extreme positions and opportunistic styles do not fit the general philosophy and tone of the Foundation and are not acceptable.
Asset Allocation	The Board of Directors considers it prudent and desirable and hereby delegates to the professional investment adviser the responsibility and discretion to develop a suitable asset allocation strategy and to invest the Foundation's assets within the limits imposed by (1) the general investment objectives, goals, and philosophy expressed above, (2) the Board of Directors, (3) the limitations on acceptable investments described below and (4) the principles set forth by the Prudent Investor Rules.
Investment Guidelines	*Fixed Income Investments*
	The purpose of fixed income investments is to provide a highly predictable source of income and to reduce the volatility of the total portfolio market value. The professional investment adviser shall be given significant discretion in setting the appropriate limitation on the percentage of the Foundation's fixed income holdings attributable to a single issuer. The Board of Directors has further observed that similarly situated organizations typically mandate that any obligations of a bank or trust company must be issued by a bank or trust company chartered by the United States or a state thereof and have assets in excess of $4 billion.
	Equity Investments
	The purpose of equity investments is to provide current income, growth of income, and appreciation of principal with the recognition that this requires the assumption of greater market volatility and risk of loss. The Board of Directors has a preference for significant diversification across industry and individual holdings. No single mutual fund or common stock should constitute the bulk of the market value of the investment portfolio.
Allowed Assets	*Fixed Income Investments*
	Fixed income investments are limited to the following investment categories: money market instruments, bond funds, certificates of deposit, commercial paper, corporate bonds, money market mutual funds, treasury bills and notes, federal agency securities, government securities, mutual funds and, generally, other cash equivalents. All corporate bonds and bond funds must be publicly traded on a major exchange.
	Junk Bonds: Investments in publicly traded junk bonds are allowed, provided that such investments are consistent with the Prudent Investor Rules, and that the Foundation's ownership interest is not so great as to exceed the limitations commonly adopted by similarly situated organizations.

(Continued)

Exhibit 6.3 (Continued)

Equity Investments

Except as specifically set forth below, equity investments shall mean publicly traded common stocks or common stock mutual funds in Subchapter C corporations listed on a major exchange to take advantage of listing requirements, disclosure rules, and to improve liquidity. Covered options may be written against common stocks held by the Foundation to increase return and/or reduce risk.

Unrelated Business Taxable Income: Prior to making an investment in an asset that is not publicly traded, such as in a limited partnership, due consideration should be given to whether such an investment would give rise to unrelated business taxable income (UBTI). If so, further consideration should be given to the impact of a for-profit federal (and possibly state) income tax liability on the return from such an investment and the concomitant federal (and possibly state) income tax filing requirements to which the Foundation would be subject. The purchase of an investment asset, such as a parcel of real estate, using borrowed funds, normally will give rise to UBTI.

Real Estate: Direct and indirect investments in real estate, such as through a managed real estate fund, are allowed, provided that such investment is consistent with the Prudent Investor Rules.

Hedge Funds: An ownership interest in a hedge fund that is not publicly traded is allowed, provided that (1) the Foundation's ownership interest in such hedge fund is not so great as to exceed the limitation on such an ownership interest as is commonly adopted by similarly situated organizations and (2) such investment is consistent with the Prudent Investor Rules.

Jeopardizing Investment Considerations	Prior to engaging in the following types or methods of investment, due consideration should be given to the tax consequences and risks associated with investments that the IRS closely scrutinizes in connection with its oversight of the jeopardizing investment rules: trading in securities on margin (which would give rise to UBTI), trading in commodity futures, investments in working interests in oil and gas wells, the purchase of "puts" and "calls" (especially in respect of uncovered options), and "straddles," the purchase of warrants, and selling short.

Reprinted with permission from Foundation Source.

that any overarching exuberance (or any other nondirective investment strategy) does not take hold. Fidelity to the IPS is a critical function of not just the IC but the full board, and having an easy to read reminder of this makes it much easier.

"I like these investment policy statement samples. They allow me to better grasp the issues involved with investing in a foundation," said Mary.

"Indeed, the IPS is a critical part of the work that the investment committee and the full board frankly will focus their time on," advised Em.

Exhibit 6.4   The Investment Policy Statement: A One-Pager

Investment Policy Statement - *Draft*
ABC Foundation

Objective: Capital Preservation and Capital Appreciation–portfolio managed to provide returns that exceed the long-term inflation rate by our stated spending rate of 5 percent.

Risk Tolerance: "Conservatively Opportunistic"—The portfolio is subject to some principal volatility, which is accepted in the pursuit of greater long-term returns.

Liquidity Constraints: All investments can be liquidated to cash in 3 days.

Legal: Uphold all laws and regulations of fiduciary investment management practices.

Taxes: Remain mindful of the excise tax and avoid any investments that generate UBTI.

Time Horizon: Perpetuity.

Unique: Avoid sectors that conduct research on animals or are serial polluters of the environment. No tobacco companies.

"But there must be more to it than that—I mean the rest of the investment management process—we can't invest on policy directives alone, right?" asked Phil.

"Of course, we have the entire concept of asset allocation and manager search to still discuss," said Em.

"And let's not forget that communication piece, for I am very interested in being kept apprised to where we are on a periodic basis," said a proactive Mary.

"Yes, that's all part of the next part of the IPS—the addendum portion," said Em.

Addendums to the Investment Policy Statement

Developing a well crafted IPS is only the first step in the process known as the Investment Management Process (see Exhibit 6.1). Once the IPS is in place and agreed to, the adviser will begin to develop an asset allocation model (although this is often done in conjunction with the IPS). From there, the implementation phase comes into focus, and finally, the all-important communication phase.

Asset Allocation Model

Bringing the investment management process full circle, we need to more fully address the foundation's stated asset allocation model.

Studies (Brinson, Beebower, and Hood, *Financial Analysts Journal*, 1992) have shown that the asset allocation model of a given investor accounts for more than 92 percent of that portfolio's variation. Variation is a fancy term for volatility or risk. Over the last two decades, this study was the Holy Grail for those in the financial advice industry—it has seemingly morphed into the conclusion that asset allocation accounts for the majority of returns in a portfolio rather than variation. Notwithstanding the importance of volatility management in a portfolio, clearly that is not the same thing as return generation. What this really speaks to is the emotionality of the individual investor—where volatility can force them into selling at a low and buying at a high. Can the sage-like folks at a foundation's IC fall victim to this same type of thing? Of course they can (as we discussed earlier), albeit maybe not as much (investing a foundation's money is not quite the same thing as your own—no matter how conscientious you take your trustee role). The point that an asset allocation strategy is a critical step in the investment management process is not debatable—it is critical and the foundation needs to address it with the gravitas it deserves.

As IC members of a foundation, we need to cast a skeptical eye toward asset allocation to ensure that it is as diversified as we require (and we should all require diversification). We need to pay particular attention to the pernicious bias known as *style drift,* where a particular fund or investment strategy was firmly in one portion of the asset allocation and then, over time, drifts to another (i.e., value managers drifting toward technology during the 1990s—that didn't end well for all involved). So it is not just having the right balance or allocation from the start, but to ensure that it stays in the correct balance throughout the period. Exhibit 6.5 illustrates a simple (wide asset definitions rather than the more detailed one you would see in the IPS) one-page (again these are good to enclose in each board member's handbook but remember to update them accordingly) asset allocation model for a foundation. Note the ranges for each asset—this speaks more to our next topic—Strategic versus Tactical Asset Allocation.

Strategic Asset Allocation versus Tactical Asset Allocation

The strategic asset allocation model (SAA) is defined through a careful assessment of the investor's objectives, risk tolerance, and other

Exhibit 6.5   Asset Allocation Model

XYZ Foundation

	Lower Limit	Upper Limit
– Cash	5%	30%
– Fixed Income		
• Short Term	5%	30%
• Intermediate Term	25%	40%
• Global Fixed Income	0%	10%
– U.S. Equity		
• Large Cap Core	5%	15%
• Large Cap Growth	5%	15%
• Large Cap Value	5%	15%
• Mid Cap	0%	15%
• Small Cap	0%	15%
– International Equity	5%	25%

constraints, coupled with his or her emotional make-up. It is this combination of art and science that provides us with the stated IPS and then, from those directives, the mixture of asset classes (SAA). But what happens when the markets move, or, better yet, when the markets are in flux? Do we feel comfortable investing a foundation's assets in a 65 percent equity and 35 percent fixed-income allocation when the average price earnings multiple is substantially above historical levels? Or when there is a palpable sense of complacency toward risk or a frothiness that makes us scratch our heads. Well, maybe not us—after all we are just members of the IC—but clearly our advisers should take this current market environment issue to heart, no? Let's go back to 1998 or 1999; the Nasdaq was flying high—a new paradigm we were told—and Internet and technology companies were all the rage. If we were to invest in a 65 percent/35 percent portfolio then how would the foundation have fared? Would it be able to maintain its grant making in the coming years? Would it have to shut its doors?

Sure, it is easy to say that in retrospect, but would we have said it then? Well, it may not have been easy to see but the handwriting was clearly on the wall. Elevated valuations, no respect to risk, leveraged buying as far as the eye could see, frothy new issues and IPOs—all telltale signs to the professional financial adviser. But it is

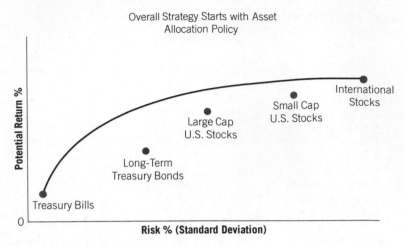

Exhibit 6.6   Asset Allocation and the Efficient Frontier

often so hard to see when you are in the midst of it all. So how will our advisers protect our foundation's portfolio? These are the types of questions that the IC needs to address to the advisers and money managers that come in and parade their portfolios in front of the IC. How do you manage risk? How do you maintain fidelity to your process and your thinking and not be swayed by the current investment theme du jour?

The tactical asset allocation model (TAA) can help in this regard. What the TAA does is the same thing as the SAA—picks up right where it left off—but before investing in that 65 percent/ 35 percent portfolio the TAA sits back and studies the market/ economic/geopolitical environment and ponders risk levels. How does valuation look on average? Are there pockets of froth that we should avoid? What can go wrong out there? Then the TAA dials up or dials down the allocations in the SAA accordingly. So, for example, if the markets were seemingly on the higher risk side of the equation, that 65 percent equity allocation might be 50 percent or 45 percent to start with, only to be increased to the stated 65 percent SAA over a period of time as markets permit.

Critics of the TAA would remind us that market timing never really works—and they are right and wrong. It never really worked during the great bull market from 1982 on, but it worked just fine during the range-bound markets of 1966 to 1982. But that misses the point: as a thoughtful member of the IC you should want your

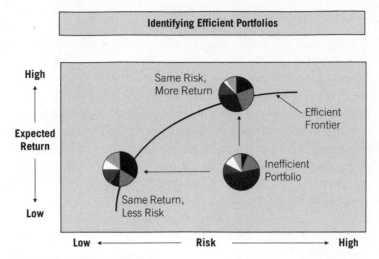

Exhibit 6.7   Identifying Efficient Portfolios

adviser to dedicate more thought to the market environment before investing, rather than just holding his nose and jumping in (with your foundation's capital at risk!). It's not timing, but rather a certain mindfulness that needs to be part of the equation, coupled with a proactive sense to carefully watch things unfold and voice those comments, concerns, and even mea culpas—it's better to cut the cord and say "I missed something" than to doggedly hold on forever just to be right)—to the IC.

Exhibits 6.6 and 6.7 speak to the process by which a professional adviser can take an inefficient portfolio and make it efficient—to get more return with the same (or sometimes even less) risk. How is this seemingly free lunch orchestrated? Well, it starts with the Efficient Frontier, a mathematical construct from the Nobel Prize–winning economist and Baruch College professor, Harry Markowitz. What Markowitz's work focuses on is the trade-off between risk and return, not for an individual security, per se, but on the mixture of these securities in a portfolio that, through correlation between the assets, lowered overall portfolio risk, thereby increasing efficiency. Again, we are looking at the science of finance and investment management to assist us in the development of a portfolio rather than adopting an often inefficient, robotic proposal that many advisers churn out at their workstations without giving deep thought to the issues (and the science) involved.

Manager Search and Implementation Phase

Once the IC members, working in conjunction with their advisers, have developed a robust investment policy statement and a well-thought-out asset allocation model then we enter the next phase: Manager Search and Implementation. Think of it this way—the IPS and asset allocation model are the blueprints in the building of your dream home; implementation (manager search is the primary part of this process) is the process of choosing the contractors to do the job. So, as many of us who have been through home-remodeling projects know, having a great plan is not the only piece of the puzzle—you also need an excellent contractor.

In choosing the managers to implement the foundation's investment policy statement, the following points are expected to be front and center:

- Managerial style—Each investment manager (as well as the adviser that chooses managers) has his or her own distinct style of investing. It is important to understand (and be able to articulate to the full board of the foundation) this style and strategy. Furthermore, on review, it is critical to hold this manager to his or her style—style drift is a dangerous tendency and should not be permitted. Also, managers need to articulate their sell discipline; that is, when and how they choose to liquidate a security in their portfolio.
- Fees—A study of how this manager is being compensated is an important factor in the choice of who we plan to trust with a portion of the foundation's assets. But we need to also dig a bit deeper and look under the hood for fees in trading, tracking error, and liquidity.
- The IC needs to judge this specific manager on its own, but also how it will work within the portfolio in total. It is nice to have a spiral staircase in the front hall, but if it is going to block the great views of the bay behind the home then any contractor worth his salt would not recommend it. It's the same with investments. Great managers might be nice, but if they are going to sway the portfolio too much to one side then the best decision often is to pass (you can always change things around in the future and re-visit this manager).

- Service matrix—The availability of managers to meet and discuss the portfolio and their current market views and thesis, and to provide salient and timely performance data, is crucial. The IC is going to need performance data in the first week or two of the new quarter—and detailed performance data at that (see Communication later in the chapter). Also in this area we need to gain a better understanding of the firm's internal controls—the size and depth of its staff, who is responsible for what area of the firm, the firm's growth rate, and how it may have changed in the past few years.
- Management—Like the contractors and architects you are hiring for your home project, you want to see their professional backgrounds, most poignantly their professional accreditations. The same goes for investment managers, and to that end, many look for the CFA designation as an arbiter of solid training and professional expertise.

Core-Satellite Approach

Many providers of institutional investment services suggest an implementation platform known as the Core-Satellite approach, where the portfolio is divided between the passive and active management schools of thought. In passive management, the portfolio is constructed to mimic the market indices and is geared in the belief that portfolio managers cannot outperform the index, so it's best to simply mimic them. In passive management (made famous by Vanguard and its founder John Bogle), the key is to minimize fees (very low-cost funds) and tracking error (the difference between the index's return and the fund designed to mimic it). Active management is firmly entrenched in the concept that good analytical homework will yield better than index returns—this above market return is known as *alpha*. Given that the market is inefficient and investors are not rational, active managers believe they can uncover mispriced securities, and in doing so formulate a portfolio that can provide substantial returns over time. The legions of active investors are hard to ignore, from Warren Buffett and Berkshire Hathaway to the folks at the Fairholme Fund and all those amazing hedge fund managers with their eye-popping long-term returns. Of course, active management is more expensive

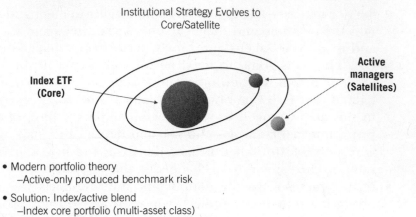

Institutional Strategy Evolves to
Core/Satellite

Index ETF
(Core)

Active
managers
(Satellites)

- Modern portfolio theory
  –Active-only produced benchmark risk
- Solution: Index/active blend
  –Index core portfolio (multi-asset class)
  –Active managers layered to enhance returns

Exhibit 6.8   The Core-Satellite Approach

than the static indexing protocol of the passive managers—but in many cases, they are worth it.

The Core-Satellite approach marries the two schools of thought—developing a passive (Core) portfolio that covers the complete investment landscape and a Satellite portfolio that searches for the best active managers. Together, these two parts of the overall portfolio provide the investor (and the IC) with the best of both worlds: a lower blended fee on the full portfolio, a diversified portfolio, and active managers seeking alpha wherever it may lie. Exhibit 6.8 illustrates (no, this is not a solar system) this platform through what many refer to as the *Core and Explore* platform.

Communication

In this, the final part of the investment management process, we rely heavily on the advisers who often act (although not always) as go-betweens in the separation of duties between advice and implementation. That is to say, in many cases the adviser will seek out the managers who will then invest the capital, and it is the job of this adviser to monitor the managers and communicate with the IC periodically. In some cases the adviser is also the manager—serving both roles is nice, for it permits a greater amount of symmetry of approach, but it is often hard to find advisers who are qualified to implement a portfolio—but most serve as the all-important "general contractor."

The function of the adviser in the Communication phase of the process is to do the following:

- Periodic check-ins with the IC of the foundation, to provide some commentary on the markets and economy in general as well as some details about where the portfolio is situated. The key here is not so much the content of the communiqué but its proactive (rather than reactive) nature and frequency. It can be a fairly simple e-mail and doesn't need to be a full blown out report.
- Full-blown reports are required, however—typically quarterly where the IC can get a view of the portfolio from under the hood so to speak. In these quarterly reports the adviser is to serve as MC and provide the following to the IC:
  - Performance attribution report showing where the returns in the portfolio came from. In other words, which pieces of the portfolio generated which returns (positive or negative)? This speaks to the issue that is often overlooked (since most investors simply care about the "bottom line") where a portfolio may have a great return, but due in large measure (or solely) to one specific security. This begs the question: "Was the manager simply lucky or does he have a verifiable process to provide strong returns?"
  - Risk assessment, which parses the portfolio down to statistics like variance and standard deviation. Also important are the portfolio's up- and downside capture ratios, which tell the investors how much upside they are getting for how much downside they are subjected to.
  - Portfolio highlights, where the IC is shown a few highlighted securities—both on the winning and losing sides—that detail the portfolio manager's thinking. The key here is the manager's risk control issues, also known as his or her *sell discipline.* Buying securities is one thing, but a defined sell discipline is a key measure for the depth of the portfolio manager's acumen.
  - Performance reporting—The IC will want to know how the foundation's portfolio performed during the period in question. The most accepted method of this reporting is the time-weighted return (TWR) method, which provides a return figure weighted over how much time the capital has been in

the portfolio. This is important, especially to the foundation that is seeing many inflows and outflows of capital throughout the period, since the TWR metric nets these effects out of the performance figure it provides. In addition, we want to see how the portfolio performed compared to a set of market indices, as well as a composite tailored to our asset allocation.

- The amount of income and cash flow generated over the period and what is expected for the balance of the year. The IC will highlight this figure to the grants committee for their work in the management of cash flows for the foundation.
- Asset allocation model—Here we want to see not only where the asset allocation currently is, but also how it has deviated from the stated asset allocation model. The deviation is an important point, for it provides a clue to the proactive stance of the adviser—*Is he simply letting things coast along or does he have a plan to insure that the foundation's assets are in a model that was accepted by the board?* Investing requires a strong sense of dynamism—one can never become too confident or too complacent.
- A discussion on the fees charged over the period, the proxies voted on, and any other administrative issues that the board should be made aware of (for example, class actions suits or other legal actions).

Communication is a critical part of the investment management process, and advisers and managers who thwart their responsibilities in this area are doomed to failure in the eyes of the IC, no matter how good their return may be. At the end of the day, the buck stops at the IC members' desks, and to that end they need to be kept aware of what is going on in the portfolio. If IC members are not getting the communication they desire from the advisers or managers there should be no third strike—*any* strikes and you are out in this ballgame. It's just that important.

■ ■ ■

"That is all very interesting—good stuff indeed," said Phil Anthony.

"Okay, so can I begin the process of making some grants?" asked an anxious Mary.

"Sure can—you guys are good to go and I hope these reports will help you and your family members for years to come. But before I leave you and as a way to celebrate this new life of yours I would like to invite you to attend a dinner party next week, where I will introduce you to a friend of mine who can share with you some stories of the great work that foundations have done over the years," said Em.

"Sounds great—look forward to it," chimed Phil and Mary.

Summary

As we move on to Part II, the Anthonys are introduced to Angelica Berrie, a fellow philanthropist who shares with them impactful stories of giving—from the simple police officer turned giver in her hometown of Chicago to the large institutional givers at the Nathan Cummings Foundation. Although every story is different the message is the same—the passion for giving is fed along the way and grows inside the philanthropist. As long as the passion is kept alive the circle is continued in the next generations.

PART

II

A PASSION FOR GIVING

Lessons in Philanthropy

When Peter Klein suggested that I contribute my experience in philanthropy to this book, I looked back on my life to frame the lessons learned from my philanthropic journey.

After growing up in Catholic convent schools in the Philippines, where the word "philanthropy" was not a part of my vocabulary, I entered a whole different world when I married New Jersey sales entrepreneur, Russ Berrie, whose success with teddy bears and Russ Trolls fueled our philanthropy.

Coming from the Catholic tradition of giving anonymously at Sunday Mass into a Jewish community that expected me to play an active and visible fund-raising role was something of a culture shock. I was welcomed into the Englewood Jewish community by a formidable fundraiser, Miriam Josephs, who laid out in no uncertain terms my responsibility as "Russ Berrie's wife." After my timid response, "but I'm not Jewish," fell on deaf ears, I dutifully agreed to host my first United Jewish Appeal Women's Division luncheon. It was the beginning of my philanthropic journey, with friendships that led me to express myself through the causes I threw my weight behind.

I discovered the satisfaction of giving, not from seeing our names on buildings but in connecting the dots between people, ideas, and issues I was passionate about.

Though my husband, Russ, encouraged me to pursue my own interests, when I joined a founding group to start a Gilda's Club in Northern New Jersey, a free social and emotional support community for families living with cancer, he told us, "I'll pay you *not* to do this!" His concern about the challenge of fund raising for a totally new nonprofit in our community was valid, but we proved him wrong and

LETTER TO THE TRUSTEES

June 7, 1998

Dear Trustee:

Over the years I have given from the Foundation or personally to many charities or institutions. To fulfill my vision, I want you to be guided by the criteria set forth in the Foundation's mission statement and from my past giving. I would like my Foundation to build success, approaching philanthropy in the same entrepreneurial spirit, which has enabled me to build my personal legacy.

I expect you to respect the areas of special interest to me, to remember that I want the Foundation to reflect my values and entrepreneurial style, investing seed money to start innovative projects, resisting the urge to shift the focus of giving into areas that are not consistent with my own personal preferences. It is my hope that whatever funds can be given should be used so that it will have an impact to make a difference in the lives of people.

However, in a rapidly changing world, the Foundation should be flexible enough to respond to unique challenges, ideas, and projects that lie beyond the identified programs areas, yet would fulfill my broad vision. In interpreting the guidelines set forth in my mission statement, I expect common sense to prevail.

Sincerely,
Russell Berrie

I went on to chair the global board of Gilda's Club Worldwide, which, at the time, had 26 clubhouses in North America. It was my first experience in the nonprofit world and taught me how I could add value by giving fully of myself beyond writing a check.

As my mentor and partner in philanthropy, Russ taught me to ask tough questions and set conditions before making a gift. He brought his entrepreneurial self into the giving equation—seeding innovative ventures with out-of-the-box leaders and purposely avoiding being "a small fish in a big pond," while never losing sight of the people whose lives he wanted to make a difference in.

His letter to the trustees of the Russell Berrie Foundation, expressing donor intent simply and clearly, continues to guide us in reflecting who he was and how we give.

My husband loved people and brought his own humanity to everything he did. He was a Type 2 diabetic, a salesman who believed all Jewish mothers should say "my son the salesman!" with as much pride as they said "my son the doctor!", and who made teddy bears for a living.

The Russell Berrie Foundation's mission statement is a personal expression of Russ's passions and aspirations, influenced by his experience living with diabetes, his humble beginnings as a toy salesman, his interest in the continuity of Jewish communal life in New Jersey and Israel, his belief in the importance of interreligious understanding, and his foresight in investing against the threat of terrorism.

When we established the Naomi Berrie Diabetes Center at Columbia University, Russ produced a teddy bear created by a mom who wanted to teach her son how to inject himself with insulin. The bear had patches on parts of the body where he could practice plunging a needle. We filled the lobby with huggable toys to create a warm and welcoming environment for families, and supplied doctors with a private stash of Russ Trolls to give away to the kids. We took great pride in the small touches that humanized the Berrie Diabetes Center: free parking for patients; diabetes care specialists like podiatrists, dentists, and ophthalmologists assembled under one roof for the convenience of working parents; nurse educators for families to learn how to deal with diabetes together; a diabetic "canteen" stocked with healthy snacks; and Halloween parties for kids who came to swap their sweets for toys.

Russ's dream of elevating sales impelled us to build the Russ Berrie Institute for Professional Sales at William Paterson University, in New Jersey, which offers the only sales degree program in the country. Its sales laboratory has a recording facility for faculty and students to observe and critique sales presentation techniques. Students from as far as New Zealand and Scotland compete in sales presentations judged by top corporate leaders who recruit the best for their companies.

We honor Russ's Jewish roots with the Berrie Fellows Leadership program, which we created after his death as a legacy gift to our community. We believe that leadership is truly the gift you leave behind! Our first two cohorts have become change agents in our community, transforming local nonprofit boards with their passion, strategic thinking skills, and innovative spirit. Alumni of the program are now shaping the curriculum and learning process, becoming mentors and role models for the next cohort.

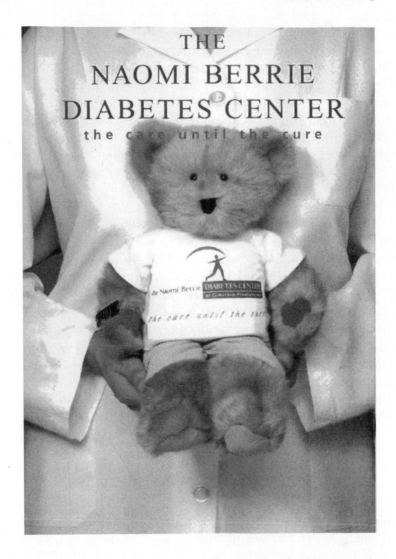

Our passion for Israel led to the creation of the Russ Berrie Nanotechnology Institute at Technion University, which produced a "nano-Bible," presented by President Shimon Peres as a gift of the Jewish people to Pope Benedict on his first visit to Israel.

The gift of nanotechnology was unique in its entrepreneurial approach, challenging the government of Israel to make an unprecedented matching dollar contribution. The government's positive response to our challenge spurred other Israeli academic institutions to participate in a "triangle matching program," which effectively tripled our investment to seed what is now the largest research and development nanotechnology platform in the country.

Marriage was the beginning of our interfaith adventure. As an intermarried couple, we celebrated the Jewish High Holidays, lit candles on Shabbat, visited Israel almost every year, and attended midnight mass at St. Patrick's Cathedral on Christmas Eve. Our mingled faiths led to the founding of the Center for Inter-Religious Understanding, with Rabbi Jack Bemporad, who taught us that "to be religious is to be interreligious." In the new reality of an increasingly interreligious world, it was clear that a new generation of spiritual leaders needed training for interfaith work. Inspired by the late Pope John Paul II's contribution to interreligious dialogue, we established the Pope John Paul II Center for Interreligious Studies at the Angelicum, a Pontifical University in Rome. Our four cohorts of interfaith fellows from 19 different countries will serve on the forefront of interreligious dialogue, building bridges between faiths so our children can live peacefully together in a better world.

After living in an active and generous Jewish community for 10 years, I was ready to consider converting when my world shifted with my husband's death in 2002. Overnight, I was a widow, vice chairman and CEO of Russ Berrie and Co., a global gift company on the New York Stock Exchange, and president of the Russell Berrie Foundation.

It was only after the company hired a new CEO that I was free to embark on the journey of lifelong learning that changed my life. Preparing for my conversion at the Shalom Hartman Institute, a center for transformational Jewish studies in Jerusalem, infused my philanthropy with the values of a 3,000-year-old tradition. Like my Jewish namesake, Ruth, I was a widow who embraced my husband's people in a journey of "becoming," learning to lead in a different way.

After Russ's death, the Berrie Foundation began its transition from a founder-led organizational culture that was often reactive in its giving, toward a more strategic proactive approach. A large part of my experiential learning was fostered by relationships with philanthropists who learned by doing, expressing values formed by life experiences that shaped their unique approaches to giving. It was an education that connected me to a network of like-minded souls who have been an invaluable resource as I learned what it meant to *be* a philanthropist.

As the foundation evolved, we sought counsel from expert practitioners in the field who expanded our thinking and helped us reflect on our past lessons to become transformational funders.

My greatest teachers are the unsung heroes who made change happen in their communities with limited resources and no expectations of recognition or reward. It is a gift to encounter such great human beings who truly make a difference in people's lives!

The ideas and advice shared by these innovators in the art of giving provide the inspiration for this section of the book. Inviting them to share the most valuable lessons for beginners, practitioners, and experienced philanthropists at any point of their philanthropic curve was an exercise in deep listening that made me look at my own practice with fresh eyes.

I hope that I listened deeply enough to translate their wisdom and experience into lessons that help you shape your most important contribution to the world.

■ ■ ■

The following chapters have been organized to complement Peter's earlier chapters on fundamental issues related to starting a philanthropic enterprise.

Chapter 7 is the essence of philanthropy as the gift of who you are. Reflecting on "What are you most passionate about?" is the starting point for your philanthropic journey.

Chapter 8 is philanthropist Ken Behring's personal story of transformation as he discovers a sense of purpose by delivering wheelchairs all over the world.

Chapter 9 is the best tutorial on philanthropy, from Peter Karoff, founder of The Philanthropic Initiative, and Joel Fleishman, author of *Give $mart: Philanthropy That Gets Results*.

Peter takes you through the philanthropic learning curve, defining characteristics of a "gifted giver," with examples from Joel and Peter of transformational gifts from visionary givers.

Chapter 10 demonstrates the power of one individual to make a difference. It does not take a million dollar check to qualify as a philanthropist, as everyday heroes Lisa Nigro and Chip Paillex show us.

Chapter 11 highlights women leading through philanthropy, inspiring other women to create a powerful network invested in shifting the odds for women of the world, who are 70 percent of the people living in poverty.

Chapter 12 explores multigenerational giving, as families grapple with issues related to wealth, learn how to transmit personal values, and empower the next generation.

Chapter 13 is about philanthropy as a voyage of discovery, featuring Scott McVay's poem inspiring us to become explorers, with the journey of musician Paul Winter and artist Aimee Morgana as examples.

Chapter 14 is former president of the Wallace Foundation's "look-back" on almost 30 years of learning, as Christine DeVita explains how foundations' best intentions of doing good are not good enough if you really intend to create change.

Chapter 15 is the intersection of heart and soul, with Amy Goldman of the GHR Foundation and Lynn Schusterman of the Charles and Lynn Schusterman Foundation expressing their giving in the best spirit of their different traditions.

Chapter 16 assembles the lessons of the philanthropic journey into a framework for a personal philosophy of giving.

CHAPTER 7

The Gift

Philanthropy as the Gift of Who You Are

Giving is offering the fruitfulness of who you are, an expression of the vitality of your being.

—Tony Weller, Organizational Shaman

Aphilanthropist is simply a "lover of humanity." Making a gift that taps into the power of our own humanity is not based on how much we have, but is deeply rooted in who we are. We connect to the source of giving by tapping into our spiritual values and passions, our deepest longing. Accessing our inner truths to align our giving with a sense of purpose gives meaning to our lives. The essence of our giving revolves around issues that resonate most within us, as we respond to the soul searching questions: "What are the issues that we would die for? What are the passions we would live for?"[1]

Giving Begins with the Self

The urge to be generous is an inward journey whose inspiration comes from introspection. "True philanthropy isn't about giving, it is about being, about being honest and true. Having the ability to compost all we thought we were into the soil of who we truly are," says Tony Weller,

---

[1]Pico Iyer, "The Soul of an Intercontinental Wanderer," *Harper's Magazine*, April 1, 1993 (from "Living in the Transit Lounge," a talk given at Yale University's Davenport College, January 1993).

"finding what makes our heart sing, our soul dance, and creating out of that our gift to the world!"

The state of being from which the impetus to give emerges is defined by Peter Karoff, founder of The Philanthropic Initiative (TPI) as "philanthropy in its purest, most rare and elusive form, the giving of oneself, one's me, for a purpose that is selfless and good, in small and large ways."[2]

Peter speaks of the personal transformation that grows from committed engagement to real change as a fundamental part of the philanthropic journey, describing the "great desire to see change occur, the discovery of our philanthropic voice and the courage to act," as "rising from our bravest and most authentic selves."[3]

Giving from that deepest self inspired Lisa Nigro, a police officer, to haul a nephew's little red wagon filled with coffee, bagels, and sandwiches, patrolling the 15th District of Chicago's crime-ridden West Side neighborhood to feed the homeless. With $30,000 of her life savings and credit cards that took 10 years to pay off, Lisa started the Inspiration Cafe, which grew into four restaurants with a service training program that puts homeless people back to work. Her goal of bridging our worlds to learn about their lives as we encounter each other on an even playing field comes from a personal sense of what really needs to change in the equation—the inner truth that needs to be addressed.

What Are You Most Passionate About?

How do we embark on our own philanthropic journey? Joel Fleishman, director of the Heyman Center at Duke University's Center for Strategic Philanthropy, suggests we begin with: "What are you most passionate about?" as the "polestar" to guide our philanthropic quest, followed by the execution question, "How much impact do you want to make on what you care most about?"

Susan Solomont of the Philanthropic Initiative describes philanthropy as a crossroads of heart and mind:

---

[2]Peter Karoff, *Strategic Philanthropy: Poetry and Practice* (The Philanthropic Initiative, November 1, 1999).
[3]Peter Karoff, *Transformation through Philanthropy: Theory, Fact, and Fiction* (The Philanthropic Initiative, October 1, 2004).

Passion starts you on your path. Your heart has to lead you to things you are passionate about. How you listen to your heart and develop strategic processes, taking what you feel deeply and expressing it, is all part of an ongoing journey. You live it! How do you choose? It includes who you surround yourself with, meeting more people, spending time learning a field . . . the path is the goal!

Starting on the path begins with yourself. Giving is an exchange of energy that requires time to reflect so we can give from a place of wholeness and integrity.

"To be a philanthropist means we must first be generous to ourselves before we can give fully of ourself to others. We need time to remember our essence limiting our original innocence, so we deliver our gifts free of conditions and judgment," says Tony Weller.

Tony's work focuses on learning to give from our essence (all we think we are and who we have become), so any "woundedness," guilt, or imbalance that causes negative energy does not get carried into our "gift exchange."

A healthy understanding of our relationship to wealth or the source of our wealth, even the nature of our relationship with the person we inherit wealth from, can color our giving. Tony's philanthropic coaching addresses the inner work of putting the pieces together—of remembering and forgiving, of healing and growth—moving toward wholeness, free of seeing ourselves as defined by material wealth.

Partnerships in philanthropy depend on alignment in this spiritual exchange, as we give from the best of ourselves and receive from those we make a gift of ourselves to, the best of themselves in return. Learning how to give, as well as how to receive, requires that internal alignment to integrate all the pieces and bring a sense of wholeness to our giving.

The interrelated structure of this "gift exchange" is expressed in the Hebrew word *natan*, which is interpreted as a "mirror word" because it is spelled the same way backward or forward and carries a dual meaning—"to give" and its equal meaning in reverse, "to receive." The reciprocity of giving that brings wholeness to both giver and receiver is also expressed in the Christian tradition, which teaches that "it is in giving that we receive." Knowing we gain the most from what we give makes us the ultimate recipient of our own generosity!

The Greatest Gift

More than money, our greatest gift as philanthropists is the "gift of time." We need time to find the space within, to get in touch with who we are so we bring the gift of our life and the fullness of our being to what we care most about. It takes time to learn, to plant seeds and wait for growth, to develop good programs, see effective results, create long-term change, to accomplish important work, to reflect on how our giving fulfills our highest aspirations.

Our philanthropic aspirations are rooted in this journey of exploration and imagination. As philanthropists, how do we cherish, nurture, share, and partake of the gift of imagination, the gift of humanity that distinguishes us from all other beings?

Tony Weller shares his vision of philanthropists as great humanists:

> As humans, we are guardians of the earth, co-creators and wisdom keepers whose interaction with all living systems on this planet ultimately affects what lives and dies. As philanthropists, social entrepreneurial angels, innovators, mentors and influential leaders, we have the amazing ability to shape the future with both tangible and intangible wealth; our gifts of time, energy, creativity and passion. Taking time out to reimagine what it means to be human at a moment when the interconnectivity of life on earth is at stake offers the opportunity to create initiatives that sustain beneficial relationships with fellow humans and the environment. Becoming role models for our children through our giving, we can liberate them from old stories of fear, hatred and hopelessness, teaching them to live a new narrative of philanthropy, powered by love, compassion, forgiveness and understanding.

To Peter Karoff, "The centrality of philanthropy to the making of a better world is the heart and soul of why you are here. Make a poem of it!"

Summary

Developing a vision for giving that is powered by our gift of imagination comes from a place of wholeness, a sense of connectedness to the world and to our environment, to the bigger emerging human story. It is the source from which we draw the creative fuel for our philanthropic journey.

The inner work of philanthropy, the introspection to reflect on who we are in how we give, brings mindfulness and intentionality to our giving practice. Giving ourselves the "gift of time" is essential.

Finding our passion, bringing our whole selves, and the giving of "one's me," are lessons Joel Fleishman, Tony Weller, and Peter Karoff share with us. Encountering ourselves as we encounter humanity deepens our souls and brings its own gift of personal transformation.

Exercise

What area of your giving is most aligned with who you are—your origins, your life experience, your personal philosophy?

If you could express your mission statement in a one-sentence poem of four lines, how would it read?

What have you learned from this lesson that you could apply to understanding what aspect of your nature stands in the way of being a better giver?

In the next chapter, Glen Macdonald, president of the Wealth and Giving Forum, introduces philanthropist Ken Behring, who shares his story about finding a sense of purpose.

CHAPTER 8

Purpose

Ken Behring's Story

Every wheelchair makes a difference, not only to the person getting it but to the family and the whole community. With a wheelchair, we give hope, we give freedom, and we give dignity.

—Ken Behring, the Wheelchair Philanthropist

Many years ago, I heard a story that illustrated so powerfully the meaning of the word *purpose* in the context of philanthropy. When real-estate developer, former owner of the Seattle Seahawks football team, and philanthropist, Ken Behring, told his story at a Wealth and Giving Forum in 2004, a copy of his speech was published by the president of the Wealth and Giving Forum, Glen Macdonald. The story still resonates many years after he delivered the speech, compelling me to seek permission to reprint it in this book as a first-person account on the meaning of purpose.

Introduction by Glen Macdonald, President of the Wealth and Giving Forum

I will never forget the moment when Ken Behring uttered the words, "I had everything money could buy, and I thought I was happy but something was missing." It was October 2004. Ken was addressing our guests at the inaugural Wealth and Giving Forum gathering in White Sulfur Springs, West Virginia. He was midway through sharing his extraordinary life story, from Depression-era kid who shot squirrels to feed his family to billionaire owner of the Seattle Seahawks.

Ken paused, his voice cracked and the natural sparkle in his eye was accentuated with some moisture. The room grew silent. Everyone fixed their gaze intently on the warm "teddy bear" of a man up on the stage and wondered what he would say next. Ken swallowed, then looked up and out into the crowd and said, "Don't wait. Don't do what I did and wait until the age of 74 to find purpose and true happiness. Please, don't wait."

At the moment, I looked around the room—heads were bowed, sniffles were audible, and there was not a dry eye in the room. It was abundantly clear to all that Ken cared about the less fortunate who benefit from his and other philanthropists' largess. But Ken also let the folks there that day know just how much he cared about them, too. Ken Behring, the wheelchair giver, the man with purpose, had touched everyone seated before him with his big heart and powerful message about purpose.

When the Wealth and Giving Forum set out to convene individuals of means and afford them opportunities to help one another figure out how best to allocate their wealth, we knew that inspiration would be a central part of awakening of one's true capacity to make a difference. Ken Behring's story illustrates well that finding purpose can come from introspection; an inward journey in which one ponders his or her true purpose as well as the best outlet for the resources, experience, and insights that one accumulates on life's journey. But as Bill Moyers and Fareed Zakaria have reminded guests at our gatherings, finding purpose can also come from looking outward at what is happening around us and sensing not only what is at stake, but what is possible if one applies his or her resources and ingenuity to combat human suffering or the ills we face collectively.[1]

When Bill Moyers addressed our guests some years after Ken, he cited such diverse "characters" as John Wesley, the nineteenth-century English evangelist, Eliot Rosewater, a fictional billionaire invention of Kurt Vonnegut, and Rachel Naomi Remen, a rather obscure physician who co-founded Commonweal. From diversity emerges a clear and compelling message. First, Mr. Moyers echoed

---

[1]Bill Moyers and Fareed Zakaria excerpts from *Reflections: Excerpted from Wealth and Giving Forum Gatherings* by Glen Macdonald (Glen Macdonald, 2005).

Ken Behring's remarks when he opened with, "I have found that the people of means who are the happiest and most deeply satisfied are those who use their money to empower others." And that without "equitable access," too many suffer initially but in the end we all lose. In fact, although self-interest may be both the prerequisite of and the foundation for doing good (witness Ken's life story), Mr. Moyers also reminded us that excessive self-interest can insulate those of means, turn them blind to the deterioration around them, and that in the end "they can become the casualties of their own privilege."

How can we avoid such insulation and complacency from setting in? One sure way is to not leave things to chance, by not assuming that somehow government institutions, universities, and modern technologies (or the like) will somehow figure a way to work itself out of the troubles confronting us.

As Fareed Zakaria warned guests at one Wealth and Giving gathering, that would indeed be a dangerous assumption and approach. Instead, he would tend to agree with Mr. Moyers's comment that, "There is 'the growing edge of things' that awaits your resources, and mine—your bare hands and mine." Or, in Wealth and Giving parlance, "that awaits our generosity."

Mr. Zakaria also counsels us that the human element like Ken Behring's humanity is a vitally important cog in the wheel. He implored our guests to pay attention to "human needs, human aspirations, human wants, and human desires" and posited that individuals who have something to give, need to step up to the responsibility and place their resources and bare hands in the service of others. It is up to human beings who choose to follow the leading footsteps of individuals like Ken Behring, who did look around, saw a suffering man, and did something about it.

At a time when philanthropy is becoming overindustrialized, with great emphasis on business-like practices and metrics, and new-fangled buzz words like scaling impact, outcome-driven programs, mission-related investing, and donor-intent permeating our thinking and habits, inspiring stories like Ken's are increasingly important to remind us that philanthropy is and must remain a human and humane endeavor where the heart rules.

Ken helps us remember that philanthropy dates back to the beginning of civilization and transcends place, time, and cultures. In fact, the term *philanthropy* is attributed to the Greek playwright Aeschylus, whose character Prometheus discovered that which makes one human: "'loves' in the sense of benefitting, caring for, nour-ishing. What Prometheus . . . 'loved,' therefore, was their human potential—what they could accomplish and become with 'fire' and 'blind hope.'"

In the Ken Behring piece that follows, you will enjoy a truly Horatio Alger-esque story about how Ken parlayed one business success into another and then another, onward and upward to a place where he owned an NFL team but also, as he puts it, a place where "something . . . was really missing." Almost by chance he discovers what was meant when, as the title of his autobiography says, "Somebody Told Me about the Word *Purpose*."

Ken's philanthropic story began when he encountered an immobile elderly gentleman alone in a hospital room in a poor area of Romania. And then came "sparks," wheelchairs, and a new journey—and with it his transformation from a charitable man to a truly philanthropic soul. Most of all, Ken found "the type of joy that comes from purpose," or as he puts it, "I'm having loads of fun."

"Somebody Told Me about the Word *Purpose*" by Ken Behring[2]

The first thing people ask me is, "How did you get into wheelchairs? What was the reason?" I was born in 1928—one of those Depression babies—and my parents were extremely poor. So I had the desire to make money. I thought money was the only thing in the world when I was growing up. We had no indoor bathroom, no water, no central heat. You want more of everything. You want more than one pair of shoes.

You try to get through that stage, but everything is about money. You don't even think about helping anybody else. When you are finally able to get the basic things, you find that you are still not satisfied. Then you come to the next stage of your life, where everything you have you want to be better. If you have a Chevrolet, you want a Cadillac. If you have one home, you want two homes. If you have two suits, you want four suits.

---

[2]This story was related by Ken Behring at the Wealth and Giving Forum in an introductory group session of the October 24, 2004 Wealth and Giving Forum session moderated by Garrick Utley and featuring Leonard Kaplan, Paul Schervish, and Kenneth Behring. Reprinted with permission from the Wealth and Giving Forum.

But still, when you finally get where there's really nothing more that money can buy, you have happiness. Now you are looking for the next stage. For me, that's when I started collecting classic cars and building a museum. I helped the University of California bring in students in paleontology and anthropology. I went to the Smithsonian and did the Mammal Hall for them with animals.

But it was all done with money. All through my life, I would give money, thinking that it was a duty rather than something that was truly coming from my heart. I purchased a football team and had that for eleven years. I was living the American dream. When you start with an outdoor bathroom and you suddenly own a professional football team—there are very few countries in the world where you can do that. I just thank God every day that I was born here.

One of the first things I purchased when I was about seven years old was a single-shot 22-caliber rifle. I would go out and shoot rabbits and squirrels. I'd bring them home, and my mother would make me clean them, and she would cook them. All winter, I had to eat these rabbits and squirrels. I really didn't like them, but I enjoyed hunting for them. It gave us food, so I had a desire always to hunt.

Later in life, I started going to Africa to hunt. Africa changed my life—seeing the people and how they live and the many things they need that they're not getting. I had everything that you could really want, that you could purchase, but I was still very unfulfilled. I knew there was something else out there.

Then somebody told me about the word *purpose*. I tried to look it up, tried to define what purpose is. I decided I would try to go out and see if I could find it. There had to be a reason why we're here besides just making money and accumulating goods and wealth.

I started taking books to Africa. We gave them to the schools, first- and second-grade English books. We took pens and paper to schools. I enjoyed taking medical supplies and whatever else I could on every trip. It became known that I would take things. I had a big airplane that I had kept from when I had the football team, an MF-80. So I was able to take a lot of supplies wherever I went.

When there was a disaster, I'd load the plane up and take it wherever the disaster was. A church got hold of me once and asked me if I'd take fifteen tons of canned meat to the Kosovo refugees. This was right after the Kosovo war, so I said I would. But when I loaded up, I still had room. Someone asked if I would take some wheelchairs and drop them off in Romania. People give me credit for thinking of wheelchairs; I wish I had been that smart. It was purely by accident that they gave me the wheelchairs and asked me to drop them off.

In Romania, we sat down and talked to the doctor who was in charge of the hospital. He said that in Third World countries, people who are disabled are discarded. They're put in the back of a hut. They're given one meal a day. People are ashamed of them. The family thinks they did something wrong because they have a disabled person. Better just to put them in the back room and hope they'll die.

At this hospital in Romania, there was an older gentleman. He had just lost his wife and then had a stroke. I was putting him in a wheelchair. That was the first time that I'd ever tried to lift somebody up and take them from a bed and put them in a wheelchair. He started to cry. Through an interpreter, he was telling me, "Now I can go outside, I can smoke, I can talk to my neighbors." And you know, the sparks flew. I thought, it means so much to this person, it makes a difference whether he really wants to live or not—something as simple as a wheelchair, a $75 investment.

I thought, maybe, just possibly, this could be the purpose that I was looking for. I had a chance to go to Vietnam, and I sent over a full container of 280 wheelchairs. We took them to Hanoi, and they got held up at the port. They told me there was a doctor at the hospital that maybe could help us get them out. I went to this hospital. I don't remember seeing anything so pathetic, so dirty, with people crowded in rooms. We went past one room, and I looked in and saw three men there who really looked odd. The doctor said, "They're lepers." I asked if I could talk to them. I had to force myself to see these people who had knobs on their arms and on their heads. They were such outcasts from the world, shoved into this little room. Nobody cared. I forced myself to touch them, to talk to them, and they showed such gratitude that somebody would care.

We did get some chairs released. We took pictures of everybody to whom we gave a wheelchair. We gave the pictures to anybody who donated $75, so they knew who had gotten the chairs, in which country, with their names and ages. One lady who wanted to thank me was typical of some older people in Vietnam. Her teeth were completely black and very broken. She said, "I'm 72 years old"—she looked a lot older than that—"I wanted to die, but I have not been able to." She was in her chair and I was sitting down. She took my hands, looked at me and smiled through those broken teeth, and she said, "Now I don't want to."

Again, it clicked: What we're doing is so simple, yet in a matter of minutes it can change a person's life. It makes a difference between wanting to live and wanting to die.

We had five chairs left, so we went back and gave them away. As I was walking out, one of the nurses said, "We've got three people in the back of the hall who are crying their eyes out; I can't control them." These were the lepers. They had heard that we were going to come back and give away wheelchairs. Because I had paid attention to them, I had built up their hope. If you give a person hope and then take it away, it's worse than their having had no hope at all. So we went all over Hanoi, and I finally found three used wheelchairs that cost 20 times what mine did. I brought them back for these three people. I don't know how God could put people in such misery as they were in. And what a difference that made in their lives. They could go outside. They could actually be living people, even if others shunned them.

Another great lesson: If you give hope to a person, you've got to follow through, because you're the only thing that they have that can make their life better.

We've given away over 300,000 wheelchairs in the past four years. We're in about 130 countries at the present time. Every wheelchair makes a difference, not only to the person getting it but to the family and the whole community, too. I truly think that we have to help the poor people if we want our world to survive. If they have no hope, they're the ones who are going to help blow this world apart.

With a wheelchair, we give hope, we give freedom, and we give dignity. A fellow in the Gaza Strip, a strong man, crawled up to me, and we got him into a wheelchair. He looked at me and said, "I'm a man."

In Honduras, a young girl was in journalism school. She got hit by a truck and lay in bed for 10 years. When she got a wheelchair, she came the very next day to show the certificate that she had re-enrolled in journalism school.

In Zimbabwe, we didn't really like the leadership, but they were kind enough to protect my plane. We have been going right into the middle of Africa for more than three years. When the natives find out we're coming, they start two days ahead, making homemade brew and pounding on the drums. It becomes a real celebration. When we get there, then they start bringing the people in. Some are in wheelbarrows, some they're carrying, some they have in wooden wagons with wooden wheels and oxen. They dump them off in front of us.

One fellow got in a wheelchair, and he started going round and round with this wheelchair. He was going as fast as he could and having a great time. But then I noticed he got out of the wheelchair and sat back on the ground. I went over and asked, "Why do you get out of the wheelchair?" He said, "Fifteen years ago, I was given a turn in a wheelchair. I crawled seventeen kilometers to get here so I could have another turn to be in a wheelchair, just to see what it felt like. Now I've had my turn, somebody else can have their turn."

In Cape Town, I had a call from some nuns. They had 237 paraplegics. A nun told me, "We only have one wheelbarrow for all these people; the only time we use them is to bury them. If there's any way we could get a few wheelchairs once in a while, we could just push them out so that they could be outside and see what life is like." That's about as bad as you can get.

In China, a little boy named Kun San was dumped in a trash can when he was a baby. An orphanage found him, and they have given him maybe seven or eight operations. He's finally where his arms and legs are almost where he can hold them down. He's got a beautiful voice, and there's a song in Chinese that he really loves. It goes, "I want my father to come home to me; if anybody knows where my father is, please tell him that I need him." He came and sat in my lap and looked up at me and said, "Are you my grandpa?" I gave the orphanage money so he can continue to go to school. Because despite being dummied and disfigured or disabled like he is, he is still able to sing, and it really inspires you.

In Guatemala, a man was in such pain that you could see it. I asked him what happened. He said he got hurt in the field. "Have you been to the doctor?" I asked. He said, "Yes, I have gangrene; the doctor gave me 30 days to take my leg off or I will die. But the doctor wants 100 dollars to cut my leg, and he wants another 25 if he has to put me to sleep." He said, "I'll go and try to raise the money, but if I can't, I'll have my family give you the wheelchair back." I counted out the money and he handed me back 25 dollars. He said, "I don't have to be put to sleep."

In Mexico, we had a lady that helped us with our laundry for about 12 years. She mentioned that she had a nephew by the name of Angel, 16 years old who had a terminal disease. He had lost his eyesight first, and then he lost his mobility. But if we could possibly give him a wheelchair, he had some years to live, and it would just make his life so much better. So I said sure. When I was down there, his parents found me and said, "Angel received his wheelchair, but he would very much like to come and thank you. Would it embarrass you or would you permit him to come?"

I said, "No, no, bring him over." I took his hands and talked to him, knowing he was blind, so he would know where I was. And then he in turn took my hands, and he looked right at me with his eyes, his blind eyes, and into my eyes he said, "I'll see you in heaven."

That's the type of joy that comes from purpose. It doesn't make any difference what you do. If you can help your fellow man—not the way I did in the beginning, by giving money—if you can really give yourself, and do it from your heart, and show people that you care, what you get back is a hundred times what you give.

Summary

This chapter's theme sounds a clarion call to all who seek a fuller definition of purpose to apply in our own lives.

Exercise

Have you experienced a similar turning point in your own journey?
What aspect of Ken's story resonated most for you and why?
What would you do in response to Ken's urging to "not wait?"
What do you feel is missing in your philanthropy?

In the next chapter, Peter Karoff, founder of the Philanthropic Initiative, describes the philanthropic learning curve to identify the stages of growth we go through as we learn how to be better givers. He defines "the Gifted Giver," with examples of transformational gifts and insights from Joel Fleishman, author of *Give $mart: Philanthropy That Gets Results*.

Resources

To learn more about Glen and Ken and the work they and their organizations do, you can refer to the following contact information.

Wealth and Giving Forum
Community Foundation of New Jersey
35 Knox Hill Road
Morristown, NJ 07936
(908) 510-5310
www.wealthandgiving.org

Wheelchair Foundation
3820 Blackhawk Road
Danville, CA 94506
(877) 378-3839
http://wheelchairfoundation.org

CHAPTER

9

The Gifted Giver

Lessons from *Peter Karoff* (Chairman and Founder of The Philanthropic Initiative) with Insights from *Joel Fleishman* (Professor of Law and Public Policy at Duke University)

> *Individual transformation is where it all begins, starting with a vision for change.*
>
> —Peter Karoff, Chairman and Founder of
> The Philanthropic Initiative (TPI)

The philanthropic quest begins with a vision for change—what you are most passionate about changing, what you care enough about to want to change, what you want to create the greatest impact on.

As Peter Karoff, poet and philanthropy guru, explains:

> The poetry of philanthropy begins with the creative imaginative surge that we feel when we are deeply moved. . . . It requires an internal readiness in your own personal process, a willingness to attempt what hasn't been done before. The soil has to be fertile, you can feed it and nurture it but cannot make it happen without finding those opportunistic moments in time when there is a real readiness to make a leap.[1]

---

[1] From "Strategic Philanthropy: Poetry and Practice Over Ten Years," a presentation at TPI's 10th Anniversary, November 1999.

Making a gift that, in the words of Lewis Hyde, author of *The Gift* (Canongate Books, 1983), "speaks commandingly to the soul and irresistibly moves us," is the initial leap we make in our philanthropic journey. Peter Karoff defines the process of getting there as a philanthropic learning curve, which has several stages.

The Philanthropic Learning Curve

The following levels in the philanthropic learning curve are adapted from a 2004 presentation of Peter's at the Morgan Library to clients of J. P. Morgan Private Bank.

Level One—You Become a Donor

A complex combination of personal and religious values, family background, business and social pressures, ego, and heartfelt response to the world around you motivates you to become a donor. Giving becomes part of your way of life, your position in the community, your yearning to be a good person. Over time, giving becomes somewhat automatic, demands on you increase, and you are on many lists. Your gifts, with few exceptions, are distributed in small amounts to an increasing number of organizations. Sound familiar?

Level Two—You Decide to Get Organized

The goal is to get control of the giving process, instead of the process controlling you. You review what you have done over the past several years, and think about what gifts have given you the most satisfaction, and what really interests you. You decide to be less reactive to requests, learn how to say no, begin to determine priorities, develop criteria, and make fewer but larger gifts.

Level Three—You Become a Learner

You realize that you don't really know enough about the issues that interest you. You roll up your sleeves, do some research, visit your community foundation, talk to experts in the field and with other donors, make site visits to relevant organizations, and survey the literature. If you cannot do all this, you hire someone to do it. Out of that process comes a clearer focus, a clearer understanding of the issue, and the organizations you support reflect that focus. You have now made a distinction between the gifts you must make, and your real philanthropy.

Level Four—You Become Issue- and Results-Oriented

You want to maximize giving and increase the chances of making a difference. You are more concerned with results and evaluation. You look harder at the underlying issues, and the ways your available resources can be best applied. You invest in the most talented nonprofit entrepreneurs. Gifts to organizations focus on building their capacity. You have become increasingly proactive and rather than simply responding to requests, you go out, or have someone go out, search for, and fund the best people and organizations.

Level Five—Your Philanthropy Is Leveraged

You develop and fund custom-designed programs that meet specific programmatic objectives. You collaborate with other donors, and you establish networks that cross domains and include public–private partnerships and collaborations with business. You attempt to create models that can be adapted, and that will attract other private and public resources. You have become increasingly competent about the issues, about what works, and about what can really make a difference.

Level Six—Alignment

Your values, your passions, and your interests are aligned! Philanthropy is among the most exciting and satisfying things you do!

Ambitious Goals and *Big* Ideas

Making the leap from giving reactively to becoming strategic and proactive is a learning process. "Foundations that believe in transformational change are learning organizations imbued with reflective consciousness," Peter says, citing a few tales of transformation.

> The Paul and Phyllis Fireman Foundation (Paul Fireman founded Reebok) had the best solution when they engaged formerly homeless women to design a plan to end family homelessness in Massachusetts and then hired them to run the program. Brilliant, obvious, and rare! How a donor thinks, how a staff

thinks, versus how the person who is living with the problem thinks.

Julian Robertson, a hedge fund legend, had the exciting idea to fund what has become the Robertson Fellows Program at University of North Carolina and Duke University. There are 120 fellows, 60 on each campus. Rivalry between the two schools is famously fueled by basketball. The program requires each fellow to live one semester on the other campus. A bus now connects the two campuses, and the culture/boundaries have been diminished, and the rich resources of each wonderful school are increasingly utilized by both student bodies.

One of Peter's favorite stories is about an anonymous donor-client who made a brilliantly leveraged gift to Cambridge College, a Boston area school that serves many first-generation minority college students. The college wanted to build an expensive new facility in Cambridge, and hired a famous architect to design it. The donor thought this was a terrible idea. Taking advantage of a down real estate market, he acquired for the college a 100,000-square-foot building with the college occupying 50,000 square feet and the balance of the building leased to others. The deal turned what was $750,000 in annual rent to a zero cost! This was equivalent to a $14 million gift, plus ownership of a valuable property—amazing leverage!

Peter shares another example of innovative thinking, citing Pierre Omidyar, founder of eBay, and his wife Pam, of the Omidyar Network, who made a hybrid endowment gift to Tufts University of $100 million, the largest in the university's history. It came with unusual conditions: that the entire amount be invested in microcredit organizations, with the annual return split, half going to scholarships and the other half to be invested back into the microcredit field. This creative use of capital was a quantum leap that provided 150,000 scholarships.

A breakthrough gift that unlocked the potential for long-term systemic change was made by the Beldon Fund. Mandated to spend down in 10 years, the fund had a sense of urgency to solve the toxic waste problem in eight different states. New laws were needed to make it happen. Leaping on it, they increased their funding to power efforts toward state legislation on advocacy issues. It was a brilliant success that changed the laws with a $40-million to $50-million investment. "The time was ripe!" according to Peter.

Peter believes that the best philanthropists are lifelong learners. He admires Bill Gates, who devours 18 to 20 books at a time, for being a great learner who doesn't assume he knows everything.

Another great learner, Frank Melville of the Melville Charitable Trust, was introduced to Peter by the Rockefeller Foundation when the trustees wanted to learn more on the issue of homelessness. The trustees embarked on a TPI-led six-month tutorial on homelessness, which resulted in the Melville Charitable Trust's decision to focus its resources on the systemic root causes of homelessness in their home state, Connecticut.

Other instances of transformational giving are provided by Joel Fleishman, co-author of *Give $mart: Philanthropy that Gets Results*:

> When John Motley Morehead Foundation awarded scholarship gifts to the University of North Carolina (full freight tuition/scholarships to 100 students/year), this direct approach effectively enabled the University to raise its standards dramatically, causing a transformational shift in the institution.

Adapting the concept of the Morehead Foundation, the Cain Foundation made a $100 million gift of Morehead-Cain scholarships to build on a successful model of merit-based scholarships. The transformative value of this gift to Chapel Hill elevated the standards and quality of students and contributed to upgrading the faculty.

Joel cites other gifts that transformed institutions:

- Sandy Weil's gift to New York University transformed a good medical school into a great medical school.
- The massive aggregation of the Howard Hughes Medical Research Institute's $8 billion capital changed the whole world of medical research.
- The Alfred P. Sloan Foundation in New York did a Census of Oceans and a Census of the Skies. Imagine a census of all living life in the oceans and heavens!

Joel asks us to imagine what we can do with real vision!

Julius Rosenwald, the founder of Sears, Roebuck, made a visionary gift to educate a whole generation of illiterate southern black youth emerging from slavery in 1924, when poor rural black kids had no places to go to school. Rosenwald's initiative adapted Andrew Carnegie's innovative approach of matching challenge grants to libraries, covering costs of opening, operations, and buying books. The brilliance of his strategy was giving half of the money to schools for black children while raising the level of education for white children.

"A genius of an idea" according to Joel's standards of gift giving, was Andrew Carnegie's concept of creating a pension fund for college teachers, the forerunner of the 401(k) fund, with teachers putting up their own money and institutions having to match them to fund the pension.

Then, there is the gift that changes a field, like the creation of the Rockefeller Institute. Modeled after the Pasteur Institute, the Rockefeller Institute has produced 30 Nobel Prize winners as of this writing and continues to set the standard for such awards in the field of research.

Among the characteristics shared by such transformational donors is having a "Point of View," according to Peter Karoff. He says, "They are focused on clear goals, with good information about the issue or program and therefore have something to say. They stay with, support, and build the capacity of the program or organization."

Another important prerequisite for transformational giving is the ability to listen.

Peter underlines the fact that big donors are not trained as listeners and the dynamic of being a great donor requires being a great listener.

Then, there is the issue of trust. As a grant maker with the power to give, Peter emphasizes the need to establish a sense of trust so recipients can be honest and tell you what they really need, which is sometimes not what you planned to give. He advises us to "think of your recipient as a partner in the effort, respect and hold them accountable to levels of performance."

He encourages philanthropists to "Dream *big*! Be visionary. Don't accept the norm, boundaries. Streeeetch! Urge grantees to be excellent—we rise to be the best! Some of the most transformational gifts have been to education, investments meant to raise the level of excellence."

In creating change, Peter cautions us to remember to put those at the center of the problem at the center of the solution. "Funders tend to jump in like a bull in a china shop with their own solutions," he explains. "When a donor knows all the answers, and is arrogant as to how things should be done, programs seldom work."

The Gifted Giver

Peter defines the art of giving as a synthesis of poetry and philanthropy and lists the characteristics of a "Gifted Giver":

> There is a "gifted giver" who in addition to money, ideas, technical assistance, advice and counsel, brings a certain attitude, a way of doing business, that adds untold value and meaning to the transaction. The "gifted giver" has the instinct that transcends the substance of the gift and in so doing becomes a catalyst for transformation. A "gifted giver" comes in many colors and hues.[2]

Peter outlines some of the transcendent gifts a "gifted giver" brings:

A Gift of Energy

An act of generosity is a kind of transaction. Someone once said there are two types of people in a meeting, those who bring energy into the room and those who take it out. The "gifted giver" is one who brings a charge into the gift transaction as opposed to draining the energy out of it.

A Gift of Truth Telling

Giving can look like a dance or a charade, where the parties pander and handle one another, are secretive, and lack the candor and the confidence to push back, to tolerate ambiguity, to tell the truth. The gifted giver understands that philanthropy is a little bit like exercise—if it isn't uncomfortable, it isn't doing the job.

A Gift of Respect

Charity can be a disguise for gaining personal or social control, and behind the kindly donor is too often an oppressor. There is no greater sign of disrespect than to abuse a position of power and the

---

[2]From *Just Money* (TPI Editions, 2006).

giver has the power. One of the biggest forms of respect is listening and the gifted giver is first and foremost a listener.

A Gift of Love

Love, so difficult to define, is the greatest motivator; it can transform, inspire, and by building confidence and self-worth make all things, even very difficult things, seem possible. A gift in the spirit of love is the most powerful way of saying, "I believe in you!" Love from a gifted giver is not soft—it is hard like a diamond.

A Gift of Justice

One view of justice is that it is nothing less than love distributed across a community or a society. Justice, whether within the rule of law, or as a doctrine of fairness, speaks to the larger issues of the human condition, those of access to economic and social opportunity. This view of justice is nonideological; the gifted giver is passionate about justice.

A Gift of Opportunity

There is an amazing amount of socially motivated leadership with great ideas, energy, political and street smarts, and potential of all sorts champing at the bit, hoping against hope that somehow, through some miracle, they can get a shot at realization. The gifted giver has antennae up for such things, eyes open to the potential of excellence, wherever it lies.

A Gift of High Expectations

Like metal to a magnet, we rise to high expectations. They push us to be the best that we can be. They encourage us to dream bigger dreams, and make us more disciplined, more thoughtful, more focused on results. The gifted giver provides the challenge and the resources to encourage and nurture high expectations.

A Gift of Courage

"We are all afraid of acts of terrorism, of a world in turmoil; we are afraid for ourselves and for our children. We are afraid of the "dark side," of the "Orks," of the "beast." A gifted giver stands with those who stand up for what they believe is right, those with their backs against the wall, those who refuse to give in to fear."

In the same vein, Peter provokes foundations to think large and challenges us to move from "doing good" to being great. In his 2008 speech to the Bill and Melinda Gates Foundation staff, he espoused his "Catechism for a Great Foundation":

Great foundations begin with the extraordinary opportunity that has been bestowed on them to use their resources with compassion, and strategy, in the relentless pursuit of better and more equitable health, social, and educational outcomes for the world. Faith and great expectations are all well and good, but they need help and support—this is not a go-it-alone trajectory. There is much at stake and no hard and fast rules of engagement, there is a large and growing community of caring that can be tapped to leverage a better world.

Integrity of the philanthropic process begins when we become a listener, a learner, or a learning organization, about others who are different, about the issues, about what works and what doesn't. Great foundations learn how to listen to the community, learn how to touch. In addition to building networks of organizations that can deliver measurable results, they build networks that are based on a culture of listening and touching. Perhaps every person of responsibility in a great foundation should spend part of every year immersed on the ground.

Great foundations believe that integrity of purpose for any social action is based on one simple condition—"If it isn't good for the community, and only good for the donor, it isn't worth doing." Anyone who doesn't understand that runs the risk of having a chair thrown at them someday. Sometimes that chair is literal, sometimes it is mud on your face, and sometimes it is because you have broken the golden rule, which is "to do no harm."

Great foundations of the future will increasingly learn how to use their cache and convening power to significantly increase communities of interest, by expanding boundaries and intersections between ideas and people and sectors.

Leadership matters—it matters across cultures, it matters across time, and it matters greatly. Virtually all lasting significant social change comes from leaders working in intersecting networks of influence. Great foundations work hard at identifying and supporting leadership.

Great foundations focus on more than problem solving and investment return, and make the time—as hard as that is—for reflection and scenario planning on the long-term reality of what will take in most cases decades to accomplish.

Great foundations, irrespective of size, resist to their core bureaucracy, remain nimble, and bring energy into a room, as opposed to taking it out.

Great foundations do more than ask the tough questions, they want—they really want—honest answers; even if those answers counter and disturb/disrupt the very assumptions the foundation holds.

Great foundations use data that drives and moves programs, but watch carefully that data expands thinking, not narrows it, and increases the opportunity for risk-taking, not the reverse.

Great foundations acknowledge that innovation in social systems does have a scientific basis—but it requires a different paradigm. Technology and new products alone will not achieve large-scale lasting impact without creative systems innovation and we don't understand how to do that well.

Great foundations work hard to develop a powerful public persona that is aligned with the mission and is fundamentally accountable and transparent to its communities of interest.

Great foundations build heart into the fabric of the culture of the organization. In addition to research, data, advisory boards, and well-thought-out theories of change, story, anecdote, poetry, and all the other aspects of human interaction that bind us together become part of the equation. Great foundations, like the best of American philanthropy, combine the heart and mind in the "search for the best in people, their organizations, and the relevant world around them."

The Transformational Gain of Giving

As we realize our power to transform people's lives, transform our communities, and transform our world, the lessons Peter shares prepare us for the experiential journey that ultimately yields the gift of our own personal transformation. "Growing our souls while we seek to transform society"[3] is the gift we gain from our giving.

The magic of that transformation is grounded in our intentionality. For those fortunate enough to have the resources to give, every day is an opportunity to awaken and learn anew, to practice acts of hope or faith or love that flow into our giving. Putting the poetry of life into the practice of our philanthropy is expressed in a poem Peter wrote:

> It isn't finished this poem called ordinary life
> Poems are hard to finish so keep pushing
> That is your job! So it finally dawned on me
> What I do what we all do is write the poem
> Every day we write the observant poem of life
> You see it isn't a matter of time but compassion
> Call it community or hope or faith or call it love.
> That is the flow that is the poem.

Summary

In this chapter, Peter Karoff and Joel Fleishman share lessons and examples of "gifted givers" who can inspire us to make our philanthropy sing! The following exercise offers a few suggestions you can try to express the joy of giving into your practice.

Exercise

Have fun expressing your mission statement in a four-line poem!
Identify what stage you are at in the philanthropic curve.
Who would you consider to be modern-day versions of philanthropic visionaries Julius Rosenwald and Andrew Carnegie?
What characteristics of the "gifted giver" would you apply to your style of giving?

In the next chapter, we find real life action heroes, Lisa Nigro and Chip Paillex, whose generosity went far beyond their ability to write a check, embodying the true spirit of philanthropy.

---

[3]Peter Karoff and Jane Maddox, *The World We Want* (Lanham, MD: AltaMira Press, 1970).

Resources

The Philanthropic Initiative (www.tpi.org):

The Philanthropic Initiative Inc. (TPI) is a not-for-profit organization offering individuals, foundations, institutions, and corporations a disciplined and results-oriented approach to philanthropy. Founded in 1989, TPI's mission is to increase the amount and impact of resources directed to the social and moral issues of our times by stimulating individual, family, and corporate giving through assisting donors in developing philanthropic strategies that are effective and rewarding. To be truly effective and rewarding, strategic philanthropy must also reflect donors' core values and concerns—empowering them to change the world by energizing their passions—whether it is through a program to nurture early childhood literacy or an innovative career education program for inner-city youth. TPI's strategy, combined with the values and passionate concerns of donors, brings about giving that makes a difference in societies and lives. It is a philanthropy that moves donors—with clear vision—toward a deeper understanding of the problems that plague our world, and guides them through the demanding process of creating meaningful change.

Peter Karoff's Reading List

- *The Networked Nonprofit: Connecting with Social Media to Drive Change* by Beth Kanter, Allison Fine, and Randi Zuckerberg (Jossey Bass, 2010): The Wiki world and especially social media are becoming huge—this book covers the basics, and the articles referenced go deeper. He especially recommends the Bernholz piece.
- *Disrupting Philanthropy: Technology and the Future of the Social Sector* by Lucy Bernholz, with Edward Skloot and Barry Varela (Center for Strategic Philanthropy and Civil Society, Sanford School of Public Policy, Duke University, 2009).
- *Working Wikily* by Diana Scearce, Gabriel Kasper, and Heather McLeod Grant (*Stanford Social Innovation Review*, Summer 2010).
- *The Digital Disruption* by Eric Schmidt and Jared Cohen (*Foreign Affairs*, November/December 2010).
- *Give $mart: Philanthropy that Gets Results* by Thomas Tierney and Joel Fleishman (PublicAffairs, 2011). This book wraps many of the ideas of strategic philanthropy with a heavy focus on donors taking responsibility for rigor and results.

- *The Foundation: A Great American Secret* by Joel Fleishman (PublicAffairs, 2009). This book is a definitive look at U.S. foundations and has extensive case studies provided on a companion web site to the book.
- *Understanding Philanthropy: Its Meaning and Mission* by Robert L. Payton and Michael P. Moody (Indiana University Press, 2008).

Books by Peter Karoff

- *The World We Want* (AltaMira Press, 2008).
- *Just Money: A Critique of Contemporary Philanthropy* (TPI Editions, 2004).

Additional Articles of Interest

- Michael Porter and Mark Kramer, "Creating Shared Value," *Harvard Business Review,* January–February 2011.
- Michael Edwards, "Philanthrocapitalism: after the goldrush," published on openDemocracy (www.opendemocracy.net).
- Lucy Bernholz, "Philanthropy and Social Investment: Blueprint," Blueprint.

Other Resources

- *Casebook for the Foundation: A Great American Secret from Duke University* (PublicAffairs, 2007). Featuring Julius Rosenwald and 100 other cases. Available online at http://cspcs.sanford .duke.edu/publications/casesforthefoundation.
- Association of Small Foundations (Washington, DC). A private foundation resource. www.smallfoundations.org.
- Council on Foundations. www.cof.org.
- Foundation Center in New York. www.foundation center.org.
- Asia Pacific Philanthropy Consortium. http://asiapacific philanthropy.org.
- National Center for Family Philanthropy (Washington, DC). http://ncfp.org.
- Wallace Foundation. www.wallacefoundation.org.

10

The Power of One

Lessons from *Lisa Nigro* (the Inspiration Corporation) and *Chip Paillex* (America's Grow-a-Row)

My favorite quote is, "Don't neglect the stranger in your midst, for unknowingly, you may have entertained an angel." That is what I think happens at Inspiration Corporation every day.
—Lisa Nigro, Founder, the Inspiration Corporation

True philanthropy goes beyond the ability to write a check. The power of one to create positive change by giving of our self in the deepest way, bringing our human experience to the solutions we create, is the essence of giving. Each act of generosity is unique because it speaks of who we are.

The gift of humanity is our moral imagination, our ability to dream and envision a better world. Bringing the best of our self to help create that world, right where we live, is a priceless gift that everyone has the power to give.

In every community, there are everyday heroes who teach us, by example, that the gift of philanthropy only requires time, energy, and imagination. Time is free and therefore priceless, yet in our busy lives it is often easier to just send a check than to take the time to participate as active citizens in making change happen.

In the Jewish tradition, we learn that even one act can transform the world, that within each of us lies the power to reshape our world.

As part of my philanthropic work, I have met amazing human beings who embody that moral principle. Their spirit of generosity is often invisible as they do things without any thought of recognition or reward. It is their readiness to act, when confronted with a problem others would leave for someone else to solve, that makes them action heroes. Their stories remind us that every day offers us an opportunity to affect one life.

The Inspiration Corporation

A former police officer, Lisa Nigro started the Inspiration Cafe with $30,000 of her life savings and credit cards that took 10 years to pay off. Her philanthropic journey begun in Chicago's crime-ridden districts, where she patrolled the neighborhood wondering how to feed the homeless. With a little red wagon borrowed from her nephew, she brought bagels and sandwiches with fresh-brewed coffee to homeless people until she earned their trust.

Soon she outgrew that wagon and equipped her Isuzu Rodeo with catering equipment, whipping up Eggs Benedict on the street until a friend had an idea to use a donated bus that they converted into a mobile café. She served breakfast on the bus every day until a local news station picked up the story. A building owner who saw her on TV offered a storefront with six months free rent, along with an offer to provide a publicist who got local celebrities to serve meals that raised $15,000.

Her inspirational story was chosen from among 2,300 applicants for a TV commercial sponsored by True North Foods, which was directed by actress Holly Hunt and premiered during the 2009 Oscars telecast. With it came a $25,000 check, which was matched by a donor, and 250 volunteers who signed up the week it aired!

The former Chicago police officer was recently honored for her community service by President Barack Obama, who awarded her the Presidential Citizens Medal at the White House.

Lisa Nigro's Story

The Inspiration Cafe in Chicago is a place where the homeless can sit down, order off a menu, get served on real plates, and be treated with dignity and respect. To get a full flavor of their mission, I went to Chicago to experience it for myself.

Dining with Lisa at one of the cafés, I am impressed by the marketing pitch on the bottom of my menu: "Dine Well. Do Good. Enjoy contemporary cuisine in a stylish setting as you change the world, one meal at a time." A fuller explanation of the mission appears on a different part of the menu.

> Cafe Too provides essential social services to Chicagoans hardest hit by homelessness and poverty. We inspire our participants to take action to improve their own lives, helping them gain valuable skills and experience that lead to employment in the food service industry. Every plate is produced by a participant in our 13-week job-training program.
>
> Each graduate gets sanitation training, employment assistance, housing assistance, and access to other services, because at Cafe Too, we serve people on both sides of the counter!
>
> Thank you for dining with us and changing lives!

Even more impressive are the restaurant's brunch specials offering:

Chicken and Sausage Etouffée

Biscuit and Gravy Skillet (corned beef hash)

Corned Beef O'Benedict (two poached eggs served over thinly sliced corned beef on a split crumpet, drizzled with stout dotted Hollandaise and served with a choice of sides)

Chocolate Chip Bread Pudding

Pancakes served with honey butter and whipped cream

Chorizo Croquette Platter

Chayote Cake Platter

Crispy Tofu Skillet

I am bowled over!

Lisa explains the mission in very personal terms, "It's all about your dignity, your choice. There are times guests send back their food and volunteers get upset, expecting them to be grateful. I tell them, it's alright, this is part of being noticed and having a voice." Her vision of bridging worlds allows us to learn about people's lives as we encounter them on a level playing field, changing the equation as we see our own humanity reflected in someone else's eyes.

Her urge to give so boundlessly of herself spawned four restaurants with a service training program that puts homeless people back to work. The organization she founded has created a place at the table for 30,000 people in need, grew the organization into a $4 million operation that offers dignity, self-sufficiency, and hope to people whose lives she helped transform. Today, Inspiration Cafe and the Living Room Cafe offer restaurant-style meals, case management, employment services, and subsidized housing units for former homeless people to rebuild their lives. Cafe Too, a culinary arts training program and full-service restaurant, employs graduates and offers breakfast, lunch, and dinner to the general public.

Lisa's life seems filled with daily miracles. She relates how she discovered that her café did not comply with the city code when celebrities came to serve meals. The City of Chicago had sent a film crew who pointed out to her that her kitchen did not have a ventilator hood. Dismayed at the discovery, she was exhilarated to hear them offer her the $10,000 needed to provide the hood!

When faced with a shortfall, she asked board members to pray and was rewarded for her faith when a $20,000 check came in shortly after. She believes that her success in overcoming obstacles comes from prayer and a deep sense of purpose, which propels her to act. Her faith gives her the courage to make the leap!

The organization she founded has become a catalyst for change. In 2010:

- The Housing Program grew to include 146 subsidized apartments housing formerly homeless people.
- Inspiration Kitchens and the Employment Project placed 160 men and women into jobs and gave 58 people further education and training opportunities.
- Community Voice Mail supplied phone numbers and message retrieval service to 1,333 homeless and phoneless individuals—providing a lifeline to jobs, housing, health care, social service providers, and family. Volunteers served 36,638 nutritious meals at Inspiration Cafe and the Living Room Cafe.
- The Supportive Services team assisted 599 people through Open Case Management and processed 207 eviction-prevention grants.

- Programs provided $295,060 in small grants for emergency and transitional needs, including $80,101 for tuition and training assistance.

In May 2011, the Inspiration Kitchens opened in Garfield Park, one of Chicago's most underserved communities. This new food service training center and 80-seat social enterprise restaurant and catering facility provides job training and placement assistance to 125 community members each year. Through a unique partnership with community organizations, half of the healthy, affordably priced meals served here are offered free to working poor families.

Lisa's gift is her ability to believe, a sense of inner knowing that something larger than herself has made all things possible. The little red wagon now hangs from the ceiling of the café, a cheerful reminder of hope!

America's Grow-a-Row

There is absolutely no reason why poverty should exist in America!
—Chip Paillex, founder, America's Grow-a-Row

After seeing a plea from the Flemington Area Food Pantry requesting home gardeners to donate excess produce, Chip Paillex cultivated his own garden and donated $3,000 worth of produce in 2002. Inspired to do more, he enlisted Jeremy and Meredith Compton of Peaceful Valley Orchards in Pittstown, New Jersey. They responded generously, offering to prep the land, provide starter seed plants and equipment, plus two acres for planting and 25 acres for gleaning on their 150-acre farm. This farm, combined with land donated by the Etter Family, was the beginning of America's Grow-a-Row.

Chip Paillex's Story: Growing, Gleaning, Giving

Families from Chip's church, Bethlehem Presbyterian, signed up to "own" the garden for a week at a time, with the responsibility for watering, weeding, harvesting, and delivering any produce directly to the food pantry. This incredibly coordinated volunteer effort continued all season long. When the Comptons offered to give them the opportunity to glean their fields of corn, 20 to 30 people would get together to pick bins full of corn (often as much as 1,000 pounds at a time!). Meanwhile, the Etter farm generated 6,000 pounds of produce, which made its way to the plates of those desperately in need.

The program expanded into a mission project, with church members and friends helping to care for the garden and glean excess produce that would otherwise have been plowed under in the normal course of farming. In 2008, it became an official not-for-profit organization, which expanded Chip's network to more than 1,000 volunteers giving 4,000 hours of their time each year to donate a million pounds of fresh food, or 4 million servings of healthy food, to soup kitchens, food pantries, crisis centers, and food banks all over the state of New Jersey.

Educating children about hidden hunger and obesity issues while exposing them to the important role that farmers and agriculture can play has been a critical element of the program. The mission of providing fresh, healthy food to those in need through a volunteer-based effort of planting, picking, rescuing, and delivering fresh produce is a unique model that educates all generations about hunger, introduces young people to farming and healthy eating, and cultivates tomorrow's leaders to give back and contribute to the sustainability of agriculture by highlighting the importance of local farms. More important, it provides them with a way to become part of the solution.

"Our planting programs involve the community—schools, church groups, youth programs, and corporate teams. Volunteers love to literally get their hands dirty in the name of feeding the hungry. They love that the program is an environmentally friendly way to feed people with healthy food. We love the fact that our volunteers are now connected with local farmers and have become champions for hunger and poverty solutions. We don't just address the hunger issue, we also help draw attention to obesity and health, the importance of farming and land preservation, the environment, poverty education, and volunteerism," Chip explains.

Grow-a-Row doesn't just give away leftover produce but actually takes orders for specific foods, planting string beans instead of zucchini at the request of a local food pantry, for example. Discovering that recipients are often new to the idea of eating fresh produce, Chip invites kids from inner cities and adults from low-income groups to the farm to pick food to take home to their families. One of the children rushed to the orchard asking, "Where's the broccoli tree?"

A young man from a group home told how, as a kid, he had to beg for food and at no point did his mother ever shop in a grocery store. He lived on rice and milk. He now comes to help because he "doesn't want anyone to have to live that way."

What started out in 2002 as a small personal garden has now become one of New Jersey's largest gleaning and food rescue programs, receiving statewide recognition in 2010 when Chip Paillex was honored as one of New Jersey's Heroes by Governor Chris Christie at the Governor's inauguration. Chip was also the recipient of the Russ Berrie Making a Difference Award in 2010, receiving a prize of $50,000.

Today, America's Grow-a-Row donates approximately 360,000 pounds of produce annually to food banks, soup kitchens, and food pantries across New Jersey. With so many community service groups, children, and corporations asking to be involved, Chip had more volunteers than he had work for. The produce distribution network continued to expand, making the organization a permanent resource in the hunger relief system. "Off the field" gleanings increased, with two ShopRite grocery stores contributing 120,000 pounds a year all year round.

Chip is proud that a nonprofit organization, which has never taken federal or state dollars, will now have the opportunity to pump a few million dollars worth of fresh produce into the welfare system once it is up and running. "We are now infusing over $475,000 worth of produce into the state for people in need," says Chip. "Imagine the possibilities once we build the infrastructure we need!"

Since 2002, America's Grow-a-Row reached a major milestone of donating 1 million pounds of fresh produce after eight years of operations. With the lease of the Compton family about to end, Grow-a-Row needed to find property to manage its large growing and gleaning program. Help materialized when two generous benefactors stepped forward to help purchase a 138-acre farm in Alexandria Township, New Jersey.

One of them was Bob Lecompte of Valley Crest Preserve Inc., who used proceeds from public funds he received when he converted 40 of his 150 acres to make a gift. What led him to give away $600,000 from the state for preserving open space and turn it around to let Grow-a-Row use, knowing that the land will later be put into a similar land preservation trust? Bob explains, "It was like money coming down from heaven to me, so I wanted to give it away to the same cause. I was not taking public money and keeping it but rolling it along so the state can use it again." The original owner of Peaceful Valley Farms, Bob expresses satisfaction at how far Chip has come, "In the beginning, Chip was our first and lone customer, renting a 30 × 30 foot plot for $300/season. People don't realize how much you can grow in a such a small piece of land!"

The other anonymous donor became involved when his daughter participated in the farm's activities. He speaks of the value of leadership and the spirit of volunteerism he saw in Chip, who was then working full time in sales and marketing for the North American Unilever Foods Corporation:

> We are investing in a leader who inspires our confidence to fund the organization. The quality of the leader was one compelling reason for making this gift. Chip demonstrates how one man can change the world one person at a time.
>
> As a funder who likes to "follow our money," we got a great deal of emotional satisfaction watching Chip operate and doing this as a volunteer. We like grantees who communicate their progress and connect us to their mission by sharing stories that give us a good feeling, knowing our gift has really made a difference in someone's life.

A 16-year-old volunteer from the Franklin Township Food Bank wrote to express how it has made a difference to a family dependent on the food bank to get their next meal, saying:

> I am definitely grateful for the people who worked hard to provide the food that I ate most nights. I also think that it's better to give than to receive because people always remember you for the things you give in life. Be it time or money, giving is the key to happiness. With more programs like Grow-a-Row, more people wouldn't have to be hungry like I was many nights. So, I will make it my duty to give more than is asked of me because I can make a difference.

For someone who had never planted anything until 10 years ago, a farm 6,000 times larger than the garden plot he started has made Chip realize he needs the goodwill of lots of volunteers to plant, harvest, and glean the fields.

In the Biblical story of Ruth, letting people glean excess produce illustrates an important "mitzvah," the virtue of giving that allows others to retain their dignity. "People want to give back," Chip emphasized. "When you know that what you pick will wind up on the plate of someone who really needs it, that's powerful!"

Summary

Lisa and Chip demonstrate the power of one to give in a way that creates ripple effects capable of transforming communities. In the following chapter, we learn from philanthropists Peggy Dulany, Monica Winsor, and Ellen Remmer how women lead through philanthropy, the growing influence of women, and the strategic importance of funding women and girls.

Resources

To learn more about Inspiration Corporation's programs and opportunities, or to get involved, visit their web site at www.inspiration corp.org.

You can also follow Lisa at www.lisanigrospeaks.com.

In addition, read *A Recipe for Hope (Stories of Transformation by People Struggling with Homelessness)* by Karen Skalitzky.

To volunteer, at America's Grow-a-Row contact:

Chip Paillex, Founder and President

Jackie Etter, VP of Development

(908) 331-2962

http://americasgrowarow.org

11

The Feminine Principle—Women Leading through Philanthropy

Lessons from *Peggy Dulany* (Founder of Synergos Institute), *Ellen Remmer* (President and CEO of the Philanthropic Initiative), and *Monica Winsor* (Vice Chair, Women Moving Millions)

This chapter focuses on the role of women in philanthropy to lead, the latest sources of data related to women's giving, and the call to action of Women Moving Millions as they invest collectively to shift the odds for women around the world, who are 70 percent of people living in poverty. Imagine what the world could be if we could change that equation!

Three women share their views on how women in philanthropy can be transformational "bridging leaders," who use their influence to be a force for change.

In a world where women do two-thirds of the world's work, receive 10 percent of the world's salaries, and own 1 percent of the means of production, creating economic empowerment opportunities to unlock their enormous potential for positive change would be transformational.[1]

---

[1]United Nations report.

"The transformative value of women giving to women is that helping women, who make up 70 percent of people living in poverty, benefits their children as well. Women are the most effective conduits through which change is made," according to Christine Grumm, president and CEO of the Women's Funding Network.[2]

Today's women givers are more likely to use their wealth to aid women in need. Women are giving to empower women and girls as a strategy for achieving sustained economic growth and productivity in communities around the world.

Women as Change Agents

The position of women and girls in any society is part of a complex social fabric, woven over many years. In the developing world, girls are the backbone of rural economies, providing labor in fields, farms, factories, and homes.

Investing in the education and empowerment of rural girls has a ripple effect. An educated girl will marry later, stay healthy, save money, build a business, educate her children, and invest in her family's education and health care. Growing up to be a driver of change, she can lift her family and society out of poverty.

By sheer numbers, women and girls who make up this untapped majority are power players of the future. Investing in women and girls to advance education, health, nutrition, and to reduce maternal and infant mortality is the key to sustainable economic and social development. The enormous impact of educated women on the growth and productivity of communities has been credited for decreased HIV/AIDS rates, increased GDP, decreased infant, child, and maternal mortality, and increased civic participation.

Queen Rania of Jordan, who received YouTube's Visionary Award for starting her own YouTube channel, focuses her messaging on why the world needs to educate girls. She believes that "education is an investment that reaps dividends because educated women expect more for their children and families—education, healthcare, and societal benefits—tipping the balance from poverty to progress."[3]

---

[2]Lisa Belkin, "The Power of the Purse," *New York Times*, August 23, 2009.
[3]www.queenrania.jo.

Consider these eye-opening facts about women:

- Women make up an estimated 70 percent of people living in extreme poverty worldwide (www.one.org).
- Two-thirds of the world's illiterate adults are women (UNICEF, Millennium Development Goals; www.unicef.org/mdg/gender.html).
- An extra year of education can increase a girl's income by 10 to 20 percent ("Plan UK," 2009; "Because I Am A Girl; The State of the World's Girls," 2009; "Girls in the Global Economy: Adding It All Up"; http://plan-international.org/girls/resources/publications.php).
- One hundred million girls in the developing world will become child brides over the next decade, with one in three girls married before she is 18 and one in seven married by the age of 15. Child marriage increases the likelihood of a girl under 15 dying in childbirth by five times, compared to a woman giving birth in her twenties. A child bride is more likely to drop out of school, reducing her opportunities for employment and perpetuating the cycle of poverty and suffering (www.girls discovered.org).
- Although women are better able to improve their lives when they own land and other assets, only 1 percent of the world's women own land (www.icrw.org).

One of the best ways to help women make the most of their opportunities is to help them save the money they earn so they can plan for their families' futures. For instance, in Malawi, a biometric-enabled bank card created by Opportunity International Bank of Malawi helps women access their savings accounts. In a society where widows become property of their husband's brothers upon their spouse's death, a woman can lose her money and property when a brother-in-law marches into the bank to claim her assets. A bank identification card ensures that no one else, not even a spouse or his relatives, can take money out of her account. It has become the number one wedding gift for brides in Malawi! In Kenya, a mobile phone-based money service called M-PESA is enabling some 13 million people to transfer and save money using their mobile phones. In the Philippines, research has shown that women with savings accounts had more of a say in how the family's money should be spent. Savings have given women new financial freedom, creating a world of opportunity for women who spent most of their lives without ever making a single financial decision. Melinda Gates of the Gates Foundation, which funded the Malawi biometric ID card, has said that "families that save for their future change not just their children's lives, but their grandchildren's, for generation after generation."[4]

USA Today's issue celebrating Women's Day quotes Claudia Kennedy, the first woman U.S. Army Lieutenant General and Member of the American Security Project, saying: [5]

> Because women have not held economic and political parity with men, it is women who hold the strongest potential to become leaders and change agents. If we can dramatically impact the economic power and influence of women, I believe we can increase global stability and alleviate poverty. The payoff is not only prosperity, but peace.

Three women who are invested in changing the ratio to achieve socioeconomic empowerment for women are Peggy Dulany, founder of Synergos Institute and the Global Philanthropy Circle; Monica Winsor, vice chair of Women Moving Millions; and Ellen Remmer, president of the Philanthropic Initiative. Their voices add weight to the case for philanthropy's focus on women and girls as change makers in global communities.

Peggy Dulany's Story

We, women, citizens, global citizens, civil society leaders, must enable others with less power to come to the table with a voice so that together we can hold our formal leaders accountable and influence the kind of societies and the world we want to see.

—Peggy Dulany, founder, Synergos Institute

Peggy Dulany's pioneering efforts through the Global Philanthropic Circle (GPC), which she founded, provide opportunities

---

[4]"Melinda Gates: Global Savings Forum," Bill & Melinda Gates Foundation, www .gatesfoundation.org/speeches-commentary/Pages/melinda-gates-2010-global -savings-forum.aspx.

[5]"Opportunity International Launches 'Banking on Women' Campaign," Opportunity International, www.opportunity.org/press-releases/opportunity -international-launches-banking-on-women-campaign.

for the inner work of philanthropy that are expressed in earlier chapters, the personal exploration of our deeper purpose to discover what keeps us from fulfilling our philanthropic aspirations. Bringing expert resources to work with GPC members experientially, Peggy leads other philanthropists to expand their personal visions into an organizational, societal, and global level. As a participant in GPC's transformative retreats, I found great value in the reflective exercises that reconnected us to our sense of purpose and inner commitment to our work.

Peggy's discovery of her deeper purpose involved the exploration of her different internal voices: as a child growing up in a world of privilege, as a member of the Rockefeller family, as a young volunteer who saw how people without connections needed what she could bring, and as a global philanthropist transformed by her encounters to develop a vision of bridging the world of resources and connections to become a convening force for good.

Peggy lives by Gandhi's exhortation to "be the change we want to see." Her transformational journey has made her a voice of inspiration. Her way of leading by "being" makes her a philanthropist who brings her consciousness to the world. Peggy's experience living and working in Rio de Janeiro sparked the idea of tapping the people who are most affected and who have the greatest motivation to solve their own problems, to empower them to be part of creating solutions.

Drawing on her power as an individual with influence, Peggy's convening role facilitates relationships between grassroots leaders and decision makers whom they would not normally have access to, and forges long-term relationships that enable communities to work together to make meaningful change occur.

Finding organizations that have been successful in partnership building through convening, facilitating, and skill building, Peggy has identified the characteristics of successful "bridging leaders" as: listening skills, empathy, ability to foster "chains of trust," relatively low ego needs, credibility within their own constituency, and ability to reach out to diverse others.

One of Peggy's "bridging heroes" is Graca Machel of Mozambique, who linked networks of African women in finance, education, agriculture, and media to increase the participation and influence of women in civil society. The resulting network built a platform from which women could act forcefully to effect government legislation on land mines and children, and empowered women in Africa to gain better-directed funding for children affected by violence and war.

In today's world, Peggy feels a greater sense of urgency for the "soft" skills that foster partnerships and alliances in global communities experiencing social change:

> As the threat of environmental change grows, conflicts and wars continue to spread, humanity and the Earth are increasingly imperiled. We need to shift the energy of our world to rebalance the feminine qualities of nurturing, conciliation, collaboration and sharing. I believe that convening, capacity building, networking, promoting and strengthening bridging leadership, bridging organizations and partnerships—represent the way forward to a world where the yin and yang is back in balance.[6]

What the world needs now, according to Peggy, is what philanthropy in its broadest sense, can offer—"love of humanity," with an added dimension of love for the planet: "Love as the critical ingredient the world needs requires us to first love ourselves, bringing our whole selves to the table as we engage with our selves, with the people we encounter and the issues we choose to involve ourselves with."

Peggy's philosophy of leading with an open heart raises the possibility of inspiring others to open their hearts to explore solutions that work for all. Peggy believes that leading from the heart, from one's passion, is almost the best assurance that what one is doing, whether philanthropically or in other parts of your life, will have the energy, the authenticity, and the passion that is much more likely to lead to concrete results.

In a world where women hold up "half the sky," Peggy believes that as women play important roles in "bridging," they need to access inner resources to rebalance the world:

> It will require personal transformation to reach into our selves to expand our consciousness of our soul's true purpose in life and of our masculine and feminine, yin-yang internal balance. For that balance is what will enable us to employ the right strategies at the right moment, personally and organizationally, to collectively rebalance societies, relationships among them and with

---

[6]Peggy Dulany's speech on "Women Leading through Philanthropy" at the Women's Philanthropy Institute conference in Chicago, 2011.

the Earth whose precious balance we are in danger of destroy-
ing, and to create more collaborative and sustainable solutions.[7]

Ellen Remmer: How Women Are Transforming Philanthropy

The feminine energy in women's philanthropy can be deceptive, as
women's "soft power" is belied by the facts. Ellen Remmer, president
of the Philanthropic Institute and board member of the Women's
Philanthropy Institute, provided the latest data on the growing influence of women.

With women worldwide asserting more economic power as
donors and philanthropists, trends in philanthropy demonstrate
their growing influence. Women now control more than half of the
private wealth in the United States. Their impact and voices will
shape the future of wealth and giving.

In addition to controlling 60 percent of the wealth in the United
States, women tend to donate more of their wealth than men do.
A Barclay's Wealth Study titled "Tomorrow's Philanthropist," released
in July 2009, showed that women in the United States give an average of 3.5 percent of their wealth to charity, while men give an
average of 1.8 percent. Further, a Fidelity Charitable Gift Fund
Survey indicated that women donors were more likely to be public about their gifts than male donors. And according to Boston
College's Center on Wealth and Philanthropy, women will inherit
70 percent of the $41 trillion in intergenerational wealth transfer
expected over the next 40 years. That enormous potential philanthropic capital will propel women to the forefront of philanthropy.[8]

In general, women give differently than men. They are less likely
to want their names on buildings and more likely to give as part of
drives that include other women. A study of more than 10,000 large
donors by the Center on Philanthropy at Indiana University suggests
that while men describe their giving as practical, women describe
theirs as emotional, an obligation to help those with less.

"Women give of their hearts as well as their checkbooks," philanthropist Helen LaKelly Hunt said. "It's not as abstract as men's
giving. The way women have reshaped the field of philanthropy is

---

[7]Peggy Dulany's speech, Chicago, 2011.
[8]Forbes.com, "Women in Philanthropy," August 18, 2009.

something we should be proud of. It's a huge accomplishment, and it's a great story."[9]

In reality, philanthropy describes how women are living their lives. We care, we nurture by instinct, we are collaborative and inclusive. Citing a study by Alice Eagly and colleagues at Northwestern University on how leadership styles of men and women differ, Ellen Remmer points out the most compelling difference:

> Women are most likely to be transformational leaders while men are more likely to be transactional leaders. Transformational leaders are defined as "those who serve as role models, mentor and empower workers and encourage innovation even when the organization they lead is already successful." And in their analysis, the transformational style was more likely to lead to good performance and organizational effectiveness.[10]

In summing up the potential for women leading through philanthropy, Ellen is emphatic, "The power and potential of women's philanthropy is infinite. All it takes is all of us!"

Monica Winsor's Story

When Robert Kennedy said, "One person can make a difference and *everyone* must try," he could have been speaking of the force behind the Women Moving Millions movement. One woman on her own can change several lives. An army of committed women can change the world.[11]

Monica Winsor, vice chair of Women Moving Millions, expresses the power of unity in collectively shifting an economic paradigm, "We are united in our passions, in our belief that women and girls are the most important agents of change on social issues anywhere in the world."

As a younger member of a family foundation, Monica Winsor grew into philanthropy feeling isolated within a narrow scope of

---

[9]"When Women Flex Their Philanthropic Power," International Museum of Women, www.mow.org.
[10]Ellen Remmer's Address to the Women's Philanthropy Network, June 24, 2008, titled "Women and Philanthropy—Transformational Leadership."
[11]*USA Today*, March 4, 2011.

family values. Seeking issues that resonated for her and like-minded people whom she could "feel at home with," she discovered the Global Philanthropy Circle. Becoming a member added an interesting new lens to her views on giving.

She considers Peggy Dulany a real mentor who infuses her spirituality into her philanthropy. "Peggy exudes the principles I'm attracted to, authenticity and deep respectful listening," says Monica. "I listened to her, watched her, and feel very humbled by how she listens and shares her wisdom to awaken our individual passions and gifts. The whole idea of linking philanthropy with personal activism is something Peggy practices powerfully. I learned from her the importance of systems change and bridging leaders."

Within the Global Philanthropy Circle, Peggy creates an intimacy that fosters authenticity within a safe space. Monica likens it to a "resonance chamber where my authentic voice could emerge and I could hear my genuine self. Being in that connected space enables members to learn how they could give more than just money. Joining the board of Synergos, which Peggy also founded, strengthened me, enhancing my personal journey as a spiritual path. I believe there is a spiritual path in philanthropy. When you have a personal connection to what you give, you are transforming yourself."

Monica Winsor's journey began as a member of a four-generation philanthropic family with foundations in the United States and Canada. Exposed to the responsibility and complexity of giving from a young age, she felt almost embarrassed talking about wealth. "Today, I derive great joy in our giving and I am motivated to take advantage of my capacity to use funds but also the access funding can provide to advocate for causes that are important to me. I just feel so grateful and can now enjoy the 'gift' of being able to give."

Finding ways to stay as authentic as she can be, Monica focuses on the value of identifying what you want to give to and feels that being grounded in spiritual practice is key to philanthropy. "It was important to me to take my spiritual practice out into the world. The idea of being willing to take risks and follow my intuition, whether or not it was popular with others, is what it takes to be a philanthropist. I am taking risks because I can. I feel very lucky to be able to do that. We can take those risks when we do what we feel most connected to."

Monica's personal journey taught her to ask a lot of questions, not just of grantees, but people she identified as leaders and mentors she could emulate. She developed her own "voice," and gained confidence in her ability to lead uniquely as a woman and to mirror that in philanthropy. As she found meaningful ways to give, "what moves my heart and really speaks to me," the issue of women and girls felt authentic.

A few years ago, Peggy Dulany hosted a meeting on women's issues that Monica attended. "It planted 'seeds in my head,'" Monica explains, "aligning something in me from long ago that I am now just articulating." That internal alignment led to her stepping into the role of vice chair of Women Moving Millions.

"I feel emotionally, spiritually, and intellectually connected to educating and elevating women, of operationalizing feminine values to create a more balanced world," Monica explains about the mission. "I like working in ways that incorporate collaboration, more lateral ways of communicating with donors. Women's funds are more democratic in that way and provide an example of a different philanthropic infrastructure. I passionately believe we have the ability and responsibility to give in ways that create connective paradigm shifts, giving not only to projects that are visible with cut-and-dried metrics but also to less simplistically measurable endeavors. As a woman, I am interested in participating in a collective movement that can shift the culture and the planet into greater balance."

At Women Moving Millions, Monica finds fulfillment and inspiration working with other women. "Coming from a patriarchal family, I find the nonhierarchical collectivity of working together refreshing!" she exclaims. "I am learning how we can create traction, moving from isolation as someone who can give away money to become more powerful in alignment with others."

Acting in unison to create opportunities for women worldwide creates forward momentum, mobilizing a global effort to invest in positive change for women and girls around the world.

Women Moving Millions is the most dramatic recent example of how women are asserting their philanthropic power in transformational ways. Initiated by sisters Helen LaKelly and Swanee Hunt, daughters of oilman H.L. Hunt, the movement was seeded with initial pledges of $6 million from Swanee and $4 million from Helen.

For the first time in history," says Helen LaKelly Hunt. "Women of wealth are giving boldly to women." Co-founders of Women Moving Millions, the Hunt sisters launched a campaign that propelled women's philanthropy to new levels by raising more than $180 million for projects that support women and girls.

The story of the Hunt sisters' philanthropic focus on giving to women is related by Helen in a speech at the International Museum of Women. She relates their upbringing as Southern Belles in Dallas who were steeped in a culture where "men handled money and women didn't ask questions." In a society where "money is power," she says. "If that's true, and women don't become financially literate, women are keeping themselves disempowered."[12]

The cultural change in the role of women as leaders and visionaries in this new path of philanthropy, making the leap from giving charitably to investing strategically in women, is the inspiring vision behind Women Moving Millions.

Summary

Coming up next is the work of multigenerational giving, issues related to transmitting family values and empowering the next generation. Sharna Goldseker, vice president of the Andrea and Charles Bronfman Philanthropies; Ruth Cummings, former chair of the Nathan Cummings Foundation; and Lance Lindblom, president of the Nathan Cummings Foundation, discuss the challenges of developing a strategic framework for family foundations.

Resources

- The Synergos Institute. www.synergos.org.
- The Global Philanthroists Circle. www.synergos.org/philanthropistscircle.
- GirlUp, a United Nations campaign that links American girls to their global counterparts to raise awareness and funds for UN Programs that help girls in developing countries. http://girlup.org.
- Coca Cola's 5 BY 20. www.thecoca-colacompany.com/dynamic/5by20.
- Visit http://10x10act.org, a global campaign to improve the lives of girls, harnessing the power of media to inform, engage, and mobilize by driving action.

---

[12]"When Women Flex Their Philanthropic Power," International Museum of Women, www.mow.org.

- Visit Women Moving Millions at www.womenmovingmillions .org.
- ONE at www.one.org.
- View reports on adolescent girls in the Girls Count series at www.coalitionforadolescent-girls.org.
- Visit the Elders at www.theElders.org, an independent group of eminent global leaders brought together by Nelson Mandela, with members like Desmond Tutu, Mary Robinson, Graca and Aung San Suu Kyi, to offer their collective influence to support peace-building and address major causes of human suffering. Achieving equality for women and girls is a major focus of their work, and they are currently building a global alliance to end child marriage, a harmful practice that affects millions of girls every year.
- Visit Girls Discovered at www.girlsdiscovered.org, including a comprehensive source of maps and data on the status of adolescent girls worldwide.
- The Women's Philanthropy Institute at the Center on Philanthropy in Indiana University is the only institution that delivers research about the spectrum of women's philanthropic activity worldwide. www.philanthropy.iupui.edu /womensphilanthropyinstitute.
- Visit Women for Women International at www.womenforwomen .org, the first large-scale private undertaking funded by Goldman Sachs that provides 10,000 underserved women in different parts of the world with educations in business. In each locale, a collaborating university selects the women, teaching them how to draft business plans, how to secure capital, and how to develop effective marketing, accounting, management and other skills. During the program and after graduation, volunteers from Goldman Sachs provide mentoring.
- Visit Queen Rania's web site at www.queenrania.jo.

CHAPTER 12

Empowering the Next Generation

Lessons from *Sharna Goldseker* (Vice President, Andrea and Charles Bronfman Philanthropies, and Director of 21/64), *Ruth Cummings* (Chair, the Nathan Cummings Foundation), and *Lance Lindblom* (President and Chief Executive Officer, the Nathan Cummings Foundation)

It is hard for young people to define their philanthropic identity when they have not fully developed their own personal identity. Without having a sense of who they are, it is impossible to figure out how they want to give.
—Sharna Goldseker, vice president, the Andrea and Charles
Bronfman Philanthropies

Sharna Goldseker's Story

- Who am I?
- What am I inheriting—what history, what values, what culture?
- Who am I distinct from that inheritance?

In Sharna Goldseker's 21 years of generational work, defining a family's philanthropic identity and values begins with delving into these questions.

Conversations revolve around questions like: What are the money messages you inherited from your family? Who did you hear them from? How do you want to carry them on in your life? These are part of the challenges in communicating family values in order to transmit them to the next generation.

Communication is critical in improving intergenerational relationships or relationships with different branches of the family. Engaging the next generation means that parents have to articulate their own values in order to transmit them clearly to their children. "Distinguishing what is inherited, who you are, distinct from the source of your inheritance, and how you translate that into philanthropy is the work you have to do before you can engage your children and create your family foundation," Sharna advises.

Learning how to work with your children as adults is a key issue in multigenerational work. Although we want to be strategic, it is really our values that shape our philanthropy and provide a sense of personal fulfillment. Communicating these values makes it easier to align actions and priorities with conscious choices about giving.

Founders often take for granted their personal history, assuming that the next generation may not be interested in their stories. Understanding the value of transmitting the family narrative from one generation to the next is a prime step in conveying the family's philanthropic legacy, develops a family communication process that helps frame conversations about governance and generational succession, and establishes a framework for families to communicate a legacy of wealth across the generations.

Engaging the next generation in philanthropy also means talking about money. Yet families often avoid the money conversation, as they are reluctant to let children know how much they have. Talking to your children about money values as a way of transmitting the values that are part of your legacy is an opportunity to tell your story, recount your origins, and discuss the forces that shaped your values and the circumstances of your life, in the context of transmitting the values that are part of your legacy.

Establishing the younger generation's emotional connection to their family history provides a sense of family continuity and builds a foundation culture that paves the way for open conversations about governance and generational succession.

Among the challenges in multigenerational work, Sharna cites difficulties working with different generations who relate to different causes. You need conversations to bridge that divide, to allow for the transmission of values. "Even if stories are different," she learned, "there is a shared value system, and even in those differences, you can develop a common language. Without the skills to knit them together, families can get lost in their differences."

Commenting on how younger generations are becoming involved in philanthropy while their parents are still active, Sharna observes that the focus tends toward developing the younger generation while the real challenge "is keeping the generation of parent funders at the table while creating room for the children without putting them at the kids' table (as with junior boards). We also need to pay more attention to the older generation and keep them engaged." She points out that, "Once you bring in the younger generation, it changes the nature of things because families don't know how to interact as peers, as professionals doing work together. They need to create a safe space where children can be among peers to ask questions and figure out who they are in the world. What they learn about themselves is valuable because it can also apply to everything in their own lives."

Providing the Tools

The challenge for families with different generational members is expressing individual core values within a collective framework. Working with more than 60 families to facilitate generational conversations, Sharna has developed tools to train families to articulate values and understand how those values motivate giving. She uses tools like the set of motivational cards, which represent different values influencing priorities in personal and philanthropic decision making. The values cards clarify who you are and what you stand for, making it easier to have discussions about what the family's core values should be.

Another facilitation tool she works with is image cards to envision your aspirations, using images to stimulate expression in ways words may not. "What life do you aspire to live?" is a visualization exercise that frees the imagination to express the essence of "being," your identity as a philanthropist who aspires to bring who you are to the world. Developing the language and vocabulary to write your own mission and vision statements, and communicating what needs to be accomplished in the future, require facilitated conversations to define shared values and achieve a defined purpose and outcome.

Together with the Association of Small Foundations at 21/64, Sharna Goldseker created the *Grandparent Legacy Project*, a resource book featuring stories of 15 philanthropists who describe how they transmitted their legacy to the next generation. Its user guide and workbook outlines steps for grandparents and grandchildren to use in capturing their family's philanthropic values. It also provides interview questions to facilitate the sharing of stories that express family values and the legacy family members want to leave behind.

21/64 is a nonprofit consulting division of the Andrea and Charles Bronfman Philanthropies, specializing in next generation and multigenerational strategic philanthropy (http://2164.net/). 21/64 offers services to individuals, families, foundations, and federations in times of generational transition, including consultations to help engage next generations in philanthropy, resource materials to help families unpack generational conversations, peer networks for younger funders, and an array of communication vehicles, resources, and facilitation tools like the values cards, Picture Your Legacy image cards, and *The Grandparent Legacy Project!* (a workbook and user guide produced with the Association of Small Foundations to help grandparents and families convey their story).

The Association of Small Foundations is a membership organization of more than 3,000 foundations that works to enhance the power of small foundation giving by providing donors, trustees, and staff of member foundations with peer learning opportunities, targeted tools and resources, and a collective voice in and beyond the philanthropic community (www.grandstreetnetwork.net).

21/64 also facilitates Grand Street, an ongoing network of next-generation family members (ages 18–28) who are involved in or will be involved in their family philanthropy one day. Participants often feel respect for their inherited family legacy but are unsure about finding their own place in the multigenerational family context. Grand Street allows participants to explore questions of their

Jewish identity, family responsibility, and philanthropic opportunity in a safe space among peers.

Four Generations of Giving: Lessons from the Nathan Cummings Foundation

After Nathan Cummings' death in 1985, most of his assets were bequeathed to the Nathan Cummings Foundation. The founder of the Sara Lee conglomerate provided only vague instructions as to its organizational purposes and operation, telling his children, "I feel it's up to you to make wise decisions."[1]

Endowed with $200 million for "charitable, eleemosynary, educational, scientific, literary, religious, and artistic purposes," the foundation needed the input of the next generation and enlisted the support of the eldest child of each sibling to plan and design the future course of the family foundation.

Ruth Cummings

Ruth Cummings was the first member of the third generation to serve as chair of the Nathan Cummings Foundation. She relates the challenges of those formative years here:

> My biggest challenge was being within a family that had no history of working together. The hierarchical family structure, with our grandfather as the "top banana," the second generation—two male children who did not have access to coaching or to their father's inner circle, and the only daughter who had access to those resources—made for complicated family dynamics that played out through the different generations.
>
> As the first board chair representing the third generation, I followed my aunt and uncle (my father had died) in the position. They had set an operational style that put unequal advantage and value on the family's orientation versus the professionals, creating a strain between the family board and professional staff. Meanwhile, the decision had been made

---

[1]Janice Petterchak. *To Share: The Heritage, Legend, and Legacy of Nathan Cummings* (Rochester, IL: Legacy Press, 2000).

and action taken to hire a very high-level professional, crea-tive, and proactive President. As a younger person, I valued the professional orientation of the enterprise, a view shared by two other family board members who were my cousins and, like me, represented the eldest in their branch of the family. This caused tension between the generations. There was a different comfort level with having a "collegial" culture with the staff as opposed to having staff "work for the board." Ultimately, this tension escalated with the addition of two professional inde-pendent board members who were not part of the family.

Family members who felt things were moving out of their control, becoming staff-driven versus family-driven, called for a meeting of only family board members and announced they wanted me to step down mid-term as Chair. I had to point out that this action was out of order and that such a decision had to go to the full board and could not be made by a group of family board members. At that time, we were considering split-ting the Foundation into three parts, according to the three family branches. Rather than bringing it to a vote of the full board, I chose to resolve the situation by stepping down to avoid having the family vote against independent trustees and staff (including the president), which would have created an impossible situation for governing.

We learned from this incident to keep the interests of the Foundation as a whole above our own personal interests, to be mindful that the Foundation is greater than the sum of its parts, and to act accordingly to honor the intention of the donor.[2]

Of the foundation's accomplishments, Ruth considers the board's decision to include independent board members and incorporate this into the bylaws as one of the most important.

"Time and again, it was their wisdom, observations, and voices that helped us move through issues that polarized family trustees."

Noteworthy steps that paved the way for the future include:

• Creating the Foundation according to the values and interests of the donor while tying the current mission and guidelines to relevant program areas that address issues of our time.

---

[2]Interview with Ruth Cummings.

- Creating a foundation inspired by Jewish values that works for a socially and economically just society, that is concerned with the health of whole communities.
- Taking on the transformation of complex problems and staying with these areas of focus for more than 20 years.
- Succeeding, even as a relatively new foundation, in engaging older and major funders in new initiatives conceived by the Foundation staff, some of which have become "mainstream," like mind-body and preventive health practices, and Jewish spirituality, as well as Jewish healing (Rabbi Rachel Cowan's work).
- Recognizing and supporting the value of contemplative practice and connecting the findings from the field to impact on creative solutions for work in other program areas.

Reflecting on the working relationship developed with four generations of the family, Ruth explains the evolution of the organizational process, from the founding stage of expressing individual desires to the institutional stage of developing the foundation culture:

> The expression of voices within the next generation begun with the creation of an "Associate" status for family members. Building a connection to the board by requiring Associates to serve on a Program Education Committee with staff and board members who review issues, policy and grants in detail, along with attending board meetings, gave the younger generation an opportunity to weigh in on discussions.
>
> What has emerged to date from the fourth generation trustees, all of whom are currently women (the oldest in her early thirties), is an interest in women's issues and leadership. Our work in Israel, which was focused on religious pluralism, has now evolved into women's leadership programs across all sectors for social and economic justice.

Learning and sharing her experience with families starting multifamily foundations, Ruth cites a few valuable lessons:

- Working with good consultants can produce good results if the goal is clear from the outset.
- Start by identifying shared values in order to work together—even just a few can launch people together.

- Initial and annual retreats that enhance working and playing together are quite effective.
- One doesn't have to like everyone or think the same way but there should be a shared sense that the overall goal is putting the mission first.

Lance Lindblom

The intergenerational development process has made the Nathan Cummings Foundation a trailblazer in the field of family philanthropy. Though each member had a different take on their grandfather's intent, the work of expressing the aspirations of each generation was the first step in a formal process that allowed a multigenerational foundation to get the board to act strategically. After realizing that a family culture of consensual voting did not always work, governance was redesigned to enable the family to act with a majority vote.

Lance Lindblom, president of the Nathan Cummings Foundation, speaks of the challenging dynamics of those early years and the process of working with different family cultures. The Nathan Cummings Foundation developed a governance framework document and a historic board resolution regarding selection of family members as trustees and associates. This was adopted in 2008 and is referred to as the "Sundance Compact." These governance documents are generously shared in the following pages with permission of the Nathan Cummings Foundation as lessons in multigenerational philanthropy.

"Once we vote, majority rules and it cannot be revisited for 3 to 5 years unless the situation changes," explains Lance Lindblom, president of the Nathan Cummings Foundation, who spoke at length on the structure of governance. He goes on to say:

> Out of 15 board members, 10 are family, two of whom exercise one of the fourth generation's vote. The governance committee does a search for outside Trustees and five nonfamily members, with elections held every three years for five nonfamily trustees, who can serve two terms but have to rotate off the board for a year before they can return.[3]

---

[3]From a personal interview with Lance Lindblom.

Nathan Cummings Foundation
Approved Governance Framework

INTRODUCTION

As the Nathan Cummings Foundation (NCF) continues to grow, and the involvement of the family continues to increase, the Foundation turned its attention to strengthening its governance systems and structures to most effectively support the work of the organization. After much discussion in its April 13–14, 2002 Retreat, and subsequently modified and approved by the Executive Committee and Board of Directors, the Nathan Cummings Foundation adopted a new Foundation Governance Framework.

WHAT IS GOVERNANCE?

Governance is the structures, systems, and processes that enable effective oversight and inform decision-making in the Foundation. There is no single best governance system. Rather, the governance system of an organization needs to reflect the unique character, operations, and needs of the organization.

The Foundation's governance system is based on a high level of engagement by Trustees, Associates, and other family members. This model of governance adds unique value to the work of the Foundation by tapping into the vision, values, and energy of family members. This high level of engagement, however, **requires a heavy investment of Foundation resources and staff time to support it.**

A primary focus of the Board's work at the 2002 Retreat was to identify ways to improve the efficiency of the governance system, in order to obtain the "maximum return on the investment" the Foundation is making in family engagement–and the family is making in the Foundation.

RETHINKING THE PROGRAM ADVISORY COMMITTEES

In the past, the Program Advisory Committee (PAC) structure was one of NCF's primary governance vehicles. The purpose of the PACs was to provide Trustees and Associates with the opportunity to:

- deepen their understanding of the Foundation's program areas;
- guide the Foundation's strategy in these areas; and
- provide oversight of the Foundation's programs.

However, the PAC structure was not effectively meeting Trustees' and Associates' expectations for involvement and oversight. Specific criticisms of the PAC structure included:

- PAC meetings are viewed as being too short and too superficial, rather than providing an opportunity for in-depth learning.

(Continued)

- The large number of people involved in PAC meetings is seen as negatively impacting the level of engagement of PAC members and reducing the time available for in-depth education and discussion.
- Lack of continuity from meeting to meeting as members and non-members drop in and out.
- The expectations of the PAC Chair, the Program Director, and the President are unclear and create confusion over roles and responsibilities.
- There are few opportunities for *active* involvement and learning by PAC members.
- Approving the docket has become a pro-forma exercise as the document is "too thick to read and not user-friendly," and because the list of individual grants does not explain how these grants are advancing the objectives of the Foundation.
- The PAC structure does not provide opportunities for leadership development, especially for the 4th generation.
- The one-year term for membership on PACs provides little time to develop a deep knowledge of the area.

Therefore, the Trustees, Associates, and other family members attending the retreat recommended replacing the PACs with a new model for program engagement, which is detailed below.

NEW MODEL FOR PROGRAM ENGAGEMENT

Determining the proper balance among the multiple areas of governance responsibility listed above–and the most effective model for carrying out these roles–was a lengthy, but productive process. The following "consensus recommendation," adopted and slightly modified by the Executive Committee and Board of Directors, was developed through the collective input of Trustees, Associates, other family members, and the President.

1. **PROGRAM TEAMS:** *Focus on Education and Engagement*
    Program Advisory Committees will be replaced by Program Teams. Program Teams will focus on building an in-depth understanding of program areas and on providing a vehicle for *active* engagement of Trustees and Associates in the Foundation's work.

    - All Trustees and Associates will **select one Program Team** as their major area of responsibility in order to promote *depth* of understanding over breadth of involvement.
    - Trustees and Associates will serve a **two-year term** on their selected Program Team, in order to provide enough time to build a deep understanding of that program area. Trustees and Associates are encouraged to rotate Program Team assignments at the end of their term so that they can build a deeper understanding of the different programs.

- Program Teams will meet **in-person once per year** (*as detailed below*). Additional communication and interaction can occur, as needed, through the use of conference calls or other means.
- Program Team meetings will **focus on education and understanding.** Potential activities include site visits, speakers, discussions, visits with grantees, etc. Teams will also focus on the implications of these learning activities on their program area.
- Each Program Team will be **led by a Team Leader**. The Team Leader will serve a **two-year term**.

The role of the Team Leader is to:
- coordinate the work of the team and team members (*trustees and associates*)
- develop education opportunities that will deepen the understanding of the program area by the team members
- identify the interests of individual team members and then delegate responsibility for specific tasks and leadership roles to team members, in line with their expressed interests and availability
- work with the team to plan, manage, and implement the education day
- work with the Program Director to plan the education day
- coordinate the logistics of team meetings and calls

2. **THE BOARD:** *Focus on Oversight and Strategy Setting*
   The Board, as a whole, will be responsible for program oversight, evaluation, and strategy setting. This will, hopefully, provide all board members and Associates with a more complete understanding of the work of the Foundation, as opposed to the program-specific focus created by the PACs.

   The board's focus will be on assessing whether the staff is effectively advancing the program objectives through the Foundation's grantmaking, not on approving individual grants.

- **Board members and Associates will receive a summary of the proposed grants in advance of the board meeting for their review.** The full docket, or program-specific sections of it, will be available **upon request** or on the NCF board website. Board members and Associates are expected to review the materials in advance of the meeting, and come to the board meeting prepared to discuss – *at the strategic level* – the proposed list of grants. Board members and Associates may also contact the Program Director to ask questions about individual grants that appear on the docket, if needed.
- At each board meeting, all **Program Directors will provide the board with a report on how the proposed grants are advancing the Foundation's objectives** within the program area (*not a review of individual grants*).

(*Continued*)

- At each board meeting, there will be an **in-depth evaluation of one program area**. This biannual evaluation will provide the opportunity to review how effective the Foundation was in advancing its objectives over the past two years, to discuss lessons learned and assess strategy.

3. **GOVERNANCE MECHANICS**
   - The Foundation will hold three (3) meetings per year *(two board meetings plus an annual retreat)*.
   - Each meeting will last two (2) full days. Additional days may be added to the retreat meeting, as desired by the board.
   - The first day of each meeting will be devoted to Program Teams. The second day will be the formal board meeting.
     - Two Program Teams will meet *concurrently* on the day prior to the board meeting *(Note: It was suggested that Interprogram and Community Grants Program Teams meet during the retreat)*.
     - Members of those Program Teams will attend their own Team Meeting. Members of the other teams, as well as other family members not currently serving on the board, are also invited to attend the Program Team meetings.
     - The Team Leader, working with team members and supported by the Program Director, will be responsible for designing the agenda for the Program Team meeting.
   - The agenda for board meetings will include:
     - Regular board business
     - Presentations by the Program Directors on how grants in each of the five program areas are advancing the program objectives (not a review of individual grants)
     - An in-depth evaluation, analysis, and strategy session for one of the program areas. Each program would be up for review about every two years.
   - The *suggested* schedule for future board meetings is April (retreat), June/July, and December.
     - All board meetings and every other retreat will be held in New York at the NCF offices.
     - A number of Board members and Associates expressed a desire for more downtime and time for reflection and family interaction at future retreats.
   - NCF staff will develop a proposal for the implementation of the new governance model for review by the Executive Committee or Board at an upcoming meeting. Implementation of the new model will begin in 2003.

SIZE OF THE BOARD

As part of its recent review of the Foundation's governance structure and systems, the Governance Committee has recommended limiting the number of Trustees and Associates, and instituting a system of rotation so that all family members who are interested and eligible in serving would have the opportunity to do so over time. It was noted that while there is enough space on the Board now for everyone who wishes to participate, the number of people who wish to participate in the future may be too large.

The proposal, and the board's discussion of it, focused on two seemingly conflicting desires:

- to create a board large enough that it provides an opportunity for all family members who are interested and eligible for service to be able to serve; and
- to create a board small enough to enable interactive discussion, full participation, and effective decision making.

The board was unanimous in its support for a maximum cap on the number of Trustees and Associates, and for the concept of rotation.

Specifically, the Trustees, Associates, and other family members attending the retreat recommended that:

1. A cap be placed on the number of Trustees and Associates that is large enough to promote involvement but small enough to be manageable (such as 20 to 25 members). (This was subsequently modified to put an absolute cap of 15 on the number of Trustees, and a temporary cap of 26 on the total number of Trustees and Associates).
2. Board meetings be open to both Trustees and Associates. It was suggested that the Trustee group be smaller in order to facilitate decision making, and the Associate group be larger in order to promote involvement.
   - Trustees have full voting rights, as well as higher expectations for participation and attendance. Associates have a full voice in the decision making process, but do not have a formal vote and have somewhat lower expectations for participation and involvement.
   - The Trustee group should contain four to seven non-family Trustees, as well as a mix of generations among the Family Trustees.
   - Membership in the Trustee and Associate groups would rotate so that any family member interested and eligible to serve would have the opportunity to do so over time. Selection of new trustees and associates would be based on objective criteria, such as position in the queue for new Trustees. Trustees could serve as Associates after rotating off the Trustee group.

(Continued)

- A few Trustees and Associates suggested that specific "very important" decisions (*to be determined*) should require the input of all the Trustees and Associates, in order to ensure that everyone has a voice in the major governance decisions of the Foundation. Other, more regular, business decisions could be made by the Trustee group alone.
3. The board continues to explore new ways for involvement in the life of the Foundation outside of the official governance system. This could include serving on the Program Teams, attending retreats, etc. This will be especially important as the family continues to expand.

RESOLVED: The following decisions made at the June 2008 Nathan Cummings Foundation Retreat regarding selection of family members as Trustees and Associates of the Foundation are hereby adopted and supersede all contradictory previous policies:

- Lineal descendants will make up the simple majority of the family representation on the Board of Trustees.
- All current trustees, associates, and direct lineal descendant family members are eligible to be considered for trusteeship, having satisfied all other relevant requirements.
- All future spouses and legal partners will be eligible to participate as associates and will be eligible to be considered as candidates for trusteeship.
- Adopted minor children of lineal descendants will be considered lineal descendants and eligible for nomination as associates and trustees.
- A nominating committee will be formed with the responsibility of selecting new trustee and associate candidates. This nominating committee will be composed of three non-family trustees and three family trustees, one from each branch of the family. The non-family trustees will be voting members on this committee and the family trustees will serve as advisors. Members of the nominating committee will serve for a term of three years.
- The Governance Committee will be responsible for nominating those Board members, family and non-family, who will serve on the nominating committee.
- The Governance Committee will develop and refine the appropriate criteria necessary for trusteeship. They will consider the already recommended criteria for family foundation stewardship proposed by the Council on Foundations. The Committee will propose these criteria to the Board for ratification at its November 2008 meeting. These criteria will then be given to the nominating committee to inform their future deliberations.
- The Governance Committee will also recommend the composition of the Nominating Committee to the Board at its November 2008 meeting.
- This Resolution and the decisions herein will be forever known and referred to as "The Sundance Compact."

Continuity comes through family members. Lindblom outlines the requirements in the following from a personal interview we had:

> To be a Board Member, you have to be 25 years old. To be an Associate, you have to be at least 18 (we have adjuncts who have to be at least 16 and are allowed to attend meetings and work on special projects to get them ready to be Associates).
>
> To prepare the next generation, a learning program was developed for third generation members and Associates over 18 years old who have all rights but voting. They make community grants to help them understand grant making in a very practical way, about 30 $5,000 grants, and report at year-end to the board on their outcomes. Board recommended grants are limited to a maximum of $50,000.
>
> The opportunity to learn together, to flesh out family beliefs and values, and to agree on governance issues to guide the way the board functions was a growth experience. Associates attend regular board meetings, with time carved out for education days. There are different levels of Associate status that allow family members who are not on the board to participate. The "Associate" structure creates involvement and allows other voices to be heard.
>
> This structured learning process channels the interests of younger generations and creates a space for their involvement and personal expression, while taking pressure off the foundation's main program focus. Given individual differences, board recommended community grants require board review and approval. This discourages trustees from bringing individual or personal projects to board meetings and makes it easier for the family to come to consensus.

Lindblom describes this mechanism as "a safety valve and exploration fund that uses trustees as scouts and explorers."[4]

These mechanisms have led to the growth and development of the Nathan Cummings Foundation. In recent years, its groundbreaking work has funded groundbreaking advocacy to innovative approaches between arts and social justice including the following initiatives:

---

[4]From a personal interview with Lance Lindblom.

- The foundation played a leadership role in coalescing arts and social justice by helping to establish the Art and Social Justice Working Group of funders and practitioners from around the country, to develop and implement common language and a shared agenda.
- It created the Jewish Social Justice Roundtable, a collaborative initiative of 23 Jewish social justice organizations.
- The foundation has changed corporate behavior through shareholder activism.
- It created Just Congregations, the reform movement's initiative to engage synagogues around the country in congregation-based community organizing—working in partnership with communities of faith for social change.
- It created the Palestinian-Israeli Women's Forum, a collaborative initiative of a diverse group of organizations and leaders advancing women as agents of change.
- It implemented the affordable Care Act Implementation Fund, a pooled fund that provides timely and strategic investments in state-based advocacy to promote effective, consumer-centered implementation of the Patient Protection and Affordable Care Act.
- It spearheaded an ecological innovation program to address climate change and a transition to a clean energy economy.

The history and lessons of the Foundation's early years are also available on their web site at www.nathancummings.org.

Summary

This chapter offers the combined expertise of Sharna Goldseker and the Nathan Cummings Foundation, as they shed light on the complex issues of multigenerational giving.

In the following chapter, Scott McVay, founding executive director of the Geraldine R. Dodge Foundation, answers the question, "What is Philanthropy?" with a lilting essay that leads to the stories of philanthropic explorers, musician Paul Winter and artist Aimee Morgana.

CHAPTER 13

Philanthropists as Explorers

Lessons from *Scott McVay* (Founding Executive Director of the Geraldine R. Dodge Foundation, and 16th President of Chautauqua Institution), *Aimee Morgana* (Founder of the N'kisi Institute), and *Paul Winter* (Founder of Music of the Earth, Inc.)

What are maps after all
but metaphors
for what we don't know?
At each juncture
of the human record of
perception of where we are
we see a little of
the near at hand
but want to know
what's over the rise
in the hill or
the far horizon at sea.
Copernicus and Kepler
gave us the first big
reorientation
Darwin and Wallace
a new map
for thinking about origins
and how we came to be.

233

Freud and Jung
poked up awareness of the unmapped unconscious
Margaret Geller
saints be praised
gave us the first map
of the universe
that others have been
fleshing out ever since.
Yes, maps are metaphors of the little we know
and a hint of where we
have to go.

—From the poem *Maps* by Scott McVay

Scott McVay's view of philanthropists as pioneers, explorers, visionaries, and eager learners casts givers in the role of voyagers, filled with curiosity and creative moral imagination. We venture out with passion as our "pole-star" to secure and uplift what we care most about. As the landscape unfolds, "maps" give us just "a hint of where we have to go."

Scott McVay's Story

The Zuni believe that maps aid our memories, give reference to our place of origin, places we visit, places we hope to go. They are references of where we are in the universe and help define our relationship to natural processes.

Maps are like relatives, they give a sense of our own personal history, relating the continuous search that is our essence, entrancing us with narratives of places we have been.

For Scott McVay—who served in the U.S. Army in Berlin as a special agent with the Counterintelligence Corps; pursued an interest in whales, dolphins, and porpoises (authored a paper in *Science* on the discovery of Songs of Humpback whales with Roger Payne); organized and led two expeditions to the Alaskan Arctic to study, record, and film the rare Bowhead whale; and travels the world to learn about natural history and human culture—philanthropy is only a part of the map of his consciousness.

Scott's favorite *Peanuts* cartoon on philanthropy is the one where Charlie Brown tells Lucy, "When I grow up, I want to be a philanthropist!" Lucy responds, "You gotta have a lot of money to be a philanthropist!" Charlie thinks a bit, a thought bubble appears over his head, and then he says, "I'll just give away other people's money."

Whether we give our own or other people's money, the spirit of exploration that leads to exciting discoveries is the wisdom Scott shares with us in his delightful and enlightening essay.

What Is Philanthropy?

Listening. Asking questions. Listening again.
Asking more questions. Listening yet again.

Hear the music of insistent birds. Hear the buzz of
insects in the sun.
Hear the rustle in the leaves as a fellow mammal moves by.
Hear the high-pitched clicks of the bat flipping here and there,
finding the evening's repast.

Listen to Bach, Beethoven, Copeland, the panflute of the Andes,
Didjeridoo of the Aborigines, the slit drum of the South Pacific.

See latent connections between seemingly disparate sectors,
recognizing patterns and possibilities to a point of understanding, then act.

Nurture beauty in the songs of Nature and the hymns of humanity.

Remember Art & Science outlast tyrants of the time.

Seek out the authentic idea or person beyond
noise of the moment.

Follow hunches and discover niches of opportunity; then stay
with them as they gather momentum in the culture.

Trust your heart and gut beyond intellect.

A New idea
typically does not
at the beginning
fit the guidelines.

Yet that's where the strategic possibilities lie.

To close where we begin, recall Confucius (551 BC–479 BC):
When the Master entered the Grand Temple, he asked questions about everything there. Someone said, "How can it be claimed that the son of Shu Lang-he knows the rites? Every time he is present he asks about everything!" When this was reported to the Master he remarked, "This is precisely the rite."

Philanthropy is a state of being, a way of seeing, a willingness to take risks and an internal readiness to make a leap. It is staying open to new ideas that make of us happy "I-don't-know-it-alls!" It is the exploration that fuels our philanthropic aspirations, but the daring adventure is discovering what we don't know, losing our way and finding unexpected gifts, seeing "patterns and possibilities" to connect the dots.

Scott's joyful interpretation of the philanthropic journey led me to connect with two inspiring explorers, whose passion and authenticity add truth to Scott's philosophy of philanthropy as a personal voyage of discovery and inspiration.

The Journey of Discovery: Aimee Morgana's Story

Discoveries can happen anywhere! Discovery is about looking at something deeply and diligently, with a desire to understand, and seeing it in a new way. Don't be afraid to do something that's never been done before.
—Aimee Morgana, researcher in interspecies
communication, artist, and teacher

Aimee Morgana is a researcher, an artist, and a teacher. When she began her career as an artist, Aimee Morgana created immersive worlds, filling boxes with bird feathers and ephemera that expressed the relationship of nature and humanity. Then she began working with living birds.

A researcher in interspecies communication, Aimee focuses on exploring the inner terrain of the animal mind and our relationships with animals. She brought home an Amazon green parrot and discovered by interacting with it that it had learned to appropriately use about 80 words. Intrigued after seeing a parrot named Alex on TV who could do simple counting and identify colors and objects presented on a tray, when her Amazon parrot died, Aimee found an African gray parrot she named N'kisi, and decided to teach this parrot language.

"Artists get to be eccentric and discover and pursue something, so I thought, why not really try to teach him!" she exclaims. With her background teaching art for 20 years, Aimee developed her own communication-based program to teach N'kisi like a child, using her experience as an art teacher to nurture creativity. N'kisi has developed a vocabulary of more than 1,580 words, far more than any other language-using animal. N'kisi uses words in context, forming sentences that express feelings, like "it hurt a lot," to describe pain after being bitten by another parrot, or "I don't want to die," and "I feel better already," when he was recovering.

Finding a way to reach N'kisi's mind was a journey of discovery. Describing the creative linguistic communication process of teaching a parrot to use human language, Aimee explains her creativity-based teaching approach: "Teaching art was a great preparation for this because with art, you can't just tell someone what to do, it's more like teaching you to do what *you* do, to express yourself." She likens her attempts to reach into a mind in darkness to Helen Keller's experiential learning.

Aimee describes how N'kisi makes connective associations, telling her to "put a battery in!" and mimicking how she puts new batteries into his toys when they stop moving. When Aimee

Photograph from: Wings Worldquest, http://explore.
wingsworldquest.org/node/481

showed him a dead lizard, his first reaction was to advise her to "put a battery in." When she explained that she couldn't do that for an animal, he went on to his next memory association—suggesting that she "light a candle." Aimee explains that after 9/11, they were looking out from her window watching people lighting candles on the street and she explained that many people had died and it was very sad, and they were lighting candles for people who had died. So, at N'kisi's prompting, Aimee lit a candle for the lizard. Recently, N'kisi has been expressing his desire to be in a book, saying "I wanna be in a book, I'm gonna be in a book, yeay!"

Aimee is awed at the capacity for relationship between her and N'kisi, "He calls me Friend." There is so much more to discover," she says, "We are not alone in terms of consciousness. There are other species out there that can relate to us with love, and can relate to us like family. This is what life on earth is about."

The Grand Symphony of Life: Paul Winter's Story

> *Perhaps the most inspiring and encouraging thing I have learned through this project has been about the universal values shared by all cultures, which we experience again each time we make music with people and talk with them about their respect for the natural world. The birds for me symbolize these universals. The motto of "Flyways" is: "migrating birds know no borders." And the music, I believe, can awaken the universal heart of humanity.*
>
> —Paul Winter, founder, Music for the Earth Inc.

A different philanthropic adventure is that of musician Paul Winter, whose Winter Solstice concerts at the Cathedral of St. John the Divine have been a holiday attraction for many years. Paul recently embarked on a multicultural journey tracking bird migration from Africa, through the Middle East, to Europe and Asia.

Paul's story of this journey originates with his love of music. It led him to an epic project that took over a decade to develop, with fieldwork in 16 countries that will culminate in a musical chronicle of the birds' long journey.

> Throughout my life, music has been a passport to the world. My college sextet was fortunate to be sent by the U.S. State

Department on a six-month tour of 23 countries of Latin America. My allurement to Brazilian music led me to then return to Brazil to live for a year. And later in the 1960s my new ensemble, which I called "Consort," was invited to play in the Israel Festival, and we fell in love with Israel much as we had Brazil.

My musical journey might have remained focused on the realms of our two-legged species had I not attended a lecture in New York in 1968 on whale songs. Mesmerized by the beauty of their singing, and by learning of the complex patterns they sing repeatedly, the whales opened the door for me to what I've come to call "The greater symphony of the Earth."

The 1970s for me were filled with explorations of the natural world and these four-legged, fin-footed, and winged musicians, and my sense of both who my community embraced, and where my home was, had expanded forever.

It was the ecological dimension of our music that led to the Consort and I being invited to be artists-in-residence at New York's Cathedral of St. John the Divine. The mission of the Dean of the Cathedral, the Very Rev. James Parks Morton, was to create a bridge between spirituality and ecology. We were given carte blanche to present any kind of event there we wanted, so I began to imagine what might be the most universal milestone we could celebrate, at the Cathedral, one which would be welcoming to any people, regardless of their religious or cultural background. It occurred to me that this might be the Winter Solstice, the great turning point of the year. So in 1980 we presented our first winter Solstice Celebration, never imagining that we would be continuing to present these annually for over three decades.

In 1991, I brought the Consort back to Israel to play in Caesarea and at the Mann Auditorium in Tel Aviv. Following the Tel Aviv concert, a man came backstage and introduced himself and asked if he could show us a video of his work with the migrating birds. His name was Yossi Leshem, and he had done his PhD on the great bird migrations that come through Israel. He was inspired by the music we had played celebrating whales and wolves, and wondered if we might consider doing something similar with the migrating birds. We were deeply inspired by his video, much of which he had made from an ultralight plane, soaring among the storks, steppe eagles, pelicans, and other species that fly over Israel.

Yossi had become renowned in Israel for finding ways to stop the collision of Air Force jets with migrating birds. He convinced the Air Force to fund a radar station at Ben Gurion airport, which he staffed with volunteers from the Society for Protection of Nature in Israel. From his studies he had good information on the 350 migrating species and the approximate times of their arrival, so with his guidance the volunteers were able to monitor their passages with the radar and then beam the Air Force to keep their jets out of particular areas and altitudes during those times. This plan succeeded in cutting plane/bird crashes by 74 percent.

He became an instant friend, and we talked about ways we might collaborate in the future.

In 1993, Yossi Leshem, now Director of the Society for Protection of Nature in Israel, invited the Consort to play for the SPNI annual convention during Passover week, in a canyon in the Negev Desert south of the village of Sde Boker. Yossi arranged for me to fly there in a motorized two-person glider from Galilee airport in the north. Piloted by a former Air Force pilot, we flew with the migrating storks, often turning off the engine to glide among hundreds of these great birds as they soared in their spiraling slow-motion ballet. From that unforgettable experience came the vision for the *Flyways* album—to create a musical chronicle of the birds' long journey, using music of each culture over which they fly.

It would be an epic project, involving field research and recording in 16 countries of the migration route, from South Africa up the Rift Valley to Egypt and through the Middle East to Turkey where the birds diverge to Europe and Asia. The vision for the *Flyways* project was so compelling that it kept Yossi and me in dialogue for over a decade, until we found time in our respective schedules to work on the fund-raising and research needed to launch the project.

We finally began fieldwork in 2006, in Ethiopia, and have since gone to 14 of the 16 countries. Having begun with the premise that the migrating birds and their habitats were endangered, we soon learned that the same was true of the indigenous cultures in many of these countries. So it has become an integrated mission, celebrating both the birds and the traditional peoples, along with the habitats that need to be protected for all to survive and to thrive.

In each country I have sought to find a soulful instrument or voice which could evoke some sense of the beauty and grace of the soaring birds, and become part of the tapestry of our "Flyways" music. We will invite musicians from each country to be part of a new international ensemble, the Great Rift Valley Orchestra, which will record the *Flyways* composition and perform it with the Paul Winter Consort in concerts around the world.

Perhaps the most inspiring and encouraging thing I have learned through this project has been about the universal values shared by all cultures, which we experience again each time we make music with people and talk with them about their respect for the natural world. The birds for me symbolize these universals. The motto of *Flyways* is: "migrating birds know no borders." And the music, I believe, can awaken the universal heart of humanity.

I have deep gratitude for the philanthropic missions of our funders, who have enabled and encouraged these journeys of exploration on the pathways of our *Flyways* project. And I'm optimistic that the forthcoming album of the *Flyways* composition, and our future concert tours and DVD of the project, will bring into the lives of many people the miracle of the migration as well as the beauty of these traditional music, and at the same time awaken in these listeners a deeper sense of their part in this grand symphony of life.[1]

Summary

Scott McVay inspires us to think of philanthropy as a voyage of exploration, with two explorers who embody his notion of philanthropists as explorers seeking new paths.

The next chapter takes us from the inspirational to the practical, with Christine DeVita, former president of the Wallace Foundation, as she reflects on her 29 years of foundation experience—lessons learned, mistakes made—and shares a strategic funding approach for effective philanthropy.

---

[1]Paul Winter's account of the making of *Flyways* was written expressly for this book.

Resources

- The N'kisi Institute, P.O. Box 30301, New York, NY 10011 www.nkisi.org, www.wingsworldquest.org.
- *Flyways* is a musical celebration of the migration of half a billion birds along the Great Rift Valley from Eurasia through the Middle East to South Africa and back. The *Flyways* composition will chronicle this extraordinary journey, using music of the cultures of the 22 countries over which the birds fly, interwoven with the actual voices of migrating birds, including cranes, eagles, bee-eaters, thrush nightingales, and many others. The project involves musical collaborations across cultures, concerts, a CD/DVD, and an educational program to raise awareness, promote peace, and assist the work of a wide range of local conservation and cultural organizations throughout the region. The *Flyways* project also supports efforts to designate the Great Rift Valley as a UNESCO World Heritage Site, bringing together in common cause the 22 states of the Great Rift Valley (http://flyways music.org).
- Music for the Earth was founded in 1976 by musician Paul Winter as a way of using the power of music to achieve conservation, social justice, and other ends.

Music for the Earth (www.musicfortheearth.org)

P.O. Box 1740

Litchfield, CT 06759

14

The Journey from Doing Good to Making Change

Lessons from *Christine DeVita* (President, the Wallace Foundation)

Change takes more than money; it requires knowledge about what works and what doesn't. The greatest contributions made by foundations come about through a combination of innovation, knowledge and public engagement. Timely knowledge is the real currency for creating social change. Foundations are well positioned to be "honest brokers" of solutions, helping foster the development of new approaches and then sharing them with the people and institutions that could benefit.

—Christine DeVita

On the eve of her retirement from the Wallace Foundation, Christine DeVita looks back on 29 years of philanthropic practice, starting as a lawyer and deputy counsel of the Readers Digest Association to being president for 24 years.

A Passion for Learning and the Arts

The Wallace Foundation, with assets of $1.4 billion in 2011, traces its origins half a century ago to founders DeWitt and Lila Acheson Wallace, who left their entire fortune to philanthropy. Staying true to its founders' passions for learning and the arts, the Wallace

Foundation adopted a new approach to philanthropy after studying results of their efforts in the 1990s.

"When we stepped back and really analyzed our first decade as a national foundation," Chris relates, "we were stunned to see that we had created about 100 different program initiatives, all related to our larger mission in the arts and education, but ultimately with no significant or long-term impact because we were spreading our resources a mile wide but an inch deep. We changed that in our second decade to invest heavily in a few big issues and stayed with them over long periods of time. As a result, we created real impact in our chosen fields" (Wallace Report 2009: "Appraising a Decade").

The conclusion was a turning point that fundamentally shifted the Wallace Foundation's focus from "doing good" to "making change," developing an approach to philanthropy that is the hallmark of its work today.

Chris shares her assessment of the foundation's shift:

> We learned our grant making had not led to as much widespread or sustained change in areas we cared most about, arts and education. Once we exited, funding was not sustained. Based on that assessment, we restructured the foundation around the concept of creating change in our chosen fields by developing and sharing effective ideas and practices. We decided to take a more systemic view of the areas in which we were working and engage directly with people who had power and authority to make more sustainable, widespread change. This common approach is used across all our program areas, in which we develop and test ideas "on the ground," gather credible, objective evidence on results of more significant innovations and then share that knowledge with the individuals and institutions that have the authority or influence to bring those effective ideas to life.

One of the Wallace Foundation's most effective knowledge-sharing initiatives is bringing grantees together to deliberate once a year, providing expert advice and helping each other problem solve. Chris points out that peer learning has been the foundation's best investment, as it happens in an atmosphere of openness conducive to learning, "Taking our dollars and smarts to bring grantees in regularly and provide technical assistance is the most effective leveraging."

After learning that arts programs needed help to increase audiences and were bedeviled by lack of credible data, the Wallace Foundation provided access to technical assistance as part of their grants, so that organizations could hone their strategies and do what they needed to do to get the right data. This dramatically improved data-driven analysis and provided information funders needed to confidently invest in arts organizations. Fifty-four arts organizations have benefited from these grants.

Learning from Mistakes

Foundations have few external barometers of how well they are performing. There are no revenue or share price indicators like in the corporate sector and unlike other nonprofits, no fundraising targets to meet, making it difficult to determine whether your foundation is performing well compared to others. Individual grantee performance is one indicator but not enough. Even if grantees are performing well, we need to ask ourselves if our work is creating the broader change we want to see, if our strategies could be improved, if our public outreach is effective, and our employee practices competitive, looking across and beyond the collective performance grantees and gathering objective data to benchmark results, policies, and practices against the foundation's overall goals, as well as its peers.

Reflecting on lessons learned, Chris cautions that "facts are friendly," and it is ok if you succeed or fail, but if you don't know what your mistakes are and don't learn from them, it is not ok to be ineffective. We should ask ourselves periodically, "what is the most disappointing grant from which I learned the most?"

Funders need to know how to speak the language of failure, to learn how to talk about it internally and publicly, to share that learning with other funders. One of the failures the Wallace Foundation learned from was something that would have seemed obvious. After spending a decade funding various improvement efforts in K through 12 public schools, they concluded that the lack of sustained change might be because they were working at the wrong "change lever." Their efforts ignored the role of leadership—the school principal. In researching past school reform efforts, they realized that no major reforms had paid special attention to the school principal. This was a clear departure from other sectors like business or the military, where leadership is understood to be a clear indicator of success. Until the government adopted the education policy of "no child left behind," which focused on effective school leaders like principals as change agents, this glaring gap had not been addressed.

To help address this issue, the Wallace Foundation began a major effort centered around school principals, part of which led to the creation of the Leadership Academy initiative with the New York City Partnership. This initiative transformed the selection process and curriculum, beginning with a summer intensive program that had scenario-based role plays. New York University did an evaluation, with the best principals put into the most difficult schools, and found that their students performed better in English and math. Kentucky State University adopted the model and it influenced many others to follow suit.

"With no shortage of worthy causes deserving foundation support," says Chris, "it is important to focus and do a few big things well. Ten percent of our grants are invested in research, evaluation, and communication to follow how ideas translate, how ideas travel."

Strategy and Listening to Feedback

Strategy is an essential part of the Wallace Foundation's approach to philanthropy—creating and executing clear, focused strategies to achieve results. Before launching a major initiative in the foundation's program, communications and evaluation staff devote time to designing a strategy for it. Ideas are put on paper in strategy charts that lay out the goal of an initiative, the rationale for it, and actions to be taken, and grantees then carry out the effort, gauging the effectiveness of expected results.

The Wallace Foundation benchmarks itself against other large foundations with assets in the range of $100 million or more. In the area of strategy, it used the 2009 report from the Center for Effective Philanthropy[1] to make a meaningful comparison on clarity

---

[1]Center for Effective Philanthropy, *2009 Report on Essentials of Foundation Strategy.*

and coherence of its strategy. Although 37 percent of CEOs and program officers at large foundations report agreement among the board, CEOs, and staff that their foundations' strategies are the most appropriate ones for achieving their goals, the Wallace Foundation's strategy is reviewed by its board, which approves strategy charts before the staff makes grant recommendations.

Other relevant performance indicators include comparisons of performance metrics used for all their strategies; whether strategy is tied to field data and if they track records of past programs and the foundation's current programs; average grant size and duration, to compare whether they are in the range determined by experts to be most effective; and their use of evaluation measures.

It seems hard to believe that in this day and age, 75 to 80 percent of private foundations do not have staff or publish financial reports, and that evaluations are not widely used by large foundations (though this is slowly changing) and are rarely made public. The 2010 Evaluation Roundtable identified 20 large foundations that actively conduct evaluations (roughly 15 percent of large foundations).

The Wallace Foundation believes in the importance of objective feedback and seeks it through anonymous surveys of grantees and thought leaders, acting on the information received to improve the foundation's performance. Assessing the foundation's overall effectiveness, not just the work of its grantees, the foundation examines its performance in five different areas: mission and impact, strategy, grantee relationships, communication, and governance.

An overlooked area of foundation learning is determining staffing expertise: what skills do you really need? Chris outlines how the inquiry-based culture central to the Wallace Foundation's approach depends on the ability of staff to objectively analyze and discuss data about whether strategies are working or whether grantees are hitting their benchmarks. She values strong analytical and evaluative thinking skills over field knowledge, because "we are not just funding our grantees' existing efforts but are often asking them to change the status quo, our staff must be skilled at helping our grantees manage change and negotiate different perspectives to reach common goals. While it is helpful to have people who have knowledge in fields your mission is focused on, you need people with evaluative and thinking skills, as others can be learned. You can always hire people from a specific field but it is harder to be critical and objective if they have loyalty to the field.

We ask our staff every year to do a critical analysis of grants in their portfolio. Their ability to engage in critical ideas made a difference in evaluating what's good, bad and indifferent in our funding areas."

Chris believes a foundation can, and should, contribute its ideas on how to improve institutions. Figuring out what approach to take and how it could be most effective, it has drawn upon the distinctive assets a national foundation, unrestrained by market forces or government-funding formulas, can employ:

- Identifying nascent problems, opportunities, and issues not yet widely recognized.
- Establishing relationships with innovative leaders in the field and investing in and strengthening their efforts.
- Gathering together groups of people—policymakers, practitioners, and researchers—who might not otherwise have the opportunity to learn from each other.
- Funding and sharing independent, objective research that seeks to capture the work of innovators and to understand problems in new ways that illuminate potential solutions (taken from the Wallace Foundation's 2010 Annual Report).

As Christine DeVita moves into a new phase of her life, she is grateful for the opportunity to continuously learn and improve. "Shaping how a foundation can learn and grow and change to do good better has been enormously exciting and fulfilling! A leader makes that happen and it is an amazing privilege to lead an organization that does that!"

Summary

Christine DeVita shares valuable lessons from her 24 years of experience leading a billion dollar foundation in developing a strategy that will have real impact.

In the next chapter, philanthropists Lynn Schusterman and Amy Goldman relate how their foundations reflect the values that inspire their giving.

Resources

- Center for Effective Philanthropy's Grantee Perception Survey—gathers data from a large anonymous sample of grantees from many foundations.
- 2009 Report, *Essentials of Foundation Strategy* (Center for Effective Philanthropy).
- *Creative Philanthropy* by Helmut Anheier and Diana Leat (Routledge, 2006). This is a study of foundations in United States, United Kingdom, and Australia.

15

Heart and Soul

Lessons from *Amy Goldman* (Chair and Executive Director of the GHR Foundation), and *Lynn Schusterman* (Chair of the Charles and Lynn Schusterman Family Foundation)

Amy Goldman and Lynn Schusterman express the best spirit of different traditions in their philanthropy, infusing their giving with values they inherited and intend to pass on to the next generation. The lessons they share illuminate our own learning journey as we connect who we are in how we give to the roots of our own tradition.

Amy Goldman's Story: Interfaith in Action

One of the obligations in being a philanthropist is responsibility, being in a position where you learn so much, to take lessons and get them out there.
　　　　　　　　　　　—Amy Goldman, Chair and Executive Director
　　　　　　　　　　　　　　　　　　　　of the GHR Foundation

When Amy Goldman became chair and executive director of the GHR Foundation in 2009, she moved from an international career in the world of finance to lead a family foundation "grounded in Catholic social values that expressed itself with entrepreneurial creativity in the spirit and practice of transformational philanthropy."

"In love with being Catholic," Amy explains the faith component that motivates the foundation's funding: "My parents personified the meaning of Catholic social values long before these were articulated as guiding principles for our foundation, as well as for so many social service organizations—both internal and external to the church. Being Catholic for them meant a priority placed on service to others, a respect for those working in the trenches, and an obligation to always consider others needs both locally and globally."

"We have taken the founding legacy of respect and love of faith to our programs," explains Amy. "We recognize that faith defines so many people and as we work to transform lives, we must include faith in the equation to succeed." One example of how the GHR Foundation does this is its interfaith action initiatives, which have specific social outcomes, with faith leaders as key players leveraging their networks to ensure engagement of the people the programs are trying to reach. Amy describes these initiatives:

> In Nigeria, one project increases training for behavior change around bed net usage, working with faith-based groups to train imams to distribute bed nets and encourage Christian ministers to preach the same message in their sermons. This double bottom line approach increases interfaith understanding while reducing malaria.
>
> In New York, we work with the Interfaith Center of New York to partner Catholic charities with local mosques throughout the city to bring Muslims and Catholics together, combining efforts like "food shelf" programs while facilitating dialogue between groups. While the results can sometimes cause tension, we are finding that problems of the group need to be tackled block-by-block, going neighborhood by neighborhood. We have also found that the feedback loop circulating between our U.S.-based and international projects keeps us in a learning mode. We are learning by doing.
>
> We learned not to divide our work geographically, as having constant conversations about what we are doing everywhere and convening our grantees to share obstacles and commonalities taught us to keep our geography broad on an issue. Our global work informs our local work. It is easy to keep initiatives in silos and we are constantly fighting against the tide to keep from working in isolation.

Partnering with Catholic congregations to boost recruitment, retention, education, and formation of Sisters in the United States and Africa, Amy's encounters with religious women fostered a deep respect for them as underutilized assets of the Catholic Church. "I didn't think of them before, yet these women seem to go where no one else does and are at the forefront of the church's work on the grassroots level, serving the poorest of the poor yet they receive little support from Catholic institutions."

One of the projects the GHR Foundation has funded is the All Africa Conference: Sister to Sister. The genesis of this initiative began with a group of African theologians, all women, who met Sister Margaret Farley at the Yale School of Divinity to discuss the suffering caused by the HIV and AIDS pandemic in Africa. They concluded that there was a need for women to gather in Africa in order to shatter the silence of shame that surrounds the pandemic. The convening of thought led the Sisters of Mercy to initiate the All Africa Conference: Sister to Sister, which brings together religious women so they can listen, learn, and empower each other to collaborate on strategies for prevention and care to address the crisis of HIV and AIDS.

The initiative addresses the issue of AIDS, the most globalized epidemic in history, and its impact on women, who make up 60 percent of the HIV positive adults in sub-Saharan Africa. The essence of the conference is the bonding that exists between Sister to Sister, affirming that African women are powerful in themselves, and coming together to overcome their lack of resources to mutually empower each other by sharing grace-filled time and support. They can then transform attitudes that impede effective responses to HIV and AIDS, increase their knowledge about related issues, develop personal and communal plans of action, and commit to building networks among themselves, others, and agencies after they convene. The model of convening has spread to 21 countries through regional conferences in Kenya, South Africa, Nigeria, Uganda, Cameroon, Zambia, and Malawi. Training programs for counselors, programs for raising awareness and fostering cooperation in schools, a local counseling program in Uganda, and opportunities for degree programs have been started.

Inheriting the legacy of her parents, the Foundation reflects her father's interest in solving complex issues, his way of engaging with the world, using his intellect and compassion. Amy says:

> I feel something is guiding me—a sense of calling. I was lucky enough by birth, and then fortunate to pursue an international

career which gave me a deeper understanding of conditions people live in. I feel an obligation and an opportunity. Working with religious and faith-based groups, whose whole lives are spent trying to solve complex, challenging, and tragic situations, working in those issues has been so inspiring—extraordinary people doing extraordinary things. This is the perfect culmination of who I am and what I can bring. I am bringing all my talents to bear on the issues we grapple with, and there is always the opportunity to learn more. My challenge has been to put my best self into it!

She sees ambitious goals, like promoting peace, through a long-term lens, knowing that the life cycle of initiatives tackling complex goals requires time to develop. Reflecting on the most valuable lessons she has gained from philanthropy, she considers listening and being open as the most important, followed by the need to be creative in making connections between grantees:

We take for granted that people know each other. As funders, making those connections could be so valuable.

We can bring people to the table. The time we spend with grantees is often inversely proportional to the grants. There are more areas to boost an organization in addition to partnership, like technical skills.

Once you find a problem that you feel compelled to solve, the difficulty of balancing intellect and heart with moral responsibility is realizing that change happens incrementally. Amy visualizes her task of working toward change as pushing a rock uphill:

Often we see a problem right in front of us that we think someone would surely try and fix, then you look around to see who else is doing it and there is only you. When you are standing right in front of an issue that confronts you, you can't hesitate and hope someone else will solve this, you just do it! Keep pushing, never give up pushing.

Her growth in philanthropy has come from encounters with grantees. "Often, our grantees are the ones who 'keep us on the path,'" she observes. Receiving a desk full of reflective letters from the nuns who are prolific and expressive correspondents, she draws comparisons to her previous life in the corporate world. "What other job could be so enriching?" she asks.

Lynn Schusterman's Story: Three Thousand Years of Jewish Giving

The Jews have been making gifts to communities wherever we are in the world for three thousand years.

—Lynn Schusterman, Chair of the Charles
and Lynn Schusterman Family Foundation

Raised in a home where giving back was a core value, Lynn Schusterman recalls accompanying her father on childhood visits to elderly folks in their community. "We used to pick peonies from our garden for little old ladies who had never written a check in their life and could not drive. My father would help widows with their finances and drive them to the grocery store. I remember him telling a struggling medical student to whom he had advanced tuition payments that he didn't expect to be repaid, but wanted him to succeed so he could 'pay it forward' by helping someone else." Lynn grew to understand that these expressions of her father's universal ideals stemmed from deeply rooted Jewish values.

As a newlywed couple with little to spare, Lynn and her late husband, Charles, impulsively responded to a desperate need to help the State of Israel survive yet another existential challenge, contributing $500 they did not have to the United Jewish Appeal. Her husband's later success in building Samson Resources Co. in Tulsa, Oklahoma, which ranks among the largest independent energy exploration and production companies in the United States, created the philanthropic capital to express the lessons she learned from her father and the values she shared with her husband.

When the Schustermans established their family foundation in 1987, they gave powerful expression to two passions that defined their distinctiveness: their enduring dedication to *tikkun olam*— repairing the world—and their commitment to enhancing the quality of life in Tulsa, Oklahoma, especially in areas of education, child development, and community service.

Born to Russian immigrants living in Tulsa, Charles Schusterman grew up in an Orthodox Jewish home while Lynn grew up in a Reform Jewish family. Although neither of them was religious, their shared journey made Lynn "fall in love with being Jewish."

Charles was convinced that Jewishness informed every aspect of his being—his family, his community, his philanthropy—and that this consciousness helped him achieve success in all dimensions of his life, as it has contributed throughout time to the achievements of other Jews.

In a handwritten note, he crystallized this thought: "Our unique history has acculturated us to do special things in the world. (Note: How else could a people so few in number have such a dramatic and positive impact on civilization?)"[1]

Lynn shared his devotion to those principles. In her written response to Warren Buffett's invitation to join the Giving Pledge, she describes why her family invests in Jewish life as "the belief that the Jewish people still have much to contribute to society and a deep sense of responsibility to ensure that the opportunity to share those gifts exist in the future."

The Schustermans felt that until a united Jewish community committed itself to transforming its major institutions into centers of excellence, the positive influence of the Jewish people would all but disappear. Their philanthropy fosters the renaissance of Jewish life and aims to engage a critical mass of Jews in North America, Israel, and the former Soviet Union so they continue to have a positive impact on the world—to serve as a "light unto nations." Jewish renewal, expressed in communal life, would ensure that modern Jews would walk in the footsteps of an ancient people, whose moral values would perpetuate an unbroken tradition of "repairing the world" in which they live.

The Schusterman Family Foundation was infused with the spirit of Charles Schusterman, who was diagnosed with chronic myelogenous leukemia (CML) at the age of 47. In the 12 years following his diagnosis, Charles applied his intellect and passion to shaping the foundation's philanthropic vision. His habit of carrying a sharpened pencil and an unlined pad to capture his ideas provided

---

[1]Schusterman Family Foundation Annual Report, www.schusterman.org.

a trail of succinct notes that reflect the philosophy behind the Foundation's philanthropic agenda. "It chronicles our past, explains our present, and illuminates our future," explains Lynn, who used those handwritten notes in the Foundation's first annual report to visualize the legacy he left.

His notes on philanthropy express Charles's desire to "help solve the problems of the twenty-first century," and his philanthropic aspirations. They include:

- "Try to do something that has not been done before . . . but that takes time . . . has more risk and takes energy and skill . . . *if* you want it done well."[2]
- "We want to be known as a thoughtful, serious, efficient foundation. By our participating with a nonprofit or recommending it, we want that to be considered a stamp of approval from others to do the same. This is positive leadership."[3]

After his death, Lynn put those thoughts into action, providing the leadership to engage young Jews through Birthright and programs for leadership development, the enrichment of Jewish life on campuses and in the former Soviet Union, and community service programs in Tulsa, Oklahoma, and Israel.

Mindful of the 3,000-year journey of her people, her husband's legacy, and the memories of their modest beginnings when they embarked on this philanthropic journey, she joined the Giving Pledge with the expressed intention:

> To devote the majority of my resources to the pursuit of the charitable agenda Charlie and I set for our family more than 20 years ago. I do so with respect and admiration for the efforts of those with whom we are engaged in similar endeavors, and in full recognition of the scope of the challenges that confront us. I also pledge to continue working to encourage others, including emerging philanthropists of all ages and all capacities, to join us in seeking to repair the world; the further we broaden our reach, the more we will benefit from the diversity

---

[2] 9/27/92 from annual report.
[3] Charity Philosophy 9/21/96 from annual report.

of people, perspectives and approaches as we strive to tackle problems of common concern. The same is true in the Jewish community, one I hope will receive greater support in the future from those with the means to assist.

Although the issues that confront all of us are daunting, we accept the teaching of Rabbi Tarfon in Pirkei Avot, "You are not obligated to complete the task, but neither are you free to desist from trying."[4]

Summary

Lynn Schusterman and Amy Goldman both respond to the challenges of "repairing the world" by bringing the best of their spiritual traditions to bear on crafting solutions that come from the source of their traditions.

The last chapter concludes our journey with a synthesis of lessons to become a "gifted giver."

---

[4]Lynn Schusterman's letter on joining the Giving Pledge.

CHAPTER

16

The Philanthropic Journey

It's only after you embark on this voyage of philanthropy that you realize how far there is to go. We're adrift in a sea of need. I don't think we can paddle aimlessly in our little boats. We'll have to stitch together sails from whatever we can find and catch the wind. On the other side of this vast ocean, there's a new world. But it's a better, more possible new world than all the new worlds we've ever known. This time we're not sailing to fill our pockets with the spices of India. . . . What we're sailing toward is our better selves.

—Alan Alda, actor, from an address delivered to the Council on Foundations' 1995 Family Foundation Conference

The voyage of discovery that leads us to our "better selves" yields the gift of self-transformation that comes from opening our hearts to humanity. We are transformed by encounters with people whose lives we touch, inspired by communities that live up to their own aspirations, and dare to imagine what else we can do as philanthropic explorers.

A Vision for Change

The philanthropic journey begins with a vision for change. Finding our way through a vast ocean of need begins with a vision connected to who we are and what we care passionately enough about to change.

Identifying our passion, the guiding "pole-star" of our inner journey, requires introspection and reflection. Giving ourselves the gift of time—time to encounter our self, to remember who we are and what we always wanted to do—reconnects us to our sense of purpose and clarifies the higher values that impact our giving. As purpose comes into focus, an emerging horizon of possibilities appears.

Discovering who we are in relation to the change we intend to create in this world allows deeper commitment and greater energy. Attention to what gets in the way of our wholeness, the barriers that interfere with our ability to act on our higher calling, is key to unleashing our creative potential so we can give from the richness of who we are. Accessing this deeper level of creativity within a wholistic framework anchors our philanthropy to a focal point from which to leverage change.

The Skills We Learn, the Gifts We Gain

In most of the conversations I had while writing this book, I heard many voices urging philanthropists to *"Listen! Listen! Listen!"* A good philanthropist needs this capacity for deep listening, to cultivate a culture of creative receptivity that allows the opening of minds and hearts to grantees who "keep us on the path." Our ability to listen enables change when we are transformed by what we hear to act from a larger whole.

This particular kind of listening, a quality of attention, awareness, and intention with transformative value is described by Dr. Otto Scharmer in his book, *Theory U: Leading from the Future as It Emerges.* He writes of the inner capacity of expanded listening that "moves your listening and playing from within to beyond yourself,"[1] He explains the levels of this deep listening process that leads to self-transformation:

Listening 1: Downloading (reconfirming your habits of thought).

Listening 2: Factual (listening by paying attention to facts and noticing new data).

Listening 3: Empathic (shifting to really feel how another feels, with an open heart to connect directly with another person from within).

---

[1]C. Otto Scharmer, *Theory U: Leading from the Future as It Emerges* (San Francisco: Berrett-Koehler Publishers, 2007).

Listening 4: Generative (experiencing a subtle profound change that transforms the listener through communion with a deeper sense of knowing and self to access knowledge of your best future possibility).

Learning to listen with an "inner ear" could unlock the full potential of philanthropy for enabling change. We bring this listening capacity to the way we "bridge" the world of access with the world of need, really listening to people at the center of problems offer their own solutions and empowering change agents who will transform their own communities.

Philanthropy is a work-in-progress. Philanthropists are lifelong learners and every day brings new opportunities for learning. We learn from our mistakes. We learn from other givers and our grant recipients. We learn by collaborating, convening, partnering, leveraging. We learn to connect the dots and see the big picture.

Philanthropy is the art of giving. The "gifted giver" adds value and meaning that transcends the substance of the gift, becoming a catalyst for transformation.

Philanthropists are the risk-takers who venture to use our resources to make long-term bets, armed with a vision for change, enlightened by experience, and inspired by our faith in humanity.

We are gutsy explorers and creative catalysts who ask ourselves:

- Do I Dare?
- Am I bold enough to Stre-e-etch, to make my philanthropy New, to make it Sing?

We are change makers, not just grant makers. While we struggle to define success, to measure outcomes, to balance doing good with making change, we mustn't lose sight of the people whose lives we want to affect, as we deepen our souls and we encounter humanity.

Our personal transformation ripples out into societal transformation and creates the systems change we want to see in the world. The ripple effect begins with ourselves. To create the change we want to see in this world, we have to "be the change." The ultimate gift we gain from our philanthropy is the gift of our own transformation as we discover our "better selves" in the process of encountering humanity.

Summary

It is our hope in writing this book that the lessons generously shared by leading innovators in philanthropy will enrich your giving practice and inspire you to sail toward your "better selves." We encourage you to spread them freely and to begin to express your passion, as Mother Teresa suggested, by "doing small things with great love!"

Resources

Dr. Otto Scharmer (www.ottoscharmer.com) is a senior lecturer at MIT and the founding chair of ELIAS, a program linking 20 leading global institutions from business, government, and civil society in order to prototype profound system innovations for a more sustainable world. The founding chair of the Presencing Institute and a visiting professor at the Center for Innovation and Knowledge Research at the Helsinki School of Economics, he serves as a consultant to global companies, international institutions, and cross-sector change initiatives in North America, Europe, Asia, and Africa. He has also co-designed and delivered award-winning leadership programs for client organizations including Daimler, PricewaterhouseCoopers, and Fujitsu.

Read Dr. Scharmer's article "Strategic Leadership within the Triad Growth-Employment-Ecology." It won the McKinsey Research Award in 1991.

Dr. Scharmer's books include *Theory U: Leading from the Future as It Emerges* (Berrett-Koehler Publishers, 2009) and *Presence: An Exploration of Profound Change in People, Organizations, and Society* (Crown Business, 2005), co-authored with Peter Senge, Joseph Jaworski, and Betty Sue Flowers. To order these books, go to theoryU.com or www.amazon.com.

You can also visit the Presencing Institute at www.presencing .com/. "Presencing" facilitates innovation and changes processes within companies and across societal systems.

And for copies of an executive summary of Dr. Scharmer's *Theory U* book, go to www.theoryU.com to download and print your own PDF file or leave your e-mail address to receive free printed booklets.

About the Authors

Peter J. Klein, CFA

Peter Klein has been the president/treasurer of the Claire Friedlander Family Foundation since it was first established in 2008. For the past 25 years, he has been employed as a financial advisor, serving his clients' objectives while researching a wide spectrum of investment solutions. Peter, a senior vice president/investments based in the UBS Melville (Long Island) New York office, and his team provide investment management and wealth management services to their clients—predominately private foundations and their founders. In 2009, he was awarded membership in the UBS "Global Circle of Excellence."

Peter is a Chartered Financial Analyst (CFA). He received his bachelor of arts degree in economics from the State University of New York-Stony Brook (1987) and earned a master of business administration degree, majoring in finance, from Baruch College-City University of New York (1995).

Peter has been an adjunct professor of graduate finance at C.W. Post College of Long Island University. He is the author of *Getting Started in Security Analysis*, published by John Wiley & Sons (1998 and 2009). Throughout his career, Peter has been called on for major television/radio appearances to discuss investment strategy, analysis, and related financial services.

His professional affiliations include: the CFA Institute, the New York Society of Security Analysts, Bronx High School of Science Alumni Association, Westinghouse (Intel) Science Talent Search Award Alumni, and the Nu-Health Advisory Board.

Peter's community service activities include: St. Patrick's School Golf Committee (Huntington, New York), St. Anthony's Father's Guild (Huntington, New York), Juvenile Diabetes Research Foundation (New York City, New York), the Rosen Family Wellness Center at Long Island Jewish Medical Center (New Hyde Park,

New York), and the Holocaust Museum & Tolerance Center of Nassau County (Glen Cove, New York).

Peter Klein and his wife, Irene, are the parents of three children, and residents of Huntington, New York.

Angelica Berrie

Angelica Berrie is president of the Russell Berrie Foundation, which has made transformational gifts to:

- Diabetes Care and Research at the Naomi Berrie Diabetes Center, Columbia University.
- Nanotechnology Research at the Russ Berrie Nanotechnology Institute, Technion University in Israel.
- Interfaith Fellowships to the Pope John Paul II Center for Inter-Religious Studies, the Angelicum in Rome.
- Ambulatory Care at the Angelica and Russ Berrie Center for Humanistic Care, Englewood Hospital in New Jersey.
- Cancer Care at the Sister Patricia Lynch Regional Cancer Care Center, Holy Name Hospital in New Jersey.
- Arts and Culture at the Russ Berrie Hall in the Bergen Performing Arts Center, Englewood, New Jersey, and the Angelica and Russ Berrie Performing Arts Center in Ramapo College, New Jersey.
- Salesmanship at the Russ Berrie Institute for Professional Sales in William Paterson University, New Jersey.
- The Russ Berrie Senior Home for Jewish Living in Rockleigh, New Jersey.
- Leadership Development with the Berrie Fellows Program through the UJA of Northern New Jersey.

Angelica currently serves as board chair of the Shalom Hartman Institute of North America, a pluralistic center of study in Jerusalem.

She chairs the board of the Center for Inter-Religious Understanding in New Jersey.

She helped found Gilda's Club of Northern New Jersey and became board chair of Gilda's Club Worldwide, a free social and emotional support network of clubhouses for families living with cancer across North America.

She is on the board of the Joint Distribution Committee and vice president of Ofanim, a nonprofit organization in Israel whose mission is to deliver high-quality supplemental education to children in the periphery using mobile classrooms.

After the death of her husband, New Jersey sales entrepreneur and philanthropist Russell Berrie, Angelica assumed the role of vice chair and CEO of Russ Berrie & Co., a global gift company listed on the New York Stock Exchange, known for its teddy bears and Russ Trolls.

She is currently CEO of Kate's Paperie, an iconic New York paper specialty retailer; a partner in Boston International, a wholesale gift company specializing in paper party goods; and chair of Global Nomad, an experiential travel design company based in Hong Kong.

Her other adventurous pursuits include skydiving and rappelling.

Angelica has been a featured speaker at the following philanthropy conferences:

- Jewish Funders Network West Coast Series: Inside the Philanthropist's Studio in Los Angeles (2011).
- University of Oklahoma's Women's Philanthropy Network Symposium on Friends, Family and Philanthropy in Tulsa, Oklahoma (2011).
- 2011 Women's Philanthropy Institute's 22nd Annual Symposium in Chicago on Women Worldwide: Leading through Philanthropy.
- Jewish Funders Network Conference in Philadelphia (2011).
- The Women's Philanthropy Institute's New York Times Knowledge Network course on Women and Philanthropy—The Time is Now, March 8–15, 2010.
- The Philanthropic Network Forum in San Francisco (2010).
- TPI's 20th year Symposium for Donors and Corporate Leaders in Boston (2009).
- CMS Philanthropy Conference in Florida (2008).

About the Participants

Anthony Weller

Anthony Weller is a leading global practitioner in the field of personal, corporate, and organizational consciousness and transformation, acknowledged as one of the best explorers and practitioners of the field worldwide. Tony has established a distinguished career helping thousands of individuals, families, and big businesses with his unique working models and multidisciplinary approach.

Over the past 20 years, Tony has worked with a select number of the world's wealthy families in the often difficult and immensely rewarding field of successful intergenerational wealth transition and a new vision for philanthropy and big business as agents for economic, social, and environmental engagement and change.

Tony is an ordained interfaith minister, working with religious conflicts, whose own philanthropy is the gifting of his time in support of individuals and organizations that focus on meaningful, manageable change for the world. With Professor James Lovelock and the Schumacher College, he sponsored 50 of the world's top climate specialists and was a keynote speaker at the pivotal Global Change conference in Dartington, England.

His passion is the reimagining of the educational process for the well-being of children, our future world leaders.

Susan Lewis Solomont

Susan Lewis Solomont lives in Madrid, Spain, with her husband, Alan D. Solomont, United States Ambassador to Spain and Andorra.

Prior to moving to Madrid, Susan was a senior philanthropic adviser at The Philanthropic Initiative (TPI) in Boston, Massachusetts, a not-for-profit consulting firm that advises individuals, family foundations, and corporations on how to design philanthropy programs that create meaning and impact.

For the past 10 years at TPI, Susan has worked with many corporate clients to help develop strategic approaches to corporate civic engagement. She has expertise in board relations and governance, program design, and program implementation and evaluation. She has helped to develop focused, thoughtful, and results-oriented approaches to charitable giving and community engagement.

Prior to joining TPI, Susan had an independent consulting company that worked with numerous not-for-profit organizations, helping them with governance, board relations, and capacity-building strategies.

She worked for 18 years as the Director of Corporate Development at WGBH, the Boston public broadcasting station, where she successfully raised funds for WGBH's premier television and radio programs, raising over $35 million annually from local and national companies.

Susan believes in being an active citizen of the community in which she lives. She has been a trustee on the boards of many leading institutions, including the Tufts University Friedman School of Nutrition, the New England Aquarium (board chair from 1999 to 2004), Women's Health Initiative at Boston Medical Center (co-chair from 2006 to 2009), Newton-Wellesley Hospital, the Citi Center for the Performing Arts (formerly the Wang Center), the Commonwealth Institute, the WGBH Board of Overseers, Boston Jewish Community Women's Fund, and Temple Beth Elohim (chair, Building Campaign, 2005–2009).

Kenneth E. Behring

Kenneth Behring is the founder and chairman of the Wheelchair Foundation and director of the China Foundation for Disabled People and the Water Leaders Foundation, and was listed in 2004 among *Forbes*'s 50 most generous philanthropists in the United States.

Born in 1928, the California businessman began his career as a car dealer in Wisconsin. He entered real estate development in the 1960s, and over the course of the next 35 years, his companies created numerous planned communities in Florida and California, including the world-renowned Blackhawk development near San Francisco.

While developing the community of Blackhawk, Ken established the Museum of Art, Science, and Culture, in partnership with the University of California at Berkeley. In the 1990s, he also established the Behring Education School at Berkeley, for the purpose of educating and qualifying former teachers to become school principals for inner-city schools.

After purchasing the Seattle Seahawks in 1988, he started the Seattle Seahawks Charitable Foundation, which benefited educational and other children's charities. Ken made Smithsonian Institution history when he donated $100 million to it, for which he was presented the prestigious Order of James Smithson in 1998.

The establishment of the Wheelchair Foundation in 2000 marks the most recent chapter in Ken's philanthropic efforts to improve the lives of disadvantaged people around the world. This was inspired by his concern for hundreds of people he has met who are unable to walk and who cannot afford a wheelchair.

He has also recently established the Water Leaders Foundation, to change the lives of millions of people in poverty around the world with comprehensive and sustainable water solutions. He aims to create an entire safe-water generation by eliminating water-related deaths and disabilities with affordable technology to turn undrinkable water into pure and healthy water.

Ken was inducted into the American Academy of Achievement in 1989, the California Building Hall of Fame in 1992, and the Bay Area Sports Hall of Fame in 1994. He serves or has served on many boards of education and philanthropic organizations, including the Medal of Honor Foundation, the Smithsonian National Board, the D-Day Museum, the Academy of Achievement, and the Shanghai Museum of Science and Technology, and was given an honorary doctorate degree by Brigham Young University.

Ken is also an honorable citizen of the Chinese cities of Suzhou and Dalian. In 2004 and 2006, he received the Magnolia award from the Shanghai municipal government. He has five sons and 10 grandchildren, and resides in Blackhawk, California, with his wife, Patricia.

Glen Macdonald

Glen Macdonald co-founded and serves as president of the Wealth & Giving Forum. He leads a team of professionals dedicated to developing innovative programs and partnerships, to fulfill the organization's mission to promote philanthropy among families of means. He has presented his perspective on philanthropy, social entrepreneurship, and the responsible deployment of capital at various conferences, including the Forum 2000 Conference in Prague in October 2006; Renaissance Weekend in Monterey, California, in September 2007; and the Forbes Family Business Conference in October 2007.

Glen is currently with the Olson Financial Group, based in Summit, New Jersey. He spent most of his private-sector career at PricewaterhouseCoopers, where he was a partner in the management consulting unit and advised companies on business strategy, marketing, sales, restructurings, process improvement, and financial management. Glen was also formerly a vice president at Adventis Corporation, a strategy consultancy, where he served as the executive in charge of the firm's New York office. His views on industry and management have appeared in a *Wall Street Journal* article and in interviews with the *New York Times, Financial Times, Chicago Tribune,* and various business journals.

Before his career in industry, Glen was a lecturer in international politics at the University of North Carolina at Chapel Hill (UNC) and a special adviser to UNESCO in Paris on technology policies in developing economies.

Glen received his BA with highest honors in political science and economics and his MA in international relations, both from UNC-Chapel Hill. He has been a recipient of several fellowships, including a Ford Foundation Fellowship at the Harvard Center for International Affairs, the French government's Chateaubriand Fellowship, and a Fulbright scholarship to conduct field research in Mexico. His research and writings have focused on economic development, foreign investment in developing economies, conflict resolution, and the formation of common markets.

Glen is a member of Year Up New York City's board of directors and serves as an adviser to several nonprofit organizations. He resides with his wife, Sylvie, and their three children in Westfield, New Jersey.

Peter Karoff

Peter Karoff is founder and chairman of The Philanthropic Initiative (TPI), a nonprofit consulting firm that works with donors to support them in achieving engaged, high-impact philanthropy. TPI provides research, planning, program design, and management services to individuals and families as well as corporate, private, and community foundation funders. In addition to its consulting practice, TPI works to encourage the growth of more effective giving through research, educational programming, and publications. Founded in 1989, TPI has worked with over 250 donors and philanthropic institutions around the world.

A fundamental tenet of TPI's work is that giving, when targeted in smart and innovative ways, can leverage constructive, sustainable change for individuals and their communities. Giving, as TPI sees it, is serious investing, driven by a donor's values, passions, imagination, skills, and ever-growing understanding of the issues.

In addition to its consulting practice, TPI works to encourage the growth of more effective giving through research, educational programming, and publications.

Peter's primary role in TPI has been in the development of the organization, its unique client base, and the evolution of the concept and language of strategic philanthropy. He writes and speaks about these ideas to donor and philanthropic communities and is an experienced facilitator of those issues. He is working on a book, *The Generous American—The Story of 200 Years of Private Action for Public Good,* and has also written *The World We Want* with Jane Maddox.

Peter holds an adjunct position at Tufts University College of Citizenship and Public Affairs.

Peter has been a trustee or board member on more than 30 not-for-profit organizations working within a range of issue areas, including national security, the environment, community development, health and human services, race and intergroup relations, and the arts. Boards have included the New England Aquarium, New England Foundation for the Arts, Newton-Wellesley Hospital, Massachusetts Association of Mental Health, Business Executives for National Security, National Poetry Series, and Fund for Urban Negro Development.

He has served as director of Blackside Productions (producer of *Eyes on the Prize*) and frequently speaks and writes on philanthropy.

He was editor of the book, *Just Money—A Critique of Contemporary American Philanthropy*. His articles on philanthropy have appeared in several publications, including *Trusts & Estates* and *World Link* magazine.

A graduate of Brandeis University, Peter received an MFA in writing from Columbia University in 1988. In 1989, he was made a Fellow of the MacDowell Colony. Peter's poems have been published in literary magazines and anthologies.

Joel L. Fleishman

Joel Fleishman is Professor of Law and Public Policy Sciences at Duke University (AB 1955, JD 1959, MA in drama 1959, University of North Carolina; LLM 1960, Yale University) and a native of Fayetteville, North Carolina. He began his career in 1960 as assistant to the director of the Walter E. Meyer Research Institute of Law at Yale. From 1961 to 1965, he served as legal assistant to the governor of North Carolina. He then returned to Yale, first as director of the Yale Summer High School, and then as associate provost for Urban Studies and Programs. In 1969, he became associate chairman of the Center for the Study of the City and Its Environment and associate director of the Institute of Social Science at Yale.

In 1971, he came to Duke as a member of the law faculty and as director of the Institute of Policy Sciences and Public Affairs, now the Sanford School of Public Policy, in which position he served until 1983. He is now Professor of Law and Public Policy and director of the Heyman Center on Ethics, Public Policy and the Professions at Duke University's Center for Strategic Philanthropy, which assembles information on foundation decision making, problems, and analytics to promote transparency of decision making. He teaches a course on philanthropy and directs the Duke Foundation Research Program on impact measurement and strategic choice making by foundations.

From 1993 until 2001, Joel was president of Atlantic Philanthropic Service Company, a component of Atlantic Philanthropies.

His principal writings deal with legal regulation and financing of political activities as well as the regulation of not-for-profit organizations. He is author of *The Foundation: A Great American Secret— How Private Money Is Changing the World* (Public Affairs Books, 2007) and co-author of a new book with Tom Tierney, *Give Smart: How to Get Results from Your Philanthropy*, published by the Bridgespan Group.

He is now serving as co-chair of Independent Sector's Committee on the Self-Regulation of Nonprofit Organizations.[1]

Lisa Nigro

Lisa Nigro is the founder and co-chair of the Inspiration Corporation, a Chicago-based nonprofit that helps people who are affected by homelessness and poverty to improve their lives and increase self-sufficiency through the provision of social services, employment training and placement, and housing.

Lisa's philanthropic work started in the 1980s, when as a police officer she was discouraged from engaging the people she met on her beat. In 1989, stymied by her inability to respond personally to people in need, Lisa quit her job with the support of her husband, Perry. She borrowed her nephew's red wagon and filled it with coffee and sandwiches, which she handed out to people on the streets in uptown Chicago, where 10 percent of the city's homeless population lived.

With her on that first day was her friend Lisa Madigan. They were able to speak with people and learn about their issues. Finally satisfied with the richness of her relationships with Chicago's homeless, Lisa wanted to do more for them; she fitted her car with a mobile kitchen and set up outdoor cafes, serving hot, nutritious meals. Eventually, the Inspiration Cafe moved to a bus and then to a storefront.

Lisa used her charisma and vision and quickly mobilized masses of volunteers. Early supporters included philanthropists Richard Driehaus and Jim Mabie. Kraft Foods funded the mobile kitchen, and real estate developer Peter Holsten offered the Inspiration Cafe its first home. The Inspiration Corporation has since grown into a $3.8 million agency, assisting thousands of individuals each year.

---

[1]Case studies on philanthropy available from Duke web site (www.sanford.duke.edu).

Today, in addition to serving as the public face and guiding spirit of the Inspiration Corporation, Lisa travels the country as a speaker on topics related to volunteerism, nonprofit management, and personal growth.

Lisa is a BS business graduate of National Lewis University (2001). Additional education includes the Institute of Spiritual Companionship and Life Purpose Institute. Lisa and Perry live in Rogers Park with their children, Emily and Nick.

Chip Paillex

Chip Paillex is the president and founder of America's Grow-a-Row, a private garden project he created back in 2002 that he formally converted into a fully operational farming nonprofit program in 2007. His responsibilities include overall strategic development, short- and long-term organizational planning, operations, distribution logistics, volume and spend management, public relations, benefactor relationship building, assisting with volunteer recruitment, and fund raising.

As a result of his personal volunteer accomplishments in this sector, Chip has also been presented the 2007 National Jefferson Award for community service, the 2008 United Way of Hunterdon County Volunteer of the Year award, as well as the 2007 Northwest New Jersey Community Action Program (NORWESCAP) Outstanding and Dedicated Service award. In 2010, Chip was publicly recognized at the inaugural swearing-in ceremony for the newly elected New Jersey governor, Chris Christie. He was cited for his contribution in building the America's Grow-a-Row organization to where it is today. Chip was also presented with the Russ Berrie Award for making a difference in 2010.

Prior to his entry into the nonprofit arena, Chip spent 17 years in sales and marketing as well as customer development for the North American Unilever Foods Corporation. There he was responsible for the strategic development of all local marketing initiatives, as well as financial analysis, in support of a $450 million regional business. His experience made him proficient in strategic business plan development, volume and fund management, supply chain management, sales team management, and overall marketing implementation. While serving under the Unilever umbrella, Chip was presented with several top sales awards across his 17-year tenure, in recognition of his ability to motivate and manage the sales teams under his direction.

For the past three years, Chip has been employed by PNC Reverse Mortgage, a division of PNC Bank, where he currently covers the central and northwest PNC Bank regions. In 2009 and 2010 he led the entire PNC Reverse Mortgage division in both unit and dollar sales.

Peggy Dulany

Peggy Dulany is chair of the Synergos Institute, an independent nonprofit organization dedicated to creating effective, sustainable, and locally based solutions to poverty. Drawing from her experience living and working in Rio de Janeiro as a young woman, she realized that the people most affected by adverse living conditions also have the greatest energy and motivation to solve their problems. The resources they lack are the connections to the economic and political realms where necessary changes can affect whole communities.

Peggy founded Synergos in 1986, to facilitate relationships between grassroots leaders and political or business leaders, people who otherwise would not have access to each other, so that they can develop long-term relationships and forge new paths in overcoming poverty.

Her career has included heading a Boston-area public high school program for dropouts for six years, and consulting with the United Nations and the Ford Foundation on health care and family planning in Brazil, the United States, and Portugal, and with the National Endowment for the Arts on nonprofit management and planning. She was senior vice president of the New York City Partnership for five years, where she headed the Youth Employment and Education programs.

Peggy is an honors graduate of Radcliffe College and holds a doctorate in education from Harvard University. She is also chair of ProVentures, a business development company for Latin America and Southern Africa. She has sat on more than 30 nonprofit and corporate boards, including Stone Barns Center for Food and Agriculture, the Rockefeller Brothers Fund, and the Africa-America Institute, among others.

Ellen Remmer

Ellen Remmer is president and CEO of The Philanthropic Initiative (TPI). Working directly with families, independent foundations, and corporations to create focused, strategic giving programs and practical governance structures, she works with community foundations and financial services firms to strengthen their capacity to help private donors realize their philanthropic goals.

Ellen has developed many of TPI's signature donor learning programs and is a frequent speaker and workshop leader on the subjects of family philanthropy, strategic giving, and women as donors. Her publications include: *What's a Donor to Do? The State of Donor Resources in America Today*; *A Primer for Families on Strategic Giving*; *Raising Children with Philanthropic Values*; *Evaluating Your Philanthropy*; and "The Dynamics of Women and Family Philanthropy," a chapter in *The Transformative Power of Women's Philanthropy* (2006).

Ellen has worked at TPI since 1993, when her own family foundation benefited from TPI's strategic planning assistance. She also serves as a board member of her family's foundation, which supports programs that help disadvantaged girls take charge of their lives. She is on the board of governors of Indiana University's Center on Philanthropy, where she chairs the Women's Philanthropy Institute's advisory committee, and is on the steering committee of Boston Funders Supporting Women and Girls. She also serves on the board of the Associated Grantmakers Program and on the Council on Foundation's Family Foundation Committee.

Ellen is a 1975 graduate of Wesleyan University and received her MBA from the Amos Tuck School of Business at Dartmouth College.

Monica Winsor

Monica Winsor is a trustee of two family foundations—the William H. Donner Foundation and the Donner Canadian Foundation. A graduate of Brown University, she is an independent consultant to individuals and social beneficiary organizations with a focus on Africa, global health, integrative health, human rights, and women's rights. She is a co-founder of and adviser to Inspired Philanthropy

Group (IPG), providing strategic philanthropic advice, innovative fund raising, and cause-related marketing to individuals, foundations, and not-for-profit organizations working together to make a sustainable and positive impact on the planet. Prior to IPG, Monica helped launch the "6 Villages: 1 Global Fight Against AIDS" campaign for FXB International, raising awareness and funding for sustainable economic development programs in Uganda and Rwanda.

Sharna Goldseker

Sharna Goldseker has 13 years of experience in the nonprofit sector, including 10 in the philanthropic field as a grant maker and as a consultant to families, foundations, and federations on next-generation and multigenerational philanthropy.

Sharna is currently vice president of the Andrea and Charles Bronfman Philanthropies (ACBP) (www.acbp.net), where she directs 21/64 (www.2164.net), a nonprofit consulting division specializing in next-generation and multigenerational strategic philanthropy. In that capacity, she facilitates Grand Street (www.grandstreetnetwork .net), a network of 70 18- to 28-year-olds who are or will be involved in their family's philanthropy; manages Slingshot (www.slingshot fund.org), a funding collaborative for Jewish funders in their 20s and 30s; speaks and consults on generational transitions using 21/64's uniquely developed tools such as the Grandparent Legacy Project; and trains other grant makers and consultants on 21/64's approach to multigenerational philanthropy.

Previous to ACBP, Sharna was a program officer at Philanthropy Advisors, a multifamily foundation office in New York, where she managed grant making in the areas of legal rights, reproductive health, social justice, and the environment. Sharna was also a project coordinator for Enterprise Homes, a subsidiary of the Enterprise Foundation, where she developed affordable rental and for-sale housing in Maryland.

Sharna graduated Phi Beta Kappa with a BA from the University of Pennsylvania with majors in urban studies and religious studies. She has a master's in public administration in nonprofit management from New York University's Robert F. Wagner Graduate School of Public Service, where she was the inaugural Charles H. Tenney

Fellow. She also has training in organizational development and group dynamics.

Sharna currently serves on the board of the Goldseker Foundation as well as the Council on Foundations' Committee on Family Philanthropy and Next Generation Task Force.

Ruth Cummings

Ruth Cummings currently works as an independent consultant focusing on creative community building—leveraging culture, creativity, and other community assets to advance the economic, social, civic, and physical development of Jerusalem.

Her lifelong interest in Jewish identity, international art and culture, and service were inspired by the values and life of her grandfather, Nathan Cummings. She is also the executor of his estate and a founding member of the Nathan Cummings Foundation since 1988. She values participating in this legacy of optimism and *tikkun olam* (repairing the world) by remaining active with these issues as a foundation trustee, a professional consultant, and a lay leader.

She also has been a founding member at the Garrison Institute (2005–2007) and member of the advisory council (2008 to the present). The Garrison Institute fosters a dynamic connection between contemplative practice and its transformative power to empower activists to effect change in environmental and social fields. Other experiences include her work at The Lab, an arts incubator for developing professional careers of Jerusalem-based performing artists; resource and program development (2008 to the present); and Bakehila ("In the Community"), an educational enrichment program conducted with post-high-school and pre-army volunteers to benefit fifth- to eighth-grade students in four disadvantaged Jerusalem neighborhoods, including Bet Safafa, an Arab-Israeli community (2008 to the present).

Ruth graduated summa cum laude from Boston University, where she earned a BA with a major in art history and a minor in French literature. She earned her MA at Columbia University Teachers College in Art and Education, and pursued further Jewish studies at Pardes Institute of Jewish Studies (1994 to 1996).

Lance E. Lindblom

Lance E. Lindblom was appointed president and CEO of the Nathan Cummings Foundation (NCF) in December 2000. Before he joined the staff of NCF, Lance served as a program officer at the Ford Foundation, focusing on democratic accountability, economic and social policy, and globalization. Prior to that position, he was the executive vice president at Soros Foundation's Open Society Institute/Open Society Fund. For 13 years, he worked at J. Roderick MacArthur Foundation, first serving as executive director from 1980 to 1984 and then as president and CEO from 1984 to 1994.

Lance has held the following governmental positions: deputy director of the Chicago Mayor's Office of Budget and Management; chief of the Special Projects Unit and senior program analyst and budget examiner at the Governor's Office of the Illinois Bureau of the Budget; and economic and program analyst at the Illinois Economic and Fiscal Commission of the Illinois General Assembly. He also was a litigator at Jenner and Block, a law firm in Chicago.

Lance graduated magna cum laude from Harvard College. He received a master's degree in public affairs from Princeton University and a JD degree from the University of Chicago Law School.

Scott McVay

Scott McVay is founding executive director of the Robert Sterling Clark Foundation and the Geraldine R. Dodge Foundation, where he led efforts in strategic grant making in education (K–12), the arts, critical issues, and the welfare of animals.

Among his initiatives at the Dodge Foundation was a national program beginning in 1983 to advance Chinese language learning in high schools nationwide, which has grown today to over 2,000 schools. Dodge's initiative on behalf of poetry, poets, and teachers has offered a biennial Poetry Festival at Waterloo Village, which made possible 26 hours on PBS, 21 by Bill Moyers (*The Power of the Word*, 1989; *The Language of Life*, 1995; and *Fooling with Words*, 1999), reaching 50 million people.

Other initiatives included backing superb teachers, encouraging able students nationwide to become teachers, supporting public school principals to become more active learners and founding the Principals' Center of the Garden State, seeing theaters and city gardens as crucibles for building community, and giving top veterinary students in North America the chance to work at the frontiers of veterinary research.

Scott worked previously for Princeton University for 11 years as recording secretary and assistant to the president (Robert F. Goheen). A graduate of Princeton in English literature, he served in the U.S. Army in Berlin, Germany (1956–1958) as a special agent with the Counterintelligence Corps.

He has an avocational interest in whales, dolphins, and porpoises and is the author of papers in *Scientific American* (1966), *Science* ("Songs of Humpback Whales," with Roger Payne, 1971), *Natural History*, the *New York Times*, and the book *Mind in the Waters* (Scribner, 2007), among others. Scott organized and led two expeditions to the Alaskan Arctic to study, record, and film the rare bowhead whale, resulting in a cover paper in *American Scientist* (1973) and a film documentary by the National Film Board of Canada (1975).

He has published chapters in books, including *Just Money: A Critique of Contemporary American Philanthropy* (TPI Editions), *The Biophilia Hypothesis* (Island Press), *33 Steps to Biology* (Scientific American), and *Child Abuse, Domestic Violence, and Animal Abuse* (Purdue University Press).

Scott is also keenly interested in bright children and youths, who are, surprisingly, often the most neglected segment of the school population, and serves on the national board of Johns Hopkins's Center for Talented Youth.

He served with enthusiasm as the 16th president of the Chautauqua Institution in Western New York State, which attracts 6,000 to 7,000 people to the grounds every day during a 2,100-event summer season.

In 2010, he and his wife, Hella, created a Poetry Trail in Greenway Meadows, in Princeton Township, as a gift to the community, that was dedicated in October by the D&R Greenway Land Trust. The trail is located on a tract of 55 acres, and honors the voices of poets reaching back over 2,000 years and into 10 lands and cultures. The poetry of women and men, alive or alive through their work, salutes the astonishing natural world that gave us rise and provides constant nurture.

He has served on the boards of the World Wildlife Fund (25 years), the Smithsonian Institution, and the W. Alton Jones Foundation. He currently serves on the boards of the Earth Policy Institute, New Jersey Network for public television and radio, TDEX (The Endocrine Exchange, Inc.), Knowles Science Teaching Foundation, Princeton Environmental Institute, and Storm King Art Center.

Scott's honors include receipt of the Albert Schweitzer Award from the Animal Welfare Institute, Joseph Wood Krutch medal from the Humane Society of the United States, Princeton University Class of 1955 Award, Lyndon Baines Johnson Award by the White House Commission on Presidential Scholars, New Jersey Council of the Humanities Citizen of the Year 1998, and an honorary doctorate at Middlebury College.

He is blessed in his marriage to Hella Susanne McVay and in his family: two daughters, Catherine and Cynthia, and three grandchildren, Philip (19), Tess (16), and Matthew (15).

Aimee Morgana

Aimee Morgana is an interspecies communication researcher, teacher, and artist. Born January 1, 1958, in New York City, she has an MFA in art. Aimee's achievements include teaching the parrot N'kisi to use human language, and exploring the inner terrain of the animal mind and our relationships with animals.

Since childhood, Aimee has had an intuitive connection with animals, and has used these insights in developing her own techniques for teaching parrots to use language. Aimee has been working with parrots since 1985. Her goal is to establish a true communicative dialogue with a member of another species. Unlike laboratory researchers, Aimee decided to give N'kisi dominance in their relationship, relinquishing control to open the door for his creativity. She wanted to find out what a parrot might actually have to say, which would reveal fascinating information about how these animals think.

Aimee's ongoing work with N'Kisi illustrates her concept of "partnership research," an approach that honors and explores the close relationships people can have with animals as friends and teachers. Aimee is part of an emerging group of conceptually based artists interested in exploring our human relationship with nature in work dealing with animals, biology, environmental concerns, and quantum aspects of consciousness. In a dynamic cross-fertilization of approaches, some of these artists have begun collaborating with scientists in new-paradigm research projects that bridge the disciplines of art and science.

Paul Winter

Paul Winter is an acclaimed saxophonist and six-time Grammy Award nominee. He was born in Altoona, Pennsylvania, in 1939, son of Paul Theodore Winter (a piano tuner and music store owner) and Beaulah Harnish Winter. He graduated with a BA in English from Northwestern University in 1961.

Paul began playing piano and clarinet as a child; in 1951 he began playing saxophone and formed his first band. In 1968 he heard Dr. Roger Payne's pioneer recording of the songs of the humpback whale. The result was a revelation, as Paul stated in a Living Music Records press release: "The poignant voice of the humpback whales changed my musical life and opened the door for me to the entire symphony of nature." The experience sparked a commitment to create a new kind of music, what Paul refers to as "earth music," in which the intricate improvisations of his ensemble are combined with the sounds of the earth.

Paul was appointed artist-in-residence at New York's Cathedral of St. John the Divine in 1980. In 1982, he composed an ecumenical Earth Mass for the Cathedral. He also initiated the immensely popular annual tradition of the Winter Consort Winter Solstice Whole Earth Christmas Celebration at the Cathedral. In 1985, Paul and the Consort released *Canyon*, a musical portrait of the Grand Canyon, recorded both at the Cathedral and during a rafting trip through the Grand Canyon itself.

In January 1993, the Paul Winter Consort performed at the Environmental Inaugural Ball in honor of President Bill Clinton. In April of that year the Consort released its 27th album, *Spanish Angel*, recorded live in Spain. The work continued Paul's dedication to artistic exploration, love of the earth, and, as Paul explained to *Wilderness* contributor Frederick Allen, his primary musical message: "simply beauty."

Currently, he has released two new albums—a compilation of material from his original group, the Paul Winter Sextet, titled *Early Winter*, and an album of new music featuring the Paul Winter Consort and the Great Rift Valley Orchestra, with calls of the birds that migrate from Africa to Eurasia. The new project, titled *Flyways*, is a musical journey through the cultures that the birds fly over.

Awards include: United Nations Global 500 Award, Award of Excellence from the United Nations Environment Program, Joseph Hutch Award from the United States Humane Society, Peace Abbey's Courage of Conscience Award, six Grammy Award nominations, and *Sun Singer* named jazz album of the year by the National Association of Independent Record Distributors (1983).

M. Christine DeVita

M. Christine DeVita joined the Wallace Foundation in 1987 and has been its president since 1989. Under her leadership, the Foundation has evolved from a collection of small family funds into one of the nation's 40 largest foundations, with assets of more than $1 billion.

The Wallace Foundation applies a unified strategy to all of its work, combining program, evaluation, and communication expertise in an effort to deliver social benefits beyond the recipients of direct grants, through the development and sharing of knowledge. Its work was profiled in *Creative Philanthropy*, by Helmut K. Anheier and Diana Leat.

Christine has spoken about innovative philanthropic practices in venues including the Council on Foundations, Grantmakers for Education, the Arts Council of Winston-Salem and Forsyth County, the New England Museum Association, Duke University, and Bates College.

She is chair of the board of directors of the Foundation Center and a member of the visiting committee of Harvard's Graduate School of Education.

Born in New York, Christine earned her BA degree magna cum laude from Queens College of the City University of New York and her JD degree cum laude from Fordham University School of Law, where she was an editor of the *Fordham Law Review*. She is admitted to practice in New York and before the United States Supreme Court.

Amy Goldman

Amy Goldman directs the work of the GHR Foundation, which invests in those providing sustainable solutions to the world's most pressing problems. Grant portfolios include international development and relief, interfaith action to address social concerns, family support for vulnerable children, and Alzheimer's disease research and patient care. Amy is a former chair and president of the Better Way Foundation, which provides funding for early childhood development for youth living in poverty in the United States and for orphaned and vulnerable children in Africa.

Amy began her career with a concentration in East Asia and was an instructor and researcher at the Fletcher School of Law and Diplomacy, at the University of California, Berkeley and at Sogang and Yonsei Universities in Seoul, Korea. She was awarded a prestigious MacArthur Fellowship in 1991–92 for continued research on the political economy of Asia. She then moved into the private sector as a senior associate at International Trade Services in Washington, D.C., where she worked on trade negotiations and investment strategies for U.S. multinational corporations.

Amy entered the field of philanthropy as Chair of the Better Way Foundation. She has served on numerous corporate, nonprofit and foundation boards. She earned her bachelor's degree from the School of Foreign Service at Georgetown University, a Master of Arts in Law and Diplomacy from the Fletcher School of Law at Tufts University, and a MS in political science from the University of California, Berkeley.

She and her husband, Philip, have three children and live in Minneapolis.

Lynn Schusterman

Lynn Schusterman is the founder of a global philanthropic network of organizations and initiatives dedicated to spreading the joy of Jewish living, giving, and learning, as well as to enhancing the quality of life in her hometown of Tulsa, Oklahoma. This network includes the Charles and Lynn Schusterman Family Foundation, the Schusterman Foundation–Israel, the ROI Community, and the Jerusalem Season of Culture.

Through her work in the fields of service learning, education, inclusivity, and the prevention of child abuse and neglect, she has bettered the lives of hundreds of thousands of people locally, nationally, and globally.

Lynn currently holds a variety of leadership positions in organizations such as BBYO, Hillel, Repair the World, and the American Jewish Joint Distribution Committee. She is also a founding member of the Birthright Israel Foundation and a leading philanthropist in the Birthright Israel program. Locally, Lynn serves on the advisory boards for the Foundation for Tulsa Schools and the Parent Child Center of Tulsa.

Her advocacy efforts include writing articles and opinion pieces for a variety of publications, including the *Jewish Week*, the *Forward*, *JTA*, *eJewish Philanthropy*, *Contact*, and *Tulsa World*. Her reflection on family philanthropy appears in *Voices from the Heartland*, a collection of essays from 50 Oklahoma women, and she also contributed to the book *A Dream of Zion: American Jews Reflect on Why Israel Matters to Them*. Her work has been profiled in the global Jewish and secular press, including the *Jerusalem Post*, *Haaretz*, the *New York Times*, the *Wall Street Journal*, and the *Huffington Post*, among others.

A mother of three and grandmother to six wonderful girls, Lynn has been a pioneer for women in philanthropy, and her charitable work stresses the importance of family, giving back to society, and helping those who help themselves.

Index